THE ICONIC INTERIOR

Private Spaces of Leading Artists, Architects, and Designers

By Dominic Bradbury | With Photography by Richard Powers | Abrams, New York

Contents

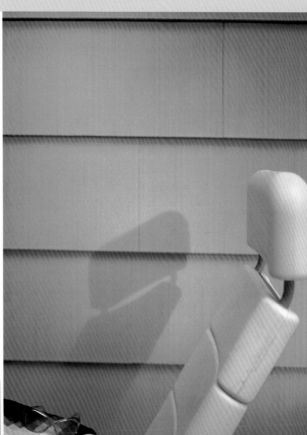

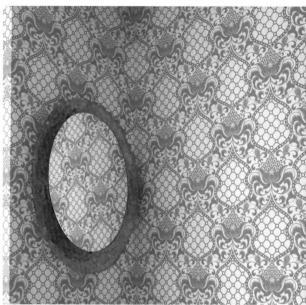

Introduction

The world of design has seen countless shifts and changes over the course of the past hundred years. The evolution of technology, engineering and design itself has affected how we all run our day-to-day lives, communicate our ideas and convey an image of ourselves. This is especially true in the context of the homes that we live in, which have been completely transformed in so many different respects. The ways in which we order our houses and apartments, the ways in which they are built and function, have all changed dramatically. The home has also become a place where we can really express ourselves, now more than ever, and a haven that we are free to shape according to our own imagination and desires.

This applies not only to the residences of a sophisticated design elite or the wealthy, as might once have been the case, but to numerous homes in different places. The explosion of interest in design and decorating personal spaces is a democratic and creative movement that leads to interiors that reflect our own passions and interests. We take delight in the process of inventing and reinventing our living spaces with colours, styles, ideas, patterns and products that entice us but also speak to others about our sense of self and individuality.

There now seems to be more interest than ever in designing and decorating the home and in shaping personal spaces. Magazines, newspapers, television programmes, design stores, websites and catalogues offer daily doses of inspiration and suggestions for the homes that we live in. Part of this feeds into a passion for property and for improving and updating living spaces so that they are worth more to future buyers, allowing progress up the property ladder. Yet beyond this practical aspect, people also aim for comfort, escapism and indulgence, and want to create a retreat in their home.

A home needs to offer many different things these days, 'a place to live' being just one of them. It should also be a place to cook and eat,

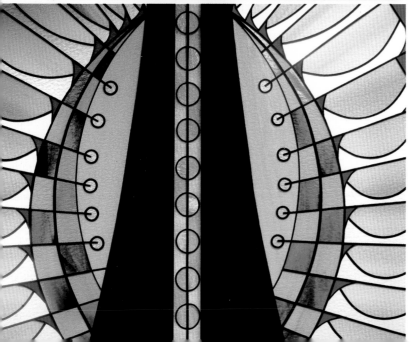

to work and play, to consume and grow, to relax and recharge. Our houses and apartments have become ever more sophisticated in the technology and engineering that helps meet all of these demands, but at the same time we want spaces that, in our eyes and hopefully the eyes of others, are beautiful, seductive and desirable beyond functional requirements.

We have become increasingly educated about design through many different sources, and gained a better understanding of the central principles used to create successful interiors. By looking at the work of designers, architects and style-makers, we develop a real sense of what we like and what we dislike, which ideas work and which might not. Part of this greater understanding comes from an appreciation of certain homes and interiors that have become iconic in one sense or another – these are spaces that sum up a design movement or define a particular style, or suggest a fresh and innovative approach to interior space that resounds through the years.

Each of these iconic interiors has a resonance and importance that reach far beyond the immediate ambitions of the designer at the time of making. They have become part of a complex, inspirational map of 20th-century design that helps spur our own imagination and encourages us to experiment with different ideas, combinations, colour choices and juxtapositions. Taking in such iconic spaces makes us braver and more confident in our own approach to design.

Given the varied ambitions for the home that have developed over time, it is no wonder that an entire industry has grown around creating sophisticated interiors moulded to our needs and desires. Just as the home has been transformed in the course of the 20th century and beyond, so has the interior design profession, and at a startling pace.

Towards the end of the 19th century, interiors were still largely the concern of artisans, craftsmen and tradesmen, particularly furniture makers, upholsterers and drapers who would happily fill the homes of their clients with as much ornament and excess as budgets would allow. There were some architects who concerned themselves with the interior as much as the design of the fabric of a house. In particular, Arts and Crafts designers such as Mackay Hugh Baillie Scott, Edwin Lutyens and Charles Voysey come to mind, who saw the two realms as closely connected and involved themselves directly with both. Yet many architects were happy to pass on a blank canvas, a crafted shell that could be filled at will with the produce of the trades and the delights of the decorative arts.

By the turn of the century, the excess of ornament (inside and outside the home) was coming under attack from many different directions, from architects such as Adolf Loos, Louis Sullivan (who coined the phrase 'form follows function') and Otto Wagner, as well as from commentators and writers such as Edith Wharton. In 1897, Wharton published a highly influential book together with architect

1901
Peter Behrens (1868–1940)
Behrens House / Mathildenhöhe
Darmstadt, Germany

Pioneering a new way of thinking about architecture and design in the early 20th century, Peter Behrens is best known for his work as artistic consultant for AEG (Allgemeine Elektricitäts-Gesellschaft/General Electric Company), where he designed everything from products and logos to the famous Turbine Hall in the company's Berlin factory (1909).

Behrens was recognized as one of the first industrial designers, but he was also a polymath – an accomplished painter, architect and designer. He represented a link between Arts and Crafts, Art Nouveau (Jugendstil) and the modern movement, with Le Corbusier, Mies van der Rohe and others working in his office.

Behrens's own home in Darmstadt was his first completed building. It was a showcase house of the Darmstadt Artists' Colony, founded at the invitation of Grand Duke Ernst Ludwig von Hessen. It was completed in 1901, in time for the Colony exhibition, and was fully catalogued as part of the show.

While the exteriors blended familiar architectural elements with a neat and rational form, the interiors represented a completely cohesive design, from the door handles down to the cutlery. The main living spaces on the ground floor could be joined for entertaining or separated for more privacy. A music room with a gilded ceiling, dark timber and panels of blue mirror glass contrasts with a dining room lifted by white furniture, an ornate ceiling with crystal electric fittings and touches of crimson. Many pieces of furniture were built in, creating a harmonious and concentrated composition.

Ogden Codman, Jr, called *The Decoration of Houses*. Wharton and Codman were both inspired by the neoclassical architecture of Europe but also appalled by what they saw as the excess of decoration that cluttered the typical late-Victorian home. 'House decoration,' they wrote, 'has come to be regarded as a black art by those who have seen their rooms subjected to the manipulations of the modern upholsterer.'[1] Wharton and Codman argued for 'simplicity' and 'harmony of line', suggesting that architecture and interiors were two sides of the same coin. Problems and excesses arose, they told their readers, when a disparity developed between the architecture of a building and its interior decoration. Wharton and Codman turned their manifesto into reality at The Mount, Wharton's country home in rural Massachusetts (see page 28). Wharton and Codman's book also struck a chord with others, such as Elsie de Wolfe and Nancy Lancaster, who soon established themselves as

1 Edith Wharton & Ogden Codman, Jr, *The Decoration of Houses*, 1897.

1903
Henry van de Velde (1863–1957)
Villa Esche / Chemnitz, Germany

Like Peter Behrens, Henry van de Velde was an artist as well as an architect and interior designer. The Belgian design pioneer was a proponent of Art Nouveau, designing furniture and interiors for Samuel Bing's influential Maison de l'Art Nouveau gallery in Paris. Throughout his career, Van de Velde retained strong links with the art world.

In 1895, Van de Velde designed a house for himself called Bloemenwerf (Flower Wharf) in Ukkel, near Brussels. The project brought him considerable attention, and his work was widely published in Germany, where he continued to work for many years, helping to shape the evolution of Art Nouveau (Jugendstil) in the country.

A good proportion of Van de Velde's work in Germany was focused on Chemnitz, where he formed a strong professional relationship with businessman Herbert Esche, co-owner of a large stocking-manufacturing plant but also a collector and patron of the arts. Van de Velde designed a number of projects for him and his family.

Shortly after his marriage, Esche commissioned Van de Velde to create a substantial family villa that would be a *Gesamtkunstwerk* (total work of art), just as Bloemenwerf had been. Van de Velde designed the structure, gardens, interiors, furniture and tableware, and reportedly even Esche's pipe. With its timber panelling, bespoke lighting and open interiors that allowed the craftsmanship and richness of materials to stand out, Villa Esche propelled Van de Velde to greater fame. The house was opened to the public in 2001.

1910

Adolf Loos (1870–1933)

Steiner House / Vienna, Austria

A pioneer and prophet of the modernist movement, in his architecture and writings Adolf Loos campaigned against what he saw as the excess of ornament that he found all around him. Turning his back on Art Nouveau and Secessionist decorational exuberance, Loos argued for a more austere, reserved and considered approach to design, most famously in his essay 'Ornament and Crime'.

The house he designed around a painting studio for the painter Lilly Steiner and her husband illustrates this approach. The simple, crisp white façade, together with the curving metallic roof and central dormer window, made a statement that was taken up by the early modernists. Although Loos was constrained by building codes, particularly on the street front, he managed to create a complex four-level building.

For Loos, there was a clear distinction to be made between the austere façade of a house and the interior, which he saw as a backdrop to the social and cultural lives of his clients and which could therefore be approached more liberally. The interior of the Steiner House is surprisingly rich, featuring a wealth of natural materials, wood-panelled walls and built-in furniture, including corner seating in the living room and Chippendale furniture in the dining room.

Other key projects from Loos's career include the Villa Müller in Prague (1928), which has been turned into a museum and opened to visitors.

pioneering figures within the new profession of interior decoration.

Elsie de Wolfe was a well-connected New Yorker, often described as the very first American professional interior decorator. Like Wharton and Codman, she was influenced by European architecture and design, and advocated simplicity, little clutter and light, fresh colours. She accepted her first commission in 1905, designing the Colony Club in New York. De Wolfe was not afraid to use pattern in the right places and happily combined antique and modern pieces. She travelled between Europe and America, and famously bought the Villa Trianon at Versailles for her French home.

By the 1920s, a number of influential decorators had established themselves successfully, treating the room as a cohesive entity in its own right, rather than a disparate collection of furniture, fabrics and *objets d'art*. In London, interior designer Syrie Maugham opened her first shop in 1922, followed by others in New York and Chicago. Eleanor Brown founded McMillen, Inc. in 1924 in New York, also arguing for 'simplicity and restraint' in the Wharton–Codman mould. She had trained both in New York and at the Parsons School of Design in Paris, which was founded in 1921 as a satellite to the American parent institution that first started life in the late 1890s. McMillen, Maugham and others catered for a high-society clientele with not one but several homes.

1914
Elsie de Wolfe (1865–1950)
The Frick Residence / New York, USA

In her decorating work Elsie de Wolfe reacted against the heavy Victorian style of her parents' generation. Her own style was feminine, fresh, light and uncluttered, and heavily influenced by French period style, with a lot of chintz and antiques, as well as more daring, contemporary touches.

De Wolfe began a career as an actress, and her interest in set design spurred on her passion for interiors. She established herself in the first decade of the 20th century and won a commission to design the interiors of the Colony Club. This success sealed her reputation as a tastemaker, and in 1913 she published her book *The House in Good Taste*. At that time De Wolfe also secured one of her most lucrative, high-profile jobs: designing the interiors of a new Manhattan mansion for the wealthy industrialist and art collector Henry Clay Frick.

De Wolfe was asked to furnish fourteen family rooms on the upper two floors of the building, which were designed in the French neoclassical style by Thomas Hastings; the grand rooms on the principal floor were designed by Sir Charles Allom.

De Wolfe's scheme for Frick included prize French antiques from buying trips to Europe in 1913. Mrs Frick's private sitting room, also known as the Boucher Room after a series of painted panels by François Boucher originally commissioned by Madame de Pompadour, is still intact today. The house is now one of New York's most popular small museums.

1925
Armand-Albert Rateau (1882–1938)
Jeanne Lanvin Apartment / Paris, France

Armand-Albert Rateau was not a typical Art Deco designer, although he made his reputation in Paris, and internationally, at the height of the style's popularity. He also took inspiration from neoclassicism, the decorative arts of Japan and China and motifs from the natural world (a menagerie of animals made their way into his furniture and interiors).

Having studied at the École Boulle, Rateau was a director of interior design firm La Maison Alavoine in Paris for many years. After serving in World War I, he set up his own company and found great success in France and abroad in the early 1920s, encouraged by key clients such as celebrated couturière Jeanne Lanvin (1867–1946).

Rateau ran his own furniture-making workshops as well as a design studio, and was asked to design the interiors of a number of Lanvin boutiques. He was also commissioned to create the interiors of her Parisian *hôtel particulier* on the rue Barbet-de-Jouy. Lanvin's bedroom features walls in a signature 'Lanvin blue', and white floral motifs stand out against the blues, while bespoke furniture and lighting incorporate sculpted supports in the shape of bronze birds.

The bedroom, bathroom and private sitting room were reassembled in the Musée des Arts Décoratifs in 1965.

Around the same time, Jacques-Émile Ruhlmann established himself as one of France's greatest design voices. By the mid-1920s Ruhlmann's Art Deco, or Moderniste, style was much in demand, with handcrafted furniture and interiors incorporating luxurious, beautifully fashioned materials such as shagreen, ebony and lizard skin as well as lacquer work and chrome. Another Frenchman, Jean-Michel Frank, was also continuing to progress the country's reputation as a centre of design excellence, reaching the height of his fame in the 1930s, when he worked for influential clients including the Vicomte and Vicomtesse de Noailles in France and Nelson Rockefeller in New York. His work was also much admired by Elsie de Wolfe, Syrie Maugham and others.

By the end of World War II, the world of design had gone through a period of great upheaval: many European designers and architects moved to the United States, and wartime technology pushed forward many innovations and materials, such as plywood, which was used

1925
Jacques-Émile Ruhlmann (1879–1933)
Hôtel d'un Collectionneur / Paris, France

Jacques-Émile Ruhlmann's work was all about luxury.
A master of the Art Deco movement, Ruhlmann understood
his market, creating furniture and interiors with extraordinary
detailing, intricate craftsmanship and exotic materials.
He would have his artisans work on a piece again and again,
rather than risk a compromise in quality, and once claimed
that many of his designs were so expensive to produce that
they lost him money.

Born in Paris, Ruhlmann took over his father's painting,
mirror and wallpaper company in 1907 and soon began
introducing his own furniture designs. In 1919, he went into
partnership with Pierre Laurent and expanded the workshops
with skilled artisans who carefully executed his designs.
His furniture displayed the sinuous qualities of the Art Deco
period, but it was rooted in traditional cabinetry and made use
of rich materials: Macassar ebony, palisander and Amboyna
burl, with detailing in shagreen, tortoiseshell and gold leaf.

For the 1925 Exposition Internationale des Arts Décoratifs
et Industriels Modernes in Paris (which gave Art Deco its
name), Ruhlmann created a pavilion with architect Pierre
Partout – the Hôtel d'un Collectionneur – a sumptuous
full-scale house arranged around a large oval salon. The
rooms were fully cohesive, luxurious and intricate spaces that
involved collaborations with leading artists and designers.

for new types of furniture as well as leg splints and military planes.
Interior decoration was slowly reinvented as 'interior design', showing
a depth of ambition that went well beyond the surface.

By the 1950s, a clear separation had established itself between the
traditionalists and the modernists, reflecting the continued diversity
of taste and style within the world of design. In England, John Fowler
famously refreshed the English country house look in collaboration with
Nancy Lancaster, and his work remains highly influential for younger
generations of designers. In the United States, Sister Parish and others
were defining a version of classic American elegance with an emphasis
on comfort and period influences. In 1962, she joined forces with
Albert Hadley, and working at Parish-Hadley became an apprenticeship
for a whole cohort of interior designers, including Mark Hampton,
who went on to achieve wide recognition in their own right.

At the same time, the modern movement was well under way
internationally, and taking architecture and interiors in a very

1926
Jean-Michel Frank (1895–1941)
Maison Noailles / Paris, France

The work of Jean-Michel Frank is characterized by a number of elements that combine within a sophisticated, easily recognizable signature. There is a formal purity and clean geometry to his furniture and interiors, which is lifted beyond austerity by highly luxurious and unusual materials and a high level of craftsmanship.

Part of Frank's reputation rested on his own designs, but he also collaborated with some of the most gifted and inventive craftsmen and artists of his age, including Alberto and Diego Giacometti. The Frank style suggests a love of neutral, organic colours, although the designer also liked to experiment with a more daring colour palette on occasion.

Throughout the late 1920s and 1930s, Frank established himself as one of the most influential designers in Europe, held in high esteem in America, where he famously worked for Nelson Rockefeller. Other clients included perfumier Jean-Pierre Guerlain, the Italian fashion designer Elsa Schiaparelli and the Vicomte and Vicomtesse de Noailles. In the world of French high society, few couples were as bohemian or controversial as the Noailles. They asked Frank to redesign the interiors of the family mansion, and he created a sequence of rooms including two sitting rooms and a smoking room featuring parchment walls, wooden panels inlaid with straw marquetry, woven grey silks and club chairs in white leather. The building is now owned by Baccarat.

1942
William Haines (1900–1973)
Howard Residence / Los Angeles, USA

Billy Haines enjoyed a successful career as a film star before moving into interior design in the early 1930s. Like Tony Duquette (see page 96), Haines was at home in the glamorous world of 1930s and 1940s Hollywood, with many stars whom he knew through his screen work becoming clients.

Much of Haines's early work was influenced by neoclassicism and a love of European antiques. But in the years after the war, his interiors and furniture came to be characterized as 'Hollywood glamour', mixing mid-century modern pieces with antiques and touches of Far Eastern design such as chinoiserie panels, and more flamboyant elements including statement chandeliers.

In the early 1940s, Haines was asked to design a home for Hollywood actress and photographer Jean Howard and her husband, Charles Feldman, that would provide comfort and a space for entertaining. The sitting room featured a generous L-shaped sofa, which took up a good section of the room, and a choice of other seating areas. The designer also made use of bold colours, using a rich emerald green for the living room walls, while mirrored panels around the fireplace helped to create an impression of greater space. Haines's work is still in circulation today in the form of his furniture collection, with many of the pieces dating back to the 1950s.

1930
Edwin Lutyens (1869–1944)
Castle Drogo / Drewsteignton, Devon, UK

Even the architect, it seems, had reservations about the idea of building a full-scale castle in the English countryside in the 20th century, but for Edwin Lutyens this unique commission became an enticing challenge.

Showing an appreciation and deep understanding of both Arts and Crafts thinking and neoclassicism, Lutyens's work represented an individual fusion of ideas that could be expressed in a number of ways, within the idiom of the English country house or the grand colonial ambition of New Delhi. At Castle Drogo, medievalism was spliced with modernity to great effect, and the gardens were designed by Lutyens's long-term collaborator, Gertrude Jekyll.

Castle Drogo was commissioned by Julius Drewe, the founder of the Home & Colonial Stores, who had made a vast fortune at an early age. Following a tenuous ancestral link to the village of Drewsteignton, Drewe bought some land in the area and asked Lutyens to design a castle. Work began in 1910 but Castle Drogo was not completed for another twenty years, as spiralling costs meant that elements had to be reduced.

Part of the glory of the interiors lies in the rich quality of light, introduced by vast windows; and dramatic open elements contrast with more intimate wood-panelled rooms. The large kitchen features a striking circular lantern skylight looking down on a round table to Lutyens's own design. Drogo is now owned by the National Trust.

different direction. In Europe and Scandinavia, architects such as Alvar Aalto and Antonio Bonet invented spaces that were open, fresh and uncluttered, with an emphasis on the character of materials and the relationship between inside and outside living. These were also designers for whom architecture and interiors were equally important, with many bespoke elements woven into the design. Similar developments were taking place in Australia, South America and other parts of the world, particularly in North America, where John Lautner, Richard Neutra and others were creating a version of the American Dream expressed in houses that celebrated the landscape, indoor/outdoor living spaces and the nature of modernity itself.

The modern movement continues to shape our approach to design, and the innovative, optimistic interiors and furniture of the 1950s in particular generate a powerful interest. In some circles the differences between modernism and traditionalism – or the contemporary versus the neoclassical, or Beaux-Arts styles – are seen

1957
William Baldwin (1903–1983)
Vreeland Apartment / New York, USA

When the celebrated magazine editor and tastemaker Diana Vreeland commissioned Billy Baldwin to design her New York apartment, she famously asked him to turn her home into a 'garden from hell'. The home that Baldwin created for the *Harper's Bazaar* editor and later American *Vogue* editor-in-chief was among the most flamboyant and colourful projects of his career and featured in many publications.

Baldwin liked his work to reflect the personalities of his clients, and in some ways this was an atypical project. One tends to think of his interiors as carefully tailored but also comfortable and welcoming. He took a considered approach to proportion and scale, and was influenced by French masters such as Jean-Michel Frank more than English country house traditionalism, but he was also an admirer of Madeleine Castaing (see page 92) and shared with her a penchant for the unexpected and intriguing juxtapositions of materials, patterns, periods and colours. Baldwin's work was immaculately thought through, but it was never dull.

Vreeland's apartment was anything but dull, with a living room dominated by flaming floral reds and a riot of pattern that continued into the bedroom and other parts of the home. Baldwin discovered the 'tree of life' fabric that dominates the sitting room on a buying trip to Spain, and much of the furniture was chosen or designed to tie in with it. The result appears much busier than other Baldwin interiors but is held together by an ordered logic. It soon became one of the most famous spaces in Manhattan.

as irreconcilable. Yet interior design is a broad and welcoming church, and the growing number of choices between particular styles and design approaches allows for greater freedom to assert individuality and character, rather than simply conveying a sense of prestige or status. This particular quality has always been part of the great charm of interior design.

As early as the 1960s, designers such as David Hicks were carving out an international reputation by cleverly combining a love of neoclassical architecture and period design with a passion for bold colours, patterns and modern elements. This eclectic but considered and intelligent approach was not quite a statement to say that 'anything goes', but it served to suggest that an openness to different kinds of influences, inspirations and design periods was a natural position to take rather than an act of iconoclasm.

Many designers and architects featured in this book – from Lina Bo Bardi to Robert Venturi and Terence Conran – have opened

1959
John Fowler (1906–1977) &
Nancy Lancaster (1897–1994)
The Yellow Room, Avery Row / London, UK

It was an extraordinary and powerful alliance: the 'prince of decorators', John Fowler, a designer respected throughout the profession for his scholarly erudition and unerring eye, and the great Anglo-American tastemaker and socialite Nancy Lancaster, who had made a name for herself on both sides of the Atlantic with her emphasis on comfort, character and atmosphere within interiors that were grounded in the English country house tradition.

When Sibyl Colefax stepped down from the London decorating firm Colefax & Fowler in 1944, Nancy Lancaster stepped in and bought the company, establishing a new partnership with Fowler. It was not always an easy association, but their work earned them both an enduring place in design history, and the company they built together continues today.

One of their most lauded and high-profile projects was the Yellow Room, created within the 19th-century building that housed the company. In the late 1950s, Lancaster decided to convert part of the building into a flat for herself, and the Yellow Room was the most accomplished element of Fowler and Lancaster's design.

With glazed walls of buttery yellow offset by a barrel-vaulted ceiling in a sable tone, the large sitting room featured yellow taffeta curtains as well as upholstered chairs and sofas in yellow and cream tones with accents of bright red. The room served as a vibrant showcase for the Colefax & Fowler look.
(Photograph by Derry Moore)

themselves to centuries of architectural and design richness. Although they come from very different backgrounds, each has absorbed and adapted a wide range of influences while pushing ahead in an individual direction and defining their own particular style, often becoming brand names in their own right. When assembling any list of iconic interiors, one is faced with this breadth and diversity of enticing signature styles.

Within the complex map of 20th-century design it is possible to see the progression of design movements from Arts and Crafts to Art Deco, to modernism and minimalism and beyond, and it is intriguing to chart the various connections between different designers and their influences. But the map is also enriched by the work of extraordinary individuals such as Tony Duquette, Piero Fornasetti and Jonathan Adler who stand out for their unique approach full of drama and vivid imagination. The individuality and adventurous spirit of such designers carry a particular resonance and encourage us to be more adventurous in our own homes.

Many of the iconic homes featured in this book are the work of interior designers and architects but a significant number were created by people from outside the interior design profession. This does not imply any weakness of interior design as a discipline, but perhaps indicates one of its strengths: the way in which it opens itself to constant reinvention and enrichment by people from all kinds of creative backgrounds.

This book also showcases interiors by artists, product designers, furniture makers and fashion designers whose work has strayed into the world of interior design and whose powerful aesthetic approach has had a significant impact beyond the confines of their own industry. One thinks of artists such as Vanessa Bell, Duncan Grant and Henry Moore, or furniture and product designers such as Wharton Esherick,

1970
Joe Colombo (1930–1971)
Colombo Apartment IV / Milan, Italy

A flamboyant and imaginative figurehead of futuristic design, Joe Colombo was way ahead of his time. Fascinated by ideas and themes that would become staples of the 21st-century home, he pioneered the development of modular and multi-functional furniture, as well as programmable lighting and even programmable homes, sensing perhaps that one day the computer would have a central place in our living spaces.

Colombo's interiors and furniture, together with his dandy image and talent for marketing and self-promotion, made him the epitome of the progressive 'playboy designer' and paved the way for contemporary design maestros such as Philippe Starck and Karim Rashid, who have created an international brand around themselves. Colombo was also a visionary who loved to experiment with new production methods and materials, especially moulded plastics, which he transformed into chairs, storage units and other pieces of furniture in bright pop colours.

His apartments in Milan also served as showcases for his work and were featured in style and design magazines. In 1970, he moved to the building of his studio and created this open, loft-style space dominated by his Cabriolet Bed and Roto Living unit, with a sinuous, sliding curtain wall to separate the two. These extraordinary pieces were multi-functional units, with the bed featuring an integrated rubber-duck-yellow canopy, radio, fan, ashtray, mirror and vanity unit.

1983
Laura Ashley (1925–1985) &
Bernard Ashley (1926–2009)
Ashley Townhouse / Brussels, Belgium

Laura Ashley is best known for reworking a version of the traditional English country look that pandered to a sense of nostalgia for a lost age. She was the 'queen of the floral print' and championed a soft, feminine approach to style and fashion, although her talents did also take her in more adventurous directions.

Ashley launched the company from her kitchen table with her husband, Bernard, in 1953, creating Victorian-style patterns for headscarves that were printed on a machine of her husband's invention. The company grew rapidly in the 1960s, with Laura Ashley looking after design and her husband steering production. What had begun as a fashion label grew further with a home furnishings range in 1981, making the patterns more widely available as textiles and wallpapers.

By the 1980s, the Ashleys' talents for creating an entire image around their brand had made them wealthy, and the company was known throughout the world. The Ashleys had a country house in Wales, but also bought homes in France, Belgium and the Bahamas, all designed in the typical Ashley style. They included this townhouse in Brussels, dominated by floral patterns and the reassuring signature look.

Often underrated as a designer and tastemaker, Laura Ashley had a profound effect on countless homes in the 1970s and 80s. The brand continues today and has been hugely influential in the development of other lifestyle brands.

1985
Lorenzo Mongiardino (1916–1998)
Peretti Tower / Porto Ercole, Italy

For Renzo Mongiardino, what mattered the most in an interior was the ambience and atmosphere. Although erudite and deeply rooted in historicism and neoclassicism, Mongiardino was not overly concerned with the authenticity and provenance of the pieces that were woven into his spaces: often the 'ancient' columns, stone walls, marble fireplaces and coffered ceilings would turn out to be an illusion, the work of specialist painters and trompe l'oeil technicians.

Mongiardino worked for the famous wealthy families of Europe and America – the Brandolinis, Rothschilds and Agnellis – but added his own element of sublime trickery and drama. His spaces were infused with the same philosophy that went into his work as a set designer for stage and film under Franco Zeffirelli, Peter Hall and Gian Carlo Menotti.

Mongiardino studied architecture in Milan alongside Giò Ponti, but soon turned his back on modernism, looking instead to the past and infusing his work with a spirit of period romance. His work was sumptuous and full of drama and playfulness, blending a mass of different influences.

Among Mongiardino's many projects were two homes for jewellery designer Elsa Peretti, best known for her work for Tiffany. One was her apartment in Rome, which took five years to create, the other this medieval tower on the Tuscan coast in Porto Ercole, where Mongiardino created the famous fireplace in the shape of a monster's face.

1991
Shoei Yoh (1940–)
Another Glass House Between Sea and Sky / Itoshima Peninsula, Fukuoka, Japan

Perched on a clifftop, Shoei Yoh's home opens out to dramatic views of the ever-changing Genkai Sea. The house is a belvedere, intimately connected to nature, water and sky. Anchored to the ground at the rear, the house projects forward on a cantilevered platform that holds the key living spaces and a terrace, all bordered with glass. The combination of these elements lends the house a seductive sense of lightness, as if the building were floating within this vivid landscape where land and ocean collide.

In the early 1970s, just after establishing his own architectural practice, Yoh built a house for himself and his family in glass and steel, partly inspired by Mies van der Rohe's Farnsworth House. Two decades later, he revisited the idea of a glass house here, on the Itoshima Peninsula, in a spot where he and his family once enjoyed picnics looking out across the water.

The house is characterized by clean lines and crisp materials and provides a sense of direct connection with the natural world through its glass walls. The main living areas are open plan so as not to disturb the simplicity and cohesion of the home: kitchen, dining area, seating and a music zone all contained within one space. The house also represents a strong alliance between architecture and engineering, and is part of an ongoing investigation into materials and form. It is emblematic of a wave of experimental, minimalist and visually striking Japanese buildings that made an international impact in the 1990s.

Russel Wright, Dieter Rams, Robin and Lucienne Day and Marc Newson, as well as figures from the fashion industry such as Bill Blass, Donna Karan and Todd Oldham, whose approach to style influenced much more than the way that we dress and whose passion for interiors led them to develop their own lines of furniture and homeware.

Interior design has never been a 'closed shop'; it has long been an unfettered form of design that allows all comers to the table, as long as they have talent and imagination. This has created rich opportunities for cross-pollination between different forms of design as well as extraordinary collaborations such as the one between Madeleine Castaing and Jean Cocteau, working together on his home at Milly-la-Forêt in France. Other highly creative partnerships include those forged between designers and enlightened clients such as Alvar Aalto and art dealer Louis Carré, who commissioned an extraordinary home in the countryside southwest of Paris, or the pioneering Haus

1995
Calvin Tsao (1952–) &
Zack McKown (1952–)
Tsao McKown Apartment / New York, USA

Designers Calvin Tsao and Zack McKown draw inspiration from all across architectural and design history. The intrinsic approach to the design of their spaces may be modernist, yet they open themselves to neoclassicism and many other influences from East to West. They see no contradiction in such openness, and their work has a pervasive clarity and sense of order while also being comfortable and atmospheric.

What is most striking about their designs is the love of detail, craftsmanship and bespoke design in intricately tailored spaces. Their own Manhattan duplex apartment, located in a 1930s building overlooking Central Park, was completely redesigned to their own taste and specifications, with the lower floor assuming the open feel of a sophisticated loft despite being anchored by a sculptural staircase of Tsao and McKown's own design.

The floors are in Brazilian cherry wood, as is the custom-made dining table. A number of other pieces, such as the sofa, are also self-designed. The overall mix is eclectic and includes 18th-century Scottish dining chairs, a Sicilian cross on one wall, a flea market daybed and Napoleonic seats bought in Paris. Banks of built-in storage give clarity to the space and also contain some of Tsao and McKown's collections of ceramics, curios, period engineering prototypes and models, as well as books. Pieces are constantly taken out for display and changed, meaning the apartment is always shifting and evolving, although its foundations remain constant.

2000
Ron Arad (1951–)
Piper Building Apartment / London, UK

A generously sized, empty shell in the Piper Building tempted Ron Arad into a rare residential commission. He is best known for his furniture designs and larger commissions such as the Design Museum in Holon, Israel, but the project presented an opportunity to craft an interior that combined sculpted architectural elements and his own furniture designs within a loose brief.

At first, it seemed that the high ceilings of the apartment would allow for a duplex, but it soon became clear that dividing the space over two floors would destroy the sense of great scale. Looking to balance the need for usable space and a desire for openness, Arad created a striking mezzanine gallery that slices through the rear of the apartment like a twisted aeroplane wing, leaving the main section closest to the Thames views free for a double-height living area. Arad compares the dynamic form of the metallic hull, which partially encloses an intimate lounge and study, to a convertible car.

The main level of the apartment is lightly divided into areas for sitting, cooking and dining, while furniture choices include a mirror-polished stainless-steel dining table and Arad's famous Bookworm library shelving. The space shows how the designer's love of biomorphic forms can successfully translate to the domestic arena.

Schminke in Löbau, Germany, which was commissioned from Hans Scharoun by a family of pasta-makers (see page 72).

The aim of this book is to showcase and celebrate the rich diversity of interior design across the 20th century. The wide-ranging list of homes featured suggests the importance of individual imagination, originality and character as well as aesthetic beauty and style. The interiors were also chosen to reflect an international and chronological mix of projects that would touch upon key stylistic movements and form an interconnected narrative of 20th-century design.

Each of the selected designers and architects was limited to one definitive project, and the choices were restricted by the need to find interiors that were well-preserved and accessible, or where archive colour photography was available. For some early 20th-century designers, the options were naturally going to be limited, given the ephemeral nature of interior space, which tends to evolve and change

2004
Seth Stein (1959–)
Robberg House / Plettenberg Bay,
South Africa

For architect Seth Stein, the Robberg House marked a
significant step towards a more international portfolio of
work as well as a more contextual approach to materials
and the way that the landscape is factored into the design.
Up until this point, Stein had been best known for a series of
crisp, urban buildings with an emphasis on clean lines and
accomplished detailing. With this South African project,
he began a series of rural houses that highlighted the setting
and the beauty of locally available materials.

The house was commissioned by fashion impresario
Lucille Lewin and her husband, Richard, who founded the
popular UK fashion chain Whistles. Stein had already worked
with the Lewins on store designs and their London home
before being commissioned to design the house at Plettenberg
Bay, looking across the Robberg Nature Reserve.

The strong, linear design of the house makes the most
of the views and indoor/outdoor connections. The spaces
are given clarity by an earthy colour palette and integrated
elements of furniture, from baths and sofas to bedside tables.
The use of organic materials, such as sandstone and panels
of banded eucalyptus wood for shutters and textured walls
around the terrace, helps soften the form of the house and
link it to the extraordinary natural beauty that surrounds it.

more significantly over the years than other forms of architecture.
My earlier book, *The Iconic House: Architectural Masterworks from 1900
to the Present* (Thames & Hudson, 2009), can be seen as a companion
volume to this one: it takes a more architectural approach to the
great houses of the 20th century, including Frank Lloyd Wright's
Fallingwater, Le Corbusier's Villa Savoye, Richard Neutra's Kaufmann
House and Mies van der Rohe's Farnsworth House.

This book focuses on the free, open and uplifting nature of
interior design and the way in which it has continually invited
new inspiration, ideas and approaches from all corners of the
globe. This aspect goes beyond fashion – many of the interior spaces
featured here have a timeless quality about them that transcends
trends, although there is a cyclical quality to design, which sees an
occasional resurgence of interest in particular periods or themes
of design.

2004
David Adjaye (1966–)
Lost House / London, UK

The Lost House is perhaps the most visually dramatic of a series of London homes designed by architect David Adjaye. They are effectively closed off from the outside world, with the focus being the quality of the interior spaces and the manipulation of light. At the Lost House, the spaces were given another dimension by the contrast of black surfaces and wall colours with shafts of natural light breaking into the heart of the building.

The house was commissioned by fashion designer Roksanda Ilincic and her husband, Philip Bueno de Mesquita. The couple had bought an unusual site on an old delivery yard positioned between former industrial buildings. With Adjaye's design, this became a secluded single-storey home bordered by a mezzanine and other hidden spaces. The open plan of the main living space was punctuated and partially divided by a central courtyard with glass walls, holding a pond (additional courtyards were positioned at either end of the house), and supplemented by skylights.

This central glass room is an art installation piece, circulating light and reflections within a context of black floors and walls. Many elements, such as the sofas and banquettes in the living area and the adjacent sunken cinema room, are integrated into the design, lending a gallery-like purity to this extraordinary and somewhat surreal home filled with optical tricks.

Interior design seeks out the eclectic and the unique from a global treasure box, and it is always open to fresh ideas. It is how designers approach and order these treasures, how they manage spaces with an eye for colour and texture, pattern, proportion, symmetry and asymmetry, light and shade that really matters. If there is a common thread to great interiors, it rests on principles of cohesion, clarity of vision and character. Disparate themes and influences can always be held together by a harmonious and intelligent approach, and this applies to many different attitudes to aesthetic and stylistic preferences.

Some of the houses in this book might appeal to readers more than others; some will delight and some may surprise, which is due to the wide-ranging nature of design styles, but all of the homes presented in this book offer something unique and special, something extraordinary that resonates through the years. These houses and apartments are essential reference points in the ongoing story of interior design.

2001
Jasper Conran (1959–)
Conran Townhouse / London, UK

There is a strong sense of both character and restraint about Jasper Conran's living spaces. His interiors are carefully edited and composed, with a freshness and lightness of touch, echoing Conran's own homeware ranges and also, to some extent, his fashion collections. Conran is one of the more accomplished fashion designers to have successfully translated his talents to the canvas of the home.

Conran's houses reflect an interest in neoclassical and period architecture combined with a more contemporary touch. This apartment was formed from the grand second-floor spaces of a Victorian townhouse (including a ballroom) built for a governor of the Bank of England, and it features high ceilings, wooden floors and architectural detailing picked out in crisp white paintwork. This is combined with elegant simplicity in the form of shutters rather than grand curtains at the windows, while a sleek Boffi kitchen sits within a neoclassical framework.

Created in collaboration with designer Ann Boyd, the former ballroom is now a sitting room, where contemporary furniture upholstered in muted mohair and linen sits alongside the grand period fireplace on simple wooden floorboards. Conran's striking collection of Elizabethan portraits adds another dimension to the spaces. It is a sophisticated and tempered fusion, tied together by fresh colours, warm textures and a modern interpretation of comfortable elegance.

The Mount / Lenox, Massachusetts, USA, 1902

As a novelist and writer, Edith Wharton needs little introduction. Her books continue to earn immense respect and affection as well as the attention of famous film-makers. Yet Wharton's very first book was not a work of fiction but a survey of interior design, *The Decoration of Houses*, published in 1897 and co-written with society architect Ogden Codman, Jr. Both were admirers of neoclassical architecture, and particularly influenced by the great country houses and gardens of Italy, France and England. Together they fought against the heavy, overbearing and excessive aspect of many Victorian interiors that betrayed the blunt, self-serving showmanship of upholsterers.

Wharton and Codman (who went on to design homes for the wealthy Vanderbilt and Rockefeller families) argued that interior decoration was in fact a branch of architecture itself and that the two should go hand in hand. They suggested that beauty and order were two sides of the same coin, and that suitability, simplicity and proportion were key.

'The great decorators, if scrupulous in the observance of *architectural* principles, were governed, in the use of ornamental detail, by the…"wise moderation" of the Greeks,' they wrote, 'and the rooms of the past were both simpler in treatment and freer from mere embellishments than those of to-day.' [1]

Wharton's approach to design was to have a profound influence, not only on the style of American homes, but the evolution of the profession of interior decoration, influencing pioneering decorators such as Elsie de Wolfe (see page 13) and Nancy Lancaster (see page 19).

Just a few years after the publication of the book, Wharton seized the chance to develop her ideas further through designing, in conjunction with Codman, a new home set in more than 40 hectares (100 acres) of rolling countryside in Massachusetts. The Mount is a neoclassical design, much influenced by Italian and English homes, with the main living spaces looking out on to terraces (where Wharton liked to play ping pong with her guests) and Italianate gardens, also created to her own design.

The main entrance is at basement level, via a rear courtyard with an entry hallway in the form of a sophisticated sunken grotto. Ascending the stairs one reaches a long gallery with terrazzo and marble floors and vaulted ceilings, running the length of the back of the house and rich in natural light. A restraint in furnishings and colour choices gives the space a sense of lightness and elegance.

The gallery feeds into the key rooms of the house, among them the large drawing room at the centre with its French fireplace and plaster ceilings.

The library alongside was more of a social space than a writing studio, as Wharton preferred to write in her bedroom suite on the floor above.

Recently restored and opened to the public, The Mount was for a time the epicentre of Wharton's world, with friends including Henry James staying a number of times. It was also a highly influential marker in the development of American design and the resurgence of interest in Beaux Arts and neoclassical style.

1 *The Decoration of Houses*, Edith Wharton & Ogden Codman, Jr, 1898.

Biography
Edith Wharton (1862–1937)

The author of *The House of Mirth* (1905), *Ethan Frome* (1911) and *The Age of Innocence* (1920), Wharton was one of the most respected American novelists of her era, and the first woman to win the Pulitzer Prize for Fiction. Also a designer and tastemaker, she created homes for herself and promoted her ideas about neoclassical architecture, interiors and garden design. She was born in New York and travelled widely with her husband until their divorce in 1913. Fully established as a novelist and social commentator, she moved to France, where she contributed to the war effort in World War I.

The crisp, neoclassical architecture of The Mount sits within generous woodland that lends the house a bucolic charm (*left* and *far left*). Wharton designed the formal gardens with a strong Italian influence that is echoed by the Palladian-style steps leading down from the terraces.

The gallery of the piano nobile (*opposite*) forms a distinctive artery linking the principal living spaces of the house. It is one of the most striking parts of The Mount, with its vaulted ceiling and terrazzo and marble floors. Wharton used the space as a gallery to display artworks.

The drawing room (*overleaf left*) sits at the heart of the building, leading to the terrace overlooking the gardens. The largest space in the house, it was used for formal entertaining and is lifted by plasterwork, natural light and calming colours. Intended for formal entertaining, it conveys a sense of drama with two wall-mounted 18th-century Belgian tapestries. The library (*overleaf right*) was designed in the French style, with recessed bookshelves.

In the dining room (*opposite far left*), paintings were integrated into the walls; the plaster work was designed by Ogden Codman, Jr, inspired by the work of 17th-century English decorative artist Grinling Gibbons. A first edition of Codman and Wharton's book *The Decoration of Houses* is displayed on the desk in the library (*opposite below right*). Upstairs, Wharton's private sitting room (*right*) sits alongside her bedroom, painted in its original colours with Italian floral panels set into the walls. Wharton completed *The House of Mirth* and *Ethan Frome* in this room.

Eliel Saarinen

Hvitträsk / Kirkkonummi, Finland, 1903

A spirit of optimism permeates the stonework and timbers of Hvitträsk. This extraordinary lakeside building, with its fairytale castle quality, was the home of Finnish designer and architect Eliel Saarinen for many years, as well as a childhood home for his son Eero, who became one of 20th-century America's most famous architects.

The house started as a kind of cooperative, bought and built in association with Saarinen's business partners, Herman Gesellius (1874–1916) and Armas Lindgren (1874–1929). In the early 1900s, Gesellius, Lindgren & Saarinen enjoyed a period of rapid success after winning a commission for the Finnish Pavilion at the 1900 World Fair in Paris. The Pavilion brought the young practice great acclaim and led to a series of major commissions, including the Helsinki railway station.

At the height of the practice's success in 1901, the three partners bought a parcel of land in a picturesque hillside location by the edge of Lake Vitträsk. Here, they designed a building that the three of them and their families could share, with enough space for offices and studios. The house was designed with an original combination of Arts and Crafts thinking, Finnish National Romantic style and Art Nouveau (Jugendstil) flourishes. The exteriors have a medieval quality, as though the house had stood here for centuries, yet the interiors form an assembly of highly individual, forward-looking rooms with an emphasis on craftsmanship, natural materials and detailing.

At the heart of the house was a large, open living room, with high timber ceilings and wooden floors, recalling a medieval great hall, while a dramatic drum-shaped fireplace sits to one side. Bespoke textiles and rugs also add warmth to the interiors. Saarinen's dining room, adjoining another living space with window seating, was inspired by ecclesiastical architecture with its vaulted ceilings. The dining area forms a more intimate evening space, lifted by ornately patterned walls and ceilings, and stained-glass windows. Saarinen designed many pieces of furniture specifically for the house, including the White Chair, which is still manufactured today.

The bedrooms, in contrast, are lighter and more feminine spaces, with many pieces of painted furniture made by Saarinen, including bedroom dressing tables, chairs and washstands. Splashes of yellows and greens integrate smoothly with the white furniture and ceilings. The airy, Scandinavian quality of these rooms contrasts not only with some of the grander living areas in the house, but also with the imposing, monastic feel of the exterior architecture.

The building itself, the practice and the three families went through many changes in a short number of years after the completion of the house. Lindgren left the practice, and the house, in 1905. Gesellius fell seriously ill in 1912 and died four years later. Hvitträsk became a summer residence for Saarinen and his wife, Loja (Gesellius's sister), and their children, while the north wing had to be rebuilt after a fire. The studio was converted into one long, large space for Saarinen after 1916, illuminated by a vast skylight.

In the 1920s, the Saarinen family moved to Cranbrook in the United States, although they continued to keep Hvitträsk, and spent the summers there, until 1949, when the house was sold to the Vuorio family (it was later opened to the public). The Saarinen House at Cranbrook can be seen as an evolution of Eliel Saarinen's thinking, with a lighter, more international and Art Deco-led approach to the interiors. Yet the two homes share a strong emphasis on craftsmanship and attention to detail while creating an atmosphere of enchantment through design.

Biography
Eliel Saarinen (1873–1950)

Finnish-born architect and designer Eliel Saarinen studied fine art, drawing and architecture in Helsinki. Together with Herman Gesellius and Armas Lindgren, Saarinen designed a series of major buildings in and around Helsinki, including the Helsinki railway station (1906) and the Finnish National Museum (1910) and also worked in furniture design. In the early 1920s he moved to the United States with his wife, Loja, and their children, and founded the Cranbrook Academy of Art, where he became president in 1932. One of his most famous buildings is the Saarinen House at Cranbrook (1930). In later years he collaborated with his son Eero Saarinen (1910–1961) and designed a series of church buildings.

The exteriors of the house (*above* and *left*) have an unusual, magical quality about them. The dining room (*opposite*) is vaulted, with a fireplace to one side. Textiles flow from the fitted sofas to the wooden floor and the dining area itself is positioned within a more intimate recess with a lower ceiling, decorated with brightly patterned ceramic tiles.

In the dining alcove (*opposite*), the dining chairs were specially designed for the space by Eliel Saarinen. The living room (*above*) has the generous proportions of a medieval great hall, with a cylindrical fireplace to one side coated in ceramic tiles, and tapestries flowing from the wall to the bench and to the floor in one fluid motion. Saarinen designed the textiles as well as various pieces of furniture. The bedroom and children's rooms, including Pipsan and Eero Saarinen's former playroom (*below*), were designed with a much lighter, more feminine approach, incorporating many bespoke pieces of furniture by Saarinen.

Louis Sorel + Tony Selmersheim

Villa Demoiselle / Rheims, France, 1908

From the beginning, Villa Demoiselle was the achievement of not just one man but a collective of like-minded specialists who shared an ambition to create something unique. The master of the project was architect Louis Sorel, who designed an innovative home with views across the city of Rheims that combined new construction techniques, Art Deco ideas and interiors infused with the more romantic spirit of Art Nouveau. Sorel collaborated with interior designer Tony Selmersheim and a carefully assembled team of gifted artisans.

The villa was commissioned in the 1900s by Henry Vesnier, the head of the Maison Pommery champagne house. Vesnier was a man of culture, who liked to keep up with new movements in art and architecture. He collected works by Corot and donated a number of his pictures to the Musée des Beaux Arts in Rheims. He also followed the work of members of 'L'Art dans tout', a loose collective of designers and architects who believed in the power of art to enrich lives and buildings on a broad scale. The collective included Henri Sauvage, Selmersheim and Sorel, to whom Vesnier turned when he decided to build an up-to-the-minute home opposite the gates of Domaine Pommery.

Sorel designed a villa that combined Art Deco elements and spatial generosity with new engineering. The frame of the house was built in concrete and metal, creating a very robust structure that was able to withstand the bombardments that shook the region in World War I. The frame was coated in brick and stone over the seven levels of the building, which included two attic storeys, a basement and a sub-basement. At the heart of the house were three floors of richly designed living space, united by a sculpted wooden staircase.

While the exterior of the villa is more reminiscent of the Art Deco period, the interiors have a more organic, Art Nouveau quality, filled with decorative references to the natural world. Selmersheim designed ornate bespoke pieces in sculpted timber, such as the stairs and the combined slipper chair and display cabinets on the landing, while Auguste Labouret created internal stained-glass windows and door panels that are one of the highlights of the house. These windows are reminiscent of translucent peacock feathers, infused with subtle greens and lavender tones.

For the generous hallway Félix Aubert created a sequence of floral patterns for the walls and ceilings, including a vine and grape motif and lattices of curling leaves. Ceiling lights and sconces are bespoke sculptures in themselves. The interiors are rich in natural light, while Sorel's floor plan offered contrasts between large, open rooms such as the main salon, the Salon d'Apparat, and the more intimate retreats such as the Salon Padouk and the Salon Cordue. The result, despite the involvement of many different eyes, was cohesive and harmonious, tied together by common colours such as pale greens and yellows for walls and fabrics that helped to lift the more imposing character of the woodwork.

In the 1930s, the house was dubbed the Villa Cochet, after Louis Cochet, a later director general of Pommery. It was used by Maison Pommery until the 1970s, when it started to disintegrate. Fortunately, conservation planners at Bâtiments de France listed the central staircase as a structure of historical importance, which stopped the house being demolished or radically converted. However, squatters moved into the building and by the turn of the century the house was a shadow of its former self.

In 2004, the house was acquired by another champagne manufacturer, Paul-François Vranken, president of Vranken Champagne and chairman and chief executive of Vranken-Pommery Monopole. With his wife, Nathalie, he led a comprehensive restoration programme, and the house is now open to the public.

Biographies

Louis Sorel (1867–1933)

Sorel studied under architect Joseph Vaudemer. In 1897, he joined the group L'Art dans tout, which had been founded two years earlier and emphasized the importance of art, decoration and craftsmanship within architecture and interior design. It counted Henri Sauvage and Alexandre Charpentier among its members. Sorel worked closely with Selmersheim and designed a number of villas and small chateaux, mostly in Paris, Trouville and Neuilly-sur-Seine. Sorel's buildings are characterized by Art Deco detailing, original motifs and generously proportioned rooms.

Tony Selmersheim (1871–1971)

The son of an architect, Selmersheim was immersed in the world of design from an early age. He studied in Paris at the École des Arts Décoratifs and at the École Guérin under Eugène Grasset. The breadth of his training gave Selmersheim an understanding of materials and craftsmanship, as well as of the importance of decoration and design. Selmersheim was the founder of the L'Art dans tout group.

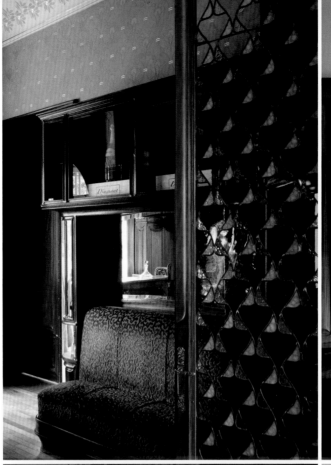

The delicate peacock-feather stained-glass windows by Auguste Labouret in the entrance hallway (*previous pages*) were carefully restored by master craftsmen with fragments of the original glass, using period black-and-white photographs for reference. The painted floral motifs by Félix Aubert that decorate the walls were also restored.

In the Salon d'Apparat (*opposite*), the floral paintwork and soft colour tones lend the room a feminine quality, which is enhanced by the lilac seating; the chandelier is a contemporary addition by Philippe Starck. The dining room (*below left*) is given a distinctive character by wall panels of yellow marble underneath an abstract fruit- and leaf-pattern wallpaper. The curtains feature a distinctive iris pattern originally designed by Edward Colonna. The bed in the Chambre de Madame (*below right*) is by Tony Selmersheim, and the chairs by the fireplace in the Salon Cordue (*above right*) are by Louis Majorelle.

Duncan Grant + Vanessa Bell

Charleston / Firle, East Sussex, UK, 1916

It was Virginia Woolf who first discovered this farmhouse at Charleston, not far from the small, picturesque village of Firle in Sussex. In 1916, she encouraged her sister, the painter Vanessa Bell, to rent the house, describing it to her as 'delightful'.

'It has a charming garden, with a pond, and fruit trees, and vegetables, all now rather run wild, but you could make it lovely,' Woolf told her. 'The house is very nice, with large rooms, and one room with big windows fit for a studio. At present it is used apparently as a weekend place, by a couple who keep innumerable animals, and most of the rooms are used by animals only….'[1]

Bell and her companion, fellow painter Duncan Grant, were looking for an escape from London as World War I raged on. Grant was a conscientious objector and could only avoid prison by working the land as a farm labourer, so Charleston offered the perfect solution for him. This was tolerated by Bell's husband, Clive (the Bells had an open marriage), and Grant's lover, David Garnett.

The relationships of the Bloomsbury set were notoriously unconventional and so too, in its own way, was Charleston, which became a country outpost for the group, with Virginia Woolf and her husband just four miles away in their own country home. Bell and Grant took Charleston on a lease, which was later renewed, and set about transforming the farmhouse, parts of which date back to the Elizabethan period, with 18th-century additions.

'It's most lovely, very solid and simple,' Bell wrote to Roger Fry, founder of the Omega Workshops, 'with flat walls in that lovely mixture of brick and flint that they use about here, and perfectly flat little windows in the walls and wonderful tiled roofs….'[2]

As well as being close companions, who went on to have a daughter together to add to Vanessa's children with Clive Bell, Grant and Bell worked together as muralists and designers, contributing designs for ceramics, textiles and painted furniture to Omega. At Charleston, their imagination and talents had free rein, as the painters began to apply themselves not just to the walls of their new country home, but to kitchen cupboards, log boxes and fire surrounds, door panels and the timber boxing around the bath tubs, while their own paintings, and those of friends, graced the walls.

The purpose of particular rooms may have evolved over the years according to the changing needs of the household, but the beauty of the interiors remained constant. The room known as Clive Bell's study initially served as a sitting room, with door panels by Duncan Grant and the decoration of the fireplace and the panelling around the window by Vanessa. The dining room features a bold geometric print by Duncan Grant in yellow, grey and black applied directly to the old wallpaper.

The Garden Room was painted a few years later, with a stencilled paisley pattern on the walls by Grant and Bell, lifted by white flowers that were added

freehand. The kneeling figures painted above the fireplace are by Grant and seem to have initially supported a mirror between them. When the mirror was accidentally cracked by the heat of an oil lamp, it was replaced by a mural of a flower basket.

In 1925, Bell and Grant added a new painting studio to the house, which they shared for many years until Vanessa finally converted one of the attic rooms into a private studio. The studio, again, became a canvas in itself with murals above the fireplace and painted furniture, although this time the walls were given a simpler, more restrained treatment to provide a backdrop to the paintings.

Throughout, one is struck by the exuberant bohemian beauty of these crafted spaces, lifted further by Grant and Bell's pictures, textiles and ceramics. Now restored and open to visitors, Charleston continues to inspire a distinctly English approach to farmhouse-style interiors. Bell and Grant's work captured the attention of designers such as Laura Ashley (see page 21) and influenced the work of paint effect specialists such as Jocasta Innes. The house continues to fascinate a wide and international audience.

1 Quoted in Quentin Bell & Virginia Nicholson, *Charleston: A Bloomsbury House & Garden*, 1997.
2 Ibid.

Biographies
Duncan Grant (1885–1978)

A post-Impressionist painter and designer, Grant was born in northern Scotland. His father was an army major and Grant spent parts of his childhood in Burma and India. He studied at the Westminster School of Art and was influenced by travels in Italy and France. He was a cousin of the writer Lytton Strachey, who first introduced him to the circle of the Bloomsbury Group. He collaborated closely with Roger Fry, the founder of the Omega Workshop, which produced painted furniture, textiles and other pieces by Grant and Vanessa Bell.

Vanessa Bell (1879–1961)

Sister of Virginia Woolf, wife of critic and writer Clive Bell and companion of Duncan Grant, Bell was a painter, textile designer and muralist. Born in London, she was home educated before studying at art school and then at the Royal Academy. Her family and close friends became the core of the Bloomsbury Group – a loose affiliation of writers, critics and artists initially based in Bloomsbury in London. She contributed many designs to Omega; murals by Bell and Grant can also still be found at Berwick Church in Sussex.

The studio (*previous page*) was designed by Roger Fry and added to the house in 1925. The walls were painted in soft, muted colours as a background for the artworks, and a long working table was placed below the high window. A bust of Virginia Woolf by Stephen Tomlin sits on an Italian chest-of-drawers placed between the two doorways, flanked by portraits by Duncan Grant.

The dining room (*opposite*), with its inglenook fireplace, is enlivened by a grey and yellow stencil pattern by Duncan Grant and Quentin Bell, added in 1939. On the Venetian side table, underneath a painting by Grant, sits a collection of plates designed by Grant for Clarice Cliff. The Garden Room (*above*) features figures above the fireplace painted on to the walls by Grant, while the floral oval replaces a broken mirror that used to hang there; the curtain fabric was designed by Grant for Allan Walton Ltd. In Vanessa Bell's bedroom (*right*) and the Green Bathroom (*far right*), furniture and bath panels become surfaces for decoration.

Coco Chanel

Chanel Apartment / Paris, France, *c.* 1920

It is one of the most famous addresses in Paris: 31 rue Cambon. This is the historic headquarters of Chanel, where the third-floor apartment created by the company's founder is still preserved to this day. It is a small, intimate space of just three rooms, but it is also a meticulously designed home full of ideas, themes and motifs that held great meaning for the owner, one of the most famous and fascinating fashion designers of the 20th century.

The apartment is accessed by an Art Deco-style mirrored staircase, which famously allowed Chanel to catch a glimpse of clients and visitors on the floor below. Its spiralling form together with the refractions of the mirror glass make for a dramatic and surreal introduction to Coco Chanel's private world.

The predominant colours of the apartment and the staircase are the beige, white and black tones most associated with her fashion collections; the walls of the apartment are painted a pale gold, and the floors and ceilings are white and cream. These colours provide a neutral canvas for a more eclectic collection of screens, *objets d'art*, ornate mirrors, carved wooden animals and furniture than one might perhaps have expected from Chanel.

Most striking are the many Asian flavours in the apartment. Chanel took her interest in Oriental art further than many of her contemporaries and collected more than thirty precious Chinese Coromandel screens dating from the 17th and 18th centuries. Eight of these dark lacquered folding screens were used in the apartment alone, as room dividers or pushed flat against a wall, forming an exotic wall coating. Chanel first discovered a taste for Chinese art together with her lover, Arthur Edward ('Boy') Capel, in the years they spent together before his death in a car accident in 1919.

The camellia, a symbol of longevity, appears on the screens and throughout the apartment. Wheat stems, another popular motif, can be seen in the form of golden sheaves and as a single stem created by Salvador Dalí. Lions, too, are a repeated favourite, showcased in the form of statuettes and recalling Chanel's pride in the fortitude that she partly attributed to being born under the sign of Leo (on 19 August 1883).

The dining room and sitting room are illuminated by numerous mirrors, which add to the impression of a dream-like, theatrical space, inhabited by curious carved animals, statuary and tokens of long-lost affairs and friendships. The chandelier in the sitting room features interlocking Cs and number 5s, and the beige suede sofa has cushions that are quilted like the iconic Chanel bag.

Yet the salon represents only part of Chanel's Parisian home life. It was a place of work and business, for receiving acquaintances, clients and journalists. At night, however, she would retreat from this highly individual apartment to a hotel suite at the nearby Ritz, where she eventually died on her own in 1971.

The apartment is sophisticated and daring, and conveys something of the spirit of the age of Art Deco. Like Chanel herself, it is also highly individual and full of surprises and eccentric touches.

Biography
Coco Chanel (1883–1971)

Chanel was the founder and creative force of one of the most famous fashion labels in the world. Born in Saumur in western France, she was sent to an orphanage at the age of twelve when her mother died and her father abandoned the family. She was encouraged to learn the trade of a seamstress and by 1910 was working as a hat-maker. She opened her first boutique in Paris, followed by a store in Deauville in 1913 when she launched her first fashion collections. Five years later, Chanel established herself as a *couturière* in Paris at the rue Cambon. In addition to her own Paris apartment, she also built a villa, La Pausa, on the French Riviera together with architect Robert Streitz in 1927.

The soothing, warm backdrop of the apartment contrasts with an eclectic and exuberant assembly of Chinese screens, wooden and bronze animals, sculptures and curios (*above*). One of Coco Chanel's favourite motifs – gilded sheaves of wheat, a symbol of prosperity – appears on the base of the glass-topped table (*opposite*). The firedogs are unique pieces by the Cubist sculptor Jacques Lipchitz.

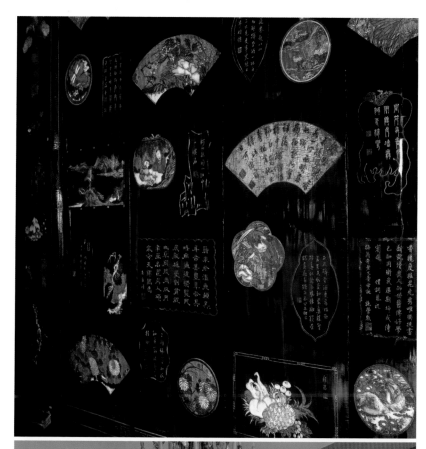

Another favourite symbol of Chanel's, the camellia, appears on one of the many Chinese lacquered screens in the apartment (*opposite*), some of which are used as a rich alternative to wallpaper when pushed against the walls, or to enclose and divide the living spaces (*right and below*).

Hollyhock House / Los Angeles, USA, 1921

Aline Barnsdall's grandfather was a true pioneer who had opened up the second oil-producing well in America and built the country's first refinery, making a family fortune. After studying drama in Europe, Barnsdall became involved in the theatre scene in Chicago and decided to build a new theatre. In 1915, she approached Frank Lloyd Wright, whose reputation was already well established at the time with projects in America and Japan, where he was building the Imperial Hotel in Tokyo.

It seems that Barnsdall was somewhat impetuous as well as unconventional, and her plans shifted and evolved constantly. Just a year later she decided to move to California and began planning a theatre in Los Angeles, where the Hollywood motion picture industry was blazing with excitement and growing at an extraordinary rate.

Barnsdall bought a 15-hectare (36-acre) parcel of land in East Hollywood, between Sunset Boulevard and Hollywood Boulevard, now known as Barnsdall Park, also dubbed Olive Hill for its olive plantation interspersed with hollyhocks and greenery. Here Barnsdall decided to commission an entire complex devoted to theatre and the arts. Wright called it a 'little principality'. There would be the theatre itself, of course, but also a restaurant, residences for staff and visiting actors, public gardens and, at the centre of the site, perched on its highest point, there would be her own home, named Hollyhock House after her favourite flower.

As Wright and his client laboured on plans for the theatre, Hollyhock House emerged as the first element of the vision to come together. Searching for a form of expression that would suit the site, the scale of Barnsdall's ambition and the character of California, Wright designed a building that was elemental, monumental and theatrical. 'Miss Barnsdall wanted no ordinary home,'[1] he said. Dominating Olive Hill, with a series of roof gardens for savouring the views of the city and the ocean, the house has the powerful appearance of a temple, drawing on Mayan and pre-Columbian influences. The structure is made of timber and stucco, but faced with blocks of cast stone – an early form of moulded concrete – with abstract hollyhock motifs.

The house aims to connect interior and exterior spaces where possible, yet it is partly turned in on itself, with sections of the building – much of it single storey, with roof terraces built above – looking in on a soothing central courtyard. Among the interior spaces the most striking is the large sitting room arranged around an extraordinary fireplace to Wright's design. A great cast-stone surround features an abstract design showing what some suggest is Barnsdall herself as an Indian princess looking out across the prairie. A water pool borders the fireplace, echoing the pools around the house, and the space is top-lit by a skylight, bringing together the elements of light, fire, water and stone.

Among the many pieces of bespoke furniture designed for the house by Wright are two vast timber-based couches, facing the fireplace at angles of forty-five degrees and anchored by vast torchieres. Despite the Mayan inspiration and the monumentality of the house, the internal spaces have the openness, light and organic craftsmanship that is associated with Wright, while at one end of the living room a pair of wall-mounted screens introduce an Oriental element, inspired by Wright's time in Japan.

Barnsdall soon grew impatient with the plans for Olive Hill. The theatre that Wright designed was never built, and just a few years later Barnsdall donated the park and its three completed buildings, including Hollyhock House, to the city of Los Angeles. The house, having been used for various purposes, is now open to the public.

The monumentalism of the design of Hollyhock, with its use of patterned cast-stone blocks, can also be seen in other Californian homes completed by Wright in the following years: the Alice Millard House in Pasadena (1924) and the Charles Ennis House (1924). They have a unique beauty, splicing past and future, but are still a world away from the organic, natural contextuality of Fallingwater.

1 Quoted in Neil Levine, *The Architecture of Frank Lloyd Wright*, 1996.

Biography
Frank Lloyd Wright (1867–1959)

One of the most influential and original architects of the 20th century, Wright designed some of America's most beloved buildings, including the Solomon R. Guggenheim Museum in New York (1959) and Fallingwater in rural Pennsylvania (1939). He studied engineering at the University of Wisconsin before moving to Chicago, where he worked at Louis Sullivan's practice, Adler & Sullivan. By the age of twenty-six, he had started his own practice, developing the Prairie Style in a series of Chicago houses and culminating in the Robie House. While drawing on the Arts and Crafts tradition and aspects of Japanese architecture, Wright was also one of the great architectural experimentalists, pioneering a uniquely American approach and embracing modern materials and technology in crafted buildings in tune with the landscape.

The sitting room fireplace (*opposite*) is a key element and focal point of the house, with bespoke furniture arranged around it. The abstract composition in cast concrete at the centre represents an Indian princess surveying a sculpted landscape and forms an integrated artwork with a pool of water at the base of the hearth.

Like many other elements in the house, from door handles to abstract hollyhock motifs cast in concrete blocks (*opposite below left*), the dining room (*opposite above*) was a unique creation, with high-backed dining chairs specially designed by Frank Lloyd Wright. The Japanese landscape screens in the living room (*right*) introduce a natural element that complements the organic tones of the timber work.

Wharton Esherick

Esherick House + Studio / Paoli, Pennysylvania, USA, 1926

There is a certain fairytale quality to Wharton Esherick's house and studio. Nestling in the woods, it is a magical building that appears as though it has grown out of the hillside itself, forming a sculpted, organic handcrafted cabin. Walking through the interiors feels like exploring the belly of some great and rare beast, with Esherick's sculpted timbers becoming its spines and bones, twisting this way and that. It is one of those houses that feels completely original – the product of a powerful and individual imagination.

Drawing on a small inheritance, Esherick first moved to a stone farmhouse nearby in 1913 with his wife, Letty. The house stood on 2 hectares (5 acres) and there Esherick painted and also farmed the land. The studio itself was begun in 1926 and, like Esherick's career, went through a number of distinct phases.

It began as a modest painting and sculpture studio, with stone and timber used in a similar way to a local barn building, but it began to evolve and grow, with Esherick adding a bedroom above the studio and later another one for his son, Peter, as well as a kitchen and dining room. In the 1960s, the living space was extended again with an adjoining silo-like addition complete with a suspended deck. Esherick's friend, architect Louis Kahn, also designed a workshop a few steps away, which eased the pressure on the multi-purpose house and studio.

Although much respected as an artist and designer, Esherick continued to struggle financially and the growing studio building gave him enough space to rent out the farmhouse while Letty and his daughters were performing with the repertory company of the Hedgerow Theatre.

The growing volumes of space allowed room for Esherick's own furniture and sculptures, with larger pieces displayed in a sunken sculpture pit, created when he found termites and had to dig down to reinforce the foundations. The furniture in the house clearly shows Esherick's interest shifting from Arts and Crafts to a more angular Expressionist-influenced style and then to highly organic freeform work.

The expanding house and studio gave Esherick free rein to express his ingenuity and craftsmanship within tailored spaces. As much as possible, Esherick used local timber from the woods around him, making use of even the smallest offcuts to carve light pulls or coat pegs in the entry hall. 'I always say that if I can't make something beautiful out of what I find in my back yard, I had better not make anything,' he said.

The form of the Esherick House and Studio evolved over decades as the artist and craftsman added to it piece by piece (*left*). The dining area alongside the kitchen (*opposite*) was added in 1940 and forms a warm, handcrafted space, with a small balcony that was added in 1965. Esherick used a medley of locally sourced timber to make everything from lampshades to handrails and salad bowls. The oak dining table dates from 1967.

Esherick stressed that his furniture should be functional as well as beautiful, with pieces as simple as a wooden spoon stamped with the maker's initials becoming working pieces of art. Also striking is the endearing attention to detail evident in the handmade door latches, in the way a timber stair rail morphs into a sinuous shelf support and in the bespoke creations made out of carved wood for air vent covers, lampshades and electric plug surrounds.

This 'Hansel and Gretel' dream house is a true delight and full of stories. It is also the most complete expression of Esherick's influential vision, which continues to inspire people today. As we rediscover the value of handmade design using natural materials, Esherick still stands out as the 'dean of American craftsmen'.

Biography
Wharton Esherick (1887–1970)

Painter, sculptor, set designer, furniture maker and interior designer, Esherick was one of the great original voices of mid-century American craft. He was born in Philadelphia and studied at the Pennsylvania Museum School of Industrial Arts and the Pennsylvania Academy of Fine Arts. He began wood carving with handcrafted frames for his own paintings and then moved into woodcuts, producing engraved book illustrations and prints. By the early 1920s, he was sculpting in wood and soon turned to furniture making. He was also commissioned to produce interiors, most notably for the Curtis Bok House in Gulph Mills (1937) and the crafted kitchen of the Louis Kahn-designed Esherick House (1961), which was commissioned by his niece.

The main studio space (*previous pages*) includes a desk made by Esherick in walnut and padauk wood in 1929 with a replacement top from 1962; the matching desk chair is also dated 1929. The drop-leaf bureau by the wall is an important early piece crafted in red oak, made between 1925 and 1927, showing the more decorative approach of Esherick's earlier work.

Throughout the house, a considerable attention to handcrafted detail is evident, from the winding stairways (*left*) to the space-saving copper sink in the bathroom (*below right*).

The bedroom/sitting room at the top of the house has a trap door. The upholstered sofa in pine and mahogany dates from 1936 and was originally made for a client.

Frank Lloyd Wright, Jr

Sowden House / Los Angeles, USA, 1926

In the 1920s Frank Lloyd Wright, Jr, helped oversee the construction of a number of his father's Californian masterpieces. It began with the Hollyhock House (see page 50), where Lloyd Wright worked with his father's assistant, Rudoph Schindler, while Frank Lloyd Wright was in Japan creating the Imperial Hotel. The Hollyhock House was the first in a series of houses that drew inspiration from Mayan and pre-Columbian ideas, becoming a 20th-century 'temple' faced with cast-concrete blocks covered with abstract motifs.

Hollyhock was followed by a sequence of four 'textile block' houses in Los Angeles, including the Charles Ennis House (1924), that used similarly monumental, ornamented concrete jigsaw pieces and with which Lloyd Wright was intimately involved. They were followed a few years later by one of his own commissions and the most famous project, the Sowden House.

Commissioned by retired painter and Hollywood photographer John Sowden and his wife Ruth, the house was designed to provide an indulgent setting suited to entertaining. Lloyd Wright drew on the experience he had gained with Hollyhock and the 'textile block' houses to create his own interpretation of an exotic, dream-like theatre of light, drama and rich textures.

Reinforced cast-concrete blocks shaped into organic, petal-like patterns form much of the house. From the street, the façade appears as a mysterious, sculpted object with the patterned blocks framing a glowing mouth of a window in pyramid formation (locals later re-christened the building the 'Jaws House'). The cave-like entrance to the building sits below this epic window, with a series of steps leading to an ornate copper door.

The living spaces are arranged around a leafy courtyard at the core of the building. This allowed Lloyd Wright to introduce a rich quality of light and explore the links between inside and outside living that fascinated him, and to create a contrast between the heavy, imposing mass of the concrete structure and the airy openness of this centre point.

A series of signature motifs provide drama to the interiors. Door and window panels make use of a repeated star design with echoes of Islamic patterns, while windows and skylights feature strongly geometric grids. Specially designed furniture showed a significant Art Deco influence, particularly apparent in the original master bedroom, where walls and furniture incorporate a repeated honeycomb pattern.

In recent years, the house has been restored and updated by designer Xorin Balbes, who has introduced a swimming pool to the courtyard and combined a number of service spaces within a more contemporary kitchen and dining area. What remains intact is the sense of high drama that the house encapsulates, which was exploited as a backdrop in Martin Scorsese's film *The Aviator*, about the life of Howard Hughes.

Lloyd Wright never managed to step out from his father's shadow completely, but he came closest with the Sowden House. His father praised the innovative use of moulded concrete, which was high praise indeed, and the house remains a monument to the golden days of Hollywood.

Biography
Frank Lloyd Wright, Jr (1890–1978)

The son of one of the most masterly and original architects of the 20th century, Frank Lloyd Wright, Jr, was born in Illinois. He studied at the University of Wisconsin and then worked with a landscape architecture practice in Boston. He moved to California in 1913 and worked as a production designer for Paramount Studios before turning to landscape design for the 1915 San Diego World's Fair. After collaborating on some of his father's Californian projects in the 1920s, Lloyd Wright designed and built a number of houses in his own right. Other projects included the Hollywood Bowl amphitheatre (1927–1928), the Institute of Mentalphysics (1957) in Joshua Tree, California, and the Wayfarers Chapel, or Glass Church, on the Palos Verdes Peninsula (1951).

Signature patterns and motifs by Lloyd Wright, Jr, appear throughout the Sowden House, which is arranged around a central courtyard. Patterns include crafted concrete blocks inside and outside (*above left and below right*), and a Moorish star motif on wooden panels and doors (*above right and below left*). Although the house is relatively modest in scale, the design and decor lend the space a fortress-like quality.

The distinctive furniture that Lloyd Wright and Sowden originally designed for the house has long disappeared, but the living spaces retain their original sense of drama, drawing light from both sides and using cast concrete to frame an intimate seating area around the fireplace (*above*). The sofa design was inspired by Lloyd Wright and the peacock chairs are bespoke. The updated bathroom (*opposite*) features a skylight of concentric circles – a motif picked up in the design of the floors – complemented by a glamorous contemporary bathtub from Diamond Spas.

Cedric Gibbons

Dolores del Río House / Los Angeles, USA, 1931

They were one of the great Hollywood couples: legendary film set designer and head of the art department at MGM, Cedric Gibbons and Dolores del Río, the sultry and seductive movie star, who was born in Mexico and took America by storm, appearing in a string of 1920s Hollywood gems, including *The Trail of '98* (1928), *Ramona* (1928) and *Evangeline* (1929). She and Gibbons married when she was at the height of her fame, having met at a party hosted by William Hearst. The couple socialized with film titans such as Greta Garbo, Errol Flynn and Marlene Dietrich.

Gibbons helped define the look of countless Hollywood films throughout the pre-war era and, by extension, influenced the Art Deco glamour of American movie theatres. He was one of the few Hollywood designers to visit the 1925 Exposition des Arts Décoratifs et Industriels Modernes (from which Art Deco took its name), and was as entranced by the Moderne style as he was by the charms of Del Río.

When it came to designing a house for Del Río and himself, Gibbons naturally took the project in hand, working alongside architect Douglas Honnold (1901–1974). The resulting building was sleek, crisp, theatrical and up to the minute, and it embraced fresh, new materials such as chrome, Bakelite and linoleum. The architecture had few of the sinuous, liner-style curves one might associate with Art Deco (Moderne) buildings; this was a more masculine design with plenty of right angles as well as lots of glass and big, open living spaces with integrated lighting schemes.

The street façade of the house is relatively closed, with the house opening up to the gardens and pool at the rear and the views of Santa Monica and the ocean beyond, with a series of elevated terraces and balconies gracing the upper level. The main living room of the three-bedroom house is also on the higher storey, taking advantage of the views and accessed by a chrome and terrazzo staircase positioned so that Del Río could make a grand entrance.

This central living space is characterized by a strong emphasis on layers of rigid horizontal lines and generous windows, with a central Art Deco-style fireplace topped by a large fitted mirror, one of many in the house. Other integrated, bespoke elements include the built-in banquette at the bottom of the stairs and a sumptuous fitted dressing room for Del Río. Among the theatrical flourishes is a ladder and trap door that linked

Gibbons's bedroom on the ground floor to Del Río's bedroom above.

By 1940, the union was starting to break down, and Del Río began a scandalous and intense affair with Orson Welles. She and Gibbons divorced a year later, and each went on to further success in their own right.

The house itself has stood the test of time and has been well cared for. In 2007, the interiors were carefully restored and updated by interior designer Michael S. Smith (see page 302), who also introduced a number of suitable pieces of furniture from the 1930s, as well as his own designs. The Dolores del Río House remains an extraordinary homage to an age of indulgence, beauty and glamour. It is a house of powerful drama that was immersed in Hollywood's golden age.

Biography
Cedric Gibbons (1893–1960)

One of the most influential Hollywood art directors of the 20th century, Gibbons was responsible for the sophisticated, glamorous look of countless Hollywood films from the 1930s and 40s. He was also responsible for the design of the iconic Art Deco-style 'Oscar' statuette for the Academy Awards. Born in Ireland to an architect father, he went to study in New York before moving into set design. Gibbons signed up with MGM and headed their art department from the 1920s until 1956, and also art directed around 150 films, including *Dynamite* (1929), *The Wizard of Oz* (1939), *National Velvet* (1944) and *Julius Caesar* (1953). He was a founding member of the Academy of Motion Picture Arts and Sciences and won eleven Academy Awards himself for his film work.

Gleaming surfaces, crisp walls and sinuous curves characterize the interiors of the house (*above and opposite*). The bespoke staircase was a key element of the design, allowing the actress to make a great entrance. Michael S. Smith restored fitted elements such as the sofa at the bottom of the stairs and sourced sympathetic furniture designs by Paul Frankl and others together with his client.

The main living room on the upper level (*above and opposite*) is a generous space for entertaining with a stepped ceiling and a mirror above the fireplace. Smith retained and restored the fitted banquettes, and the table in front is by Donald Deskey. The dining room (*below*) features an Art Deco-style rug by Keshishian.

Brinkman + Van der Vlugt

Sonneveld House / Rotterdam, The Netherlands, 1933

The world of avant-garde modernist architecture is not often seen as a colourful one. Yet colour did make its way into many pioneering buildings of the 1930s, including the Sonneveld House in Rotterdam, which is lifted by a sophisticated use of texture and tone, as well as advanced engineering, imaginative, luxurious touches and high-tech gadgets.

The master bathroom is a generous composition of vibrant turquoise tiles, including a shower with ten separate water jets. The kitchen is well appointed and functional, and lifted by a chess-board tiled floor, red doors and patterned hand-printed curtains in red, white and grey. In the studio, a built-in sofa in a vibrant blue is juxtaposed with fitted cupboards in a creamy yellow. The warmth of the interiors is in contrast with the crisp, white exteriors of the three-storey house, which echoes the sleek form of ocean liners, complete with elevated balconies in the place of decks, and topped with a roof garden.

The house was commissioned by Albertus Sonneveld and his wife, Gésine, who had two daughters known as Puck and Gé. Sonneveld was the deputy managing director of the Van Nelle company and worked in the tobacco division. As part of his job, Sonneveld often took the great ocean liners of the day to travel to America to inspect tobacco shipments, staying in smart hotels and acquiring a taste for luxury and modern design.

The family asked architect Van der Vlugt to design a bespoke house on a leafy plot of land devoted to a new development of villas on the edge of Land van Hoboken. Van der Vlugt and his partners had developed the Van Nelle Factory and a house for a company colleague (Van der Leeuw House, 1929) around the same time, so architect and client were already familiar with each other, and the concrete- and steel-framed building was designed according to the needs of the Sonnevelds.

The ground floor was dedicated to a large entrance hall, bedrooms and a bathroom for two servants and a flexible studio for Puck and Gé. The middle floor was essentially one large open-plan space, illuminated by a 17-metre (56-foot) stretch of windows overlooking the garden. This living area included a lounge, complete with a Steinway piano, a library and a dining room. A sliding leatherette wall could be used to separate the library and lounge, while curtains could section off the dining area, creating easy options for how the space could be used. A kitchen and pantry are set apart, while bedrooms and two bathrooms are located on the top floor of the house.

The Sonnevelds were content to commission new furniture and fittings by Van der Vlugt and others, bringing with them only a few personal possessions from their old home. Many pieces are fitted and bespoke, including the dining table, which features a secret bell for calling the servants. Many of the tubular steel chairs, tables and beds, as well as much of the lighting, were designed by Willem Hendrik Gispen (1890–1981) or chosen from the Gispen company catalogues.

The fabrics for curtains and upholstery were ordered from Metz & Co. department store – which worked closely with the artist Bart van der Leck on their colour range – as were the rugs, which were mostly made in Morocco. Linoleum in a variety of tones was also used in the more utilitarian parts of the house. Colour choices for doors, cupboards and walls were gently tied in with the Metz & Co. palette.

The Sonneveld House, which is now open to the public, conforms to the principles advanced by Dutch modernism (known as Nieuwe Bouwen) as well as the ideas proposed by Le Corbusier. It is also one of the warmest and most seductive houses of the 1930s, with thoughtful and considered interiors that formed a tailored home for the Sonneveld family but were also innovative, flexible and suffused with luxury.

Biography
Leendert Cornelis van der Vlugt (1894–1936)

Born in Rotterdam, Van der Vlugt studied architecture at the Academy of Arts and Technical Sciences. In 1920 he joined the office of architect Michiel Brinkman. After Brinkman's death, his son Johannes Brinkman (1902–1949) took charge of the firm and asked Van der Vlugt to become a partner. They were the creative force behind buildings such as the Van Nelle Factory (1931) and the Feyenoord Stadium (1937), both in Rotterdam. With designer W. H. Gispen and others Van der Vlugt founded the *Opbouw* magazine, promoting modernist architecture and design. He died at a young age.

Crisp and white on the outside, the Sonneveld House is a warm and bright space on the inside. The library (*opposite*) can be separated by a leatherette curtain. The red chairs by the fireplace are replicas of an original in a fabric designed by artist Bart van der Leck.

The kitchen (*opposite*) is warm as well as functional, characterized by its red floor tiles, radiators, dining chairs and geometric curtains by Metz & Co. designed by Elise Djo-Bourgeois. It was fitted with one of ten telephones installed throughout the house. The servants would have eaten their meals at the small table in the alcove at the far end of the room.

Different rooms are marked by a colour-led approach. The dining room (*above left*) includes a yellow carpet, blue curtains and touches of red all put together by Bart van der Leck. Shades of green and aquamarine blue define the dressing room (*above right*) and the luxurious bathroom (*below left*), while the master bedroom (*below right*) includes yellow and golden tones in the curving back wall behind the bed. The bedroom also featured an inbuilt radio and bell for calling servants.

Hans Scharoun

Haus Schminke / Löbau, Germany, 1933

With all the energy, imagination and hope invested in Haus Schminke, one might think that Fritz Schminke and his family deserved more than just six years of peaceful living in their dream home. The house is one of the greatest examples of the modernist style in Germany, a rare gem designed by architect Hans Scharoun that was lifted far above the ordinary by a powerful sense of dynamism and originality.

It was the result of an extraordinary collaboration between architect and patron, and completely suited to the way that the Schminke family wanted to live. They had long dreamed of building a house on the green edge of Löbau, a town east of Dresden, not far from the Czech and Polish borders. The family owned the pasta factory Loeser & Richter, and by the early 1930s, after the arrival of their four children, Fritz and Charlotte Schminke turned to Hans Scharoun to turn the dream into reality. They were soon seduced by his ideas.

The Schminkes asked for 'a modern house for two parents, four children and one or two occasional guests.'[1] They wanted the house to connect to the garden and draw in natural light and asked for a building that would be simple to maintain. Beyond this Scharoun was free to make design decisions.

The architect was a great believer in working from the inside outwards, creating spaces that were highly tailored to his clients' needs, but he also stressed the importance of context. Ultimately, Scharoun pushed the house into the sloping site at an angle, so that the elongated structure thrusts outwards like the bow of a ship and into the garden, with the main living room, adjoining solarium and curved deck-like terraces making the most of the views across the countryside.

Haus Schminke was subsequently dubbed the 'pasta steamboat', with its white, sleek form reminiscent of the great ocean liners that Scharoun would see as a child leaving port for New York from his home town of Bremerhaven. Although highly intellectual in style, the maritime elements suggest a certain playfulness, with porthole windows in the playroom and miniature bull's-eye windows with crimson glass punctuating the door to the terrace.

Throughout the house one senses a vibrant ingenuity, with a considered approach to practicality, flexibility and ergonomics. On the ground floor, the services, a hard-working Frankfurt Kitchen and maid's quarters were positioned to the rear of the house. To one side of the hallway was the playroom, which could be separated off with a sliding curtain, while four colour-coded storage lockers were designed for the children.

Sliding doors also allowed the main living room at the heart of the house to be lightly separated from both the hallway and a large conservatory that led out on to the lower terrace. To one side of the conservatory Scharoun designed an internal winter garden, complete with a miniature pond, to indulge Charlotte Schminke. 'One is exposed to nature and its elements, but is not at their mercy',[2] he said.

Upstairs, the children's bedrooms were conceived as functional spaces, with storage provided by a long stretch of cupboards lining the outside landing. The parents' bedroom was more generously designed to serve also as a second sitting room connected with the first-floor terrace.

Completed in 1933, Haus Schminke was one of Scharoun's favourite buildings as well as one of his finest, but the house itself was requisitioned by the Russian Red Army in 1945 and later confiscated. It served as a youth club for decades until full ownership was finally passed to the city of Löbau. In the late 1990s, Haus Schminke was carefully restored with the help of Scharoun's archives, and opened to the public.

1 Quoted from the Haus Schminke website, www.stiftung-hausschminke.eu
2 Ibid.

Biography
Hans Scharoun (1893–1972)

Born in Bremen, Scharoun studied at the Technical University of Berlin before serving in World War I. Over the following years he taught at the Breslau Academy for Arts and Crafts, joined the Glass Chain and Der Ring groups, and worked on a number of residential and housing projects. Unlike many of his colleagues, Scharoun stayed in Germany during the 1930s and World War II. His work was reduced under the Nazi regime, which led him to focus on reconstruction projects. Scharoun continued to teach in Berlin after the war and was finally able to undertake projects on a larger scale, such as the Berlin Philharmonic Concert Hall (1963) and the German Embassy in Brasília (1969). A number of key buildings, such as the German Maritime Museum in his home town of Bremerhaven (1975), were completed after his death.

A key aspect of Scharoun's design for the ship-like house was the strong sense of connection between the interiors and gardens, with the 'bow' of the ship pushing out into the landscape (*above and left*). The architect also created a winter garden within the house as part of the conservatory (*opposite*), with a dramatic, bespoke lattice ceiling with integrated lighting globes.

The playroom (*left*) sits next to the entrance hall and can be lightly partitioned off with a sliding curtain. Playful elements include the porthole window, picked out in red, and the colour-coded lockers for the children. The main living room (*opposite*) is a flexible space at the centre of the house, with sliding doors that can be used to separate the room from both the entrance hall and the conservatory. Originally, the ceiling would have been yellow and the floors covered with a blue velour carpet.

The compact, ergonomic kitchen (*overleaf left*) features original elements from Margarete Schütte-Lihotzky's innovative Frankfurt Kitchen, designed in 1926. For the bedroom upstairs (*overleaf right*), Scharoun was asked to design two separate beds, one facing the terrace and the other the centre of the room.

Dorchester House / Herne Hill, London, UK, 1936

H. C. Morrell made quite an impact in the area of Herne Hill in the 1930s. He built a dramatic block of Art Deco-inspired flats, played a part in the construction of the Temple Bowling Club nearby and built houses for his mother and others. He also commissioned the 'House of Tomorrow', which was shown at the Ideal Home Show in 1935. All of these were designed by architects Kemp & Tasker, who were well known for a series of Art Deco cinemas built in the heyday of 1930s theatre design.

Their greatest collaboration was the house designed for Morrell himself, also located in Herne Hill. It was a more ambitious design than the Ideal Home Show entry, tailored to the needs of the Morrell family, and sitting in a generous plot of land close to a brick apartment block that Morrell completed around the same time.

Set among generous gardens, with a rear veranda and roof terraces, this was a lavish two-storey townhouse that also included a modest roof annex. The interiors were designed in Art Deco style with an emphasis on luxurious materials, exquisite detailing and numerous integrated, built-in elements. The marble and onyx master bathroom was a high point – extraordinary care was taken with the stonework and integrated lighting, which even included an illuminated shower head.

The fireplaces throughout the house were also beautifully conceived, with the fire surround in the master bedroom including integrated lighting that echoed the ingenuity of Kemp & Tasker's cinema designs. Most delightful of all is the entrance hall and staircase, which form a dramatic centre point to the house, with a coat room and rest room neatly tucked away on either side of the front door. The lighting, switches, door handles and banisters were all especially designed for the house, along with many pieces of bespoke furniture, including a billiard table and scoreboard in the games room.

With just two previous owners, the house still retained many period features and some of its original furniture when it was acquired by architectural designer Mike Rundell. Rundell sensitively restored and updated the house, keeping the layout largely unchanged. The original kitchen was long gone, however, so Rundell created a combined kitchen and dining area from two rooms at the rear of the house.

'It was designed as a practical and elegant family home, and I wanted to preserve it as such,' says Rundell. 'It is almost unique. There are very few intact examples of private, bespoke Art Deco design in the UK. Eltham Palace (see Bradbury/Powers, *The Iconic House*) is similar in atmosphere but considerably larger in scale, while other examples

are rare and usually heavily restored or recreated. This house is completely original.'

Rundell sourced and designed furniture and fabrics sympathetic to the interior to create a seamless blend of contemporary living and Art Deco style, which was in many ways very much ahead of its time. The house retains a sense of original daring and intelligent elegance.

Biography
Kemp & Tasker

Leslie H. Kemp and Frederick E. Tasker were best known for their series of Art Deco cinemas, mostly built in and around London in the 1930s. These included Odeon cinemas in Chadwell Heath, Greenwich and Romford, and the Ritz Cinema in Luton. Other projects included residential commissions, the Temple Bowling Club in Herne Hill and various motor car showrooms. Their entry for the Ideal Home Show in 1935 was reproduced in a number of locations in London and across the UK and Ireland.

The area of the front entrance (*opposite left*), with its tiled steps and oak front door, is complemented by the entrance hall and staircase (*right*). The parquet floors and detailing of the stairs and lobby area – which includes a coat room and closet neatly tucked away next to the front door – are part of the original design of the house. In the dining room, the rosewood table sits in front of a new set of sliding timber doorsleading to the kitchen (*opposite right*), designed in a sympathetic style by Mike Rundell.

In the sitting room (*opposite*), the fireplace, floors and mouldings all date from the 1930s. Mike Rundell designed the sofa and armchair, and the artworks include pieces by Damien Hirst and Sam Taylor-Wood. The Art Deco elements in the bedroom and onyx bathroom (*above*) are original, including the illuminated fireplace with echoes of the theatrical style seen in Kemp & Tasker's Art Deco cinemas.

Patrick Gwynne

The Homewood / Esher, Surrey, UK, 1938

For modernist architect Patrick Gwynne, designing a house was about much more than making a pure architectural statement. Gwynne was just as interested in the interiors of his houses, in addition to being a talented landscape designer, so his buildings became cohesive, all-encompassing creations with a high degree of sophistication throughout.

This was especially true of his most famous building, The Homewood, in Surrey. Although he acknowledged a debt to Le Corbusier's Villa Savoye from 1931 (see Bradbury/Powers, *The Iconic House*), The Homewood was an enticing house of warmth in its own right, devoted to a luxurious lifestyle, rather than a 'machine for living'. The interiors are sumptuous in comparison with some modernist houses, enriched by a considered use of natural materials, textured finishes and bespoke ergonomic furniture, much of it designed by Gwynne himself.

Gwynne was only in his early twenties and working in the office of Canadian-born, pioneering modernist architect Wells Coates when he started work on The Homewood. It was commissioned by his parents, who had grown frustrated by the position of their Victorian country home alongside a busy road. The persuasive Gwynne encouraged them to knock down the house and build another to his own design elsewhere on the 3.2-hectare (8-acre) estate, tailored to the needs of the family. They agreed on a quiet spot bordered by woodland, and his parents sold some land in Wales to help fund the building. Wells Coates offered advice and Gwynne's friend Denys Lasdun designed an oval pool in the grounds, yet the design was very much a 'Patrick Gwynne original' and became the passion of his life.

Rather like the Villa Savoye, the main living spaces of the house were raised on a series of pillars, with enough space underneath the house for parking. A spiral staircase marked the point where the main body of the house met an adjoining wing with six bedrooms. The living area was designed as one large, expansive space with maple floors and a dramatic sequence of floor-to-ceiling windows looking out across the trees. An elegant folding screen could be used to separate off the dining area at one end of the space, while service areas including a bespoke kitchen packed with ingenious features and the staff quarters were pushed to the back of the house.

This generous living space was softened by timber-panelled walls, with textile wall coverings used in some places, and a marble fireplace. There are touches of playfulness in details such as a

folding cocktail table swinging out neatly from a slot in the panelled walls. New technologies were seamlessly woven into the design – there are glow-in-the-dark light switches, concealed cinema screens and other innovations.

The house was completed just before World War II and was used by the family for a short time only. By the end of the war both of Gwynne's parents had died and he inherited his own creation, which served as his home until his death, when it was bequeathed to the National Trust.

The house was adapted by Gwynne at various points to suit a more informal way of life, and The Homewood accommodated these changes graciously. The interiors have been gloriously preserved, including the furniture that Gwynne designed for the house, and retain a spirit of a Scandinavian-style organic beauty spliced with progressive modernity. The Homewood proved that the English country house could be both modern and beautiful.

Biography
Patrick Gwynne (1913–2003)

Born in Porchester, Hampshire, Gwynne was the son of a naval commander who would have liked him to become an accountant. But Gwynne saw Amyas Connell's early modernist High and Over house (1930) on a school trip while at Harrow, and the experience helped steer him on a course towards architecture. He trained with architectural practice Coleridge Jennings before working with Wells Coates alongside Denys Lasdun. After the war, when he served with the RAF building airfields, Gwynne worked on a number of private houses, including residences for actors Jack Hawkins and Laurence Harvey. He also designed the Serpentine Restaurant in Hyde Park (1964) and an extension to the York Theatre Royal (1967).

The living room (*opposite above*) features many bespoke elements and pieces of furniture designed by Gwynne, including the desk and leatherette sofa at the far end of the room underneath a painting by Stefan Knapp; through the open doorway one can see the top of the spiral staircase and a mural by Peter Thompson. In the kitchen (*opposite below left*), the island and circular trolley table are one-off Gwynne designs, and the stairs (*opposite below centre*) are made of concrete with a terrazzo finish.

Lubetkin Penthouse, Highpoint II / Highgate, London, UK, 1938

The views from the terrace of Berthold Lubetkin's penthouse, perched on top of his Highpoint II tower, are among the best in London. On a clear day you can see the landmarks of London spread out before you to the borders of the city. Even from inside the 7.6-metre (25-foot) sequence of retractable windows of the living room offers an enticing vista across Hampstead Heath and beyond.

But it is the interiors of the apartment, where Lubetkin spent a significant portion of his life from 1939 until 1955, that offer the greatest delights. Under a sweeping parabolic concrete ceiling, painted a pale sky blue, the architect created a home full of surprises, layered with furniture to his own design.

Lubetkin was originally commissioned by businessman Sigmund Gestetner to design Highpoint I, which was completed in 1935. Gestetner owned a company making office equipment and had thought of creating a new kind of tower block to house his workers. Highpoint I was so ground-breaking and original in many respects – from the design and construction to the detailing and generous landscaping around the building – that Gestetner and Lubetkin in a way became victims of their own success. Faced with great demand for the sixty-four flats, Gestetner sold them not to his own workers but to a more middle-class market.

Later, Lubetkin persuaded Gestetner to buy the plot next door and they began working on Highpoint II. Over the years this morphed into a collection of just twelve apartments and maisonettes crowned by Lubetkin's own penthouse, which was added at a later stage, complete with a large roof terrace. The penthouse became a social hub for artists and other architects, including sculptor Alexander Calder and Le Corbusier, who came to visit and praised Highpoint as 'an achievement of the first rank'.

From the entrance hall the apartment opens out into a large open-plan living and dining room leading to two bedrooms and a kitchen. Light floods in from large windows to either side and through slim skylights positioned in the vaulted roof. Tiled chocolate-brown floors and built-in travertine shelves contrast with highly textured walls coated in rough-cut lengths of pine timber around the entrance hall and a more intimate corner of the room with a lower ceiling around the fireplace.

In 1997, the apartment was acquired by designer Ou Baholyodhin who collaborated with conservation specialist and Lubetkin biographer John Allan of Avanti Architects on the restoration of the penthouse. Allan reinstated bookcases along one wall, and Baholyodhin discovered that Lubetkin had coated the walls flanking the entrance to the kitchen in a collage of colourful panels that were taken from children's toy theatre scenes. The designer visited the curator of Pollock's Toy Museum, who painstakingly identified the scenes and managed to source duplicates.

Similarly, Lubetkin's original rug was remade, and Baholyodhin also went to see Lubetkin's daughter, who had inherited much of the original furniture from the apartment. She was persuaded to return the two Norwegian yew and cowhide chairs to Highpoint that Lubetkin had designed especially for the penthouse.

The penthouse retains the character seen in early images taken in the 1930s. This was not a purely functional space nor simply a modernist design statement – it was a living family home of warmth, individuality and character.

Biography
Berthold Lubetkin (1901–1990)

Born in Georgia, Lubetkin studied art in Moscow and continued his studies in Berlin and later Paris, where he worked in the studio of Auguste Perret. He moved to London in 1931 and a year later co-founded Tecton Architects. In the 1930s, Lubetkin designed a series of sculpted zoo buildings in reinforced concrete, as well as residential projects. Post-war work in social housing projects followed, but Lubetkin became bitterly disillusioned with British conservatism and retreated from architecture. Key buildings include Six Pillars in Dulwich (1935) and the Finsbury Health Centre (1938) in London, the penguin pool at London Zoo (1934), and his own country home, Bungalow A, at Whipsnade, Bedfordshire (1935).

Rustic planks of pine add warmth to the entrance area of the penthouse with its bespoke built-in bench and to the area around the fireplace (*right and opposite*). The wood and cowhide chairs by Lubetkin sit on a rug based on an original design by him. Designer Ou Baholyodhin managed to source duplicates of the original wallpaper pattern – taken from children's toy theatre scenes – for the wall by the entrance to the kitchen (*overleaf above right*). Other furniture pieces include a 1950s plywood Cherner chair by Paul Goldman and a Charles Eames fibreglass rocking chair, placed alongside a Navajo rug.

Henry Moore

Hoglands / Perry Green, Hertfordshire, UK, 1940

As well as paintings, sculpture and tribal treasures, Henry Moore liked to collect buildings. His Hertfordshire estate kept growing over time to include barns and studios, outbuildings and cottages, but the focus was always on his own house, Hoglands, which was at the heart of a small community that developed within the green and pleasant hamlet of Perry Green.

The house itself is a timber-framed medieval building that was, however, much adapted and changed over the centuries. Moore and his wife, Irina, first moved into Hoglands in 1940, after their home in London was damaged in the Blitz, and the new home soon became the nerve centre of Moore's working life as well as a family home. Over the years Moore extended his estate until it included a series of studios within 28 hectares (70 acres), while his staff were housed in cottages in the village. Hoglands itself was where Moore worked in a modest home office with his secretary, Mrs Tinsley, and where he relaxed and welcomed visitors, including Julie Andrews, the musician Mstislav Rostropovich, Lord Snowdon and W. H. Auden, as well as countless collectors and curators.

The house was extended in the late 1950s, creating enough space to hold the large sitting room that dominates the house. This became perhaps the most beloved room in the house, featuring a yellow carpet and furniture from Heal's and Clement Joscelyne. It served as a canvas for an extraordinary collection of ethnic art, mostly sourced from various London dealers, including an antelope mask from Burkina Faso and a Luba helmet mask from the Congo. There are *objets trouvés* and natural curios including a narwal horn, shells and polished stones. Added to this was a collection of Impressionist art, with paintings by Gustave Courbet and Édouard Vuillard.

This eclectic and fascinating assembly of pieces sometimes provided inspiration for Moore's own work as a sculptor and artist – it was a powerful composition that spoke of Henry and Irina Moore's talents in many areas of design and showed their passion for elements such as African art that were integrated into interior spaces by many designers in the years that followed.

'My father installed his own exhibitions, more than any artist I know of,' says Moore's daughter, Mary. 'So he and my mother knew how to place things because they did it every day. Every day they were thinking about it. Later on he did have money to buy work by artists that he was interested in, but

I wouldn't say that the sitting room was designed around art. They did things together in terms of the interiors and made modernist choices – certain colours, certain textures – even though it's a period house.'

There is a modesty to many of the other rooms in the house, such as the study and galley-style kitchen, both of which were dressed in curtain textiles to Moore's own design. Moore took an interest in textiles in the 1940s, although this was overshadowed by the epic success of his sculptures. The dining room is a more formal, traditional space, dominated by antiques bought by Irina Moore.

Now managed by the Henry Moore Foundation, the house has been restored as it as was in the 1970s and opened to the public. It is a place where imagination and design, family life and art all came together under the same roof.

'Work and family life were one,' says Mary Moore. 'At my seventh birthday party at the house, one of the games was my father guessing the weight of my guests. Who has ever heard of a party game like that? We all took it for granted and he was always right. It was to do with being a sculptor and knowing what bulk and form are all about. If you are going to achieve the amount my father achieved then you just don't switch off.'

Moore's Top Studio (*below*), built alongside the main house, was one of a growing series of buildings that contained Moore's work at Perry Green. In the entrance hall to the farmhouse itself (*opposite*), a bronze cast of A'a from Rurutu in the Austral Islands sits on a plinth. The piece is a copy of an original wood statue held by the British Museum. The open double doors lead to the sitting room.

Biography
Henry Moore (1898–1986)

Moore was born in Castleford, West Yorkshire, the son of a mining engineer. He began modelling in clay and carving at school, and decided to become a sculptor at an early age. After serving in World War I, Moore became the first student in sculpture at the Leeds School of Art, before moving to the Royal College of Art. He became one of Britain's most revered, respected and successful post-war sculptors and artists, with his work being collected and exhibited internationally.

Reproduced by permission of the Henry Moore Foundation and the Henry Moore Family. Most of the objects shown are on loan from the Henry Moore Family Collection.

The sitting room (*opposite*) is the most generously proportioned room in the house, with large windows introducing strong natural light and connecting the space with the garden. It is also home to an eclectic personal collection of art and statuary, including a 14th-century Italian mourning angel on a plinth. Other pieces include the Gustave Courbet painting *La Grotte de la Loue* from 1856 above a console cabinet (*above*) and a Bobo horned antelope mask (*right*) from Burkina Faso.

Maison Jean Cocteau / Milly-la-Forêt, France, 1947

It was a unique and intriguing combination – the avant-garde poet, writer, artist and film-maker Jean Cocteau and one of the greatest and most imaginative interior designers of the 20th century, Madeleine Castaing. In the picturesque town of Milly-la-Forêt, not far from Fontainebleau, the two worked together on creating a home with a very special charm and character – the Maison Cocteau.

It was not the first time that Cocteau and Castaing collaborated. They shared a common circle of friends, particularly artists and writers, as well as a shared patron, the socialite Francine Weisweiller. Castaing decorated the Weisweillers' villa, Santo-Sospir, in Saint-Jean-Cap-Ferrat, and Cocteau added his own distinctive mark in the form of murals that graced many of the key living spaces.

The two friends also had other things in common. They were both tempted by the world of high society but they were never snobs. Both were highly creative and eclectic, Cocteau being principally a writer who thought like an artist and Castaing an artist of a particular kind who counted literature as a key influence, even noting down the furnishings of rooms as described in the novels that she read. The two of them perfected their respective distinctive and powerful voices, and at Milly-la-Forêt these two voices combined in harmony.

Cocteau bought the 17th-century stucco, stone and brick house in 1947. It offered the poet a true 'refuge', a retreat from the pace of Parisian life. The location of the house is certainly quite magical: from the picture-postcard centre of the town it is a short walk to the Notre Dame de l'Assomption church, where one finds a sleepy cul de sac, at the end of which sits Cocteau's home. Behind the high stone walls that enclose the grounds a whole new world is revealed, with the house overlooking a sequence of gardens intersected by a moat and interconnected channels.

Cocteau asked Castaing to help him design the interiors of the house. The sitting room is dominated by a bespoke abstract wallpaper applied in reverse and a typically eclectic mix of furniture, with a large mahogany armoire at one end and a large oval table nearby, covered in books, from where one can look out into the gardens. Upstairs, the walls of Cocteau's study are coated in a Castaing favourite – leopard print wallpaper. Unusually, the wallpaper is also applied to the ceiling, and the pattern repeated on a daybed and even a lampshade, giving the room the feeling of a more enclosed and intimate space well suited to the notion of the study as an almost womb-like, concentrated retreat.

In the adjoining bedroom, the canopy bed is positioned on a diagonal facing the window, and a chair made with animal horn – another Castaing trademark – sits beneath a wall mural of a pastoral landscape by Jean Marais.

Castaing once said of her clients that 'if the people are worth the trouble, inspiration invariably comes. I always tell clients that, above all, we should not try to recreate a room as it was during another epoch…. I don't like to work for people who want an interior to improve their standing in the eyes of others. But, for a certain kind of people, I do like to create a mirror in which they can recognize themselves.'[1]

Maison Cocteau has recently been restored and opened to the public, showcasing the layers upon layers of treasures, paintings and curios. The mix is so seamless that it is almost impossible to say where Castaing's work ended and Cocteau's began.

1 Quoted by Adam Lewis in *The Great Lady Decorators: The Women Who Defined Interior Design, 1870–1955*, 2009.

Biographies
Jean Cocteau (1889–1963)

A poet, writer, artist, filmmaker and playwright, Cocteau was an avant-garde auteur who excelled in many different media. Among his best-known works are the novel *Les Enfants Terribles* (1948) and the film *Beauty and the Beast* (1946). Cocteau himself insisted that he was primarily a poet, but his films and artworks were also highly influential.

Madeleine Castaing (1894–1992)

Castaing was one of the most original voices in 20th-century French design and an important influence on designers such as Billy Baldwin, Jacques Grange and Albert Hadley. The daughter of an engineer, she married the art critic Marcellin Castaing, who bought her a neoclassical manor house in Lèves, near Chartres, which she had noticed as a child and later spent part of her life restoring. Castaing founded a famous antiques store in Paris and originated the idea of room sets in her boutique. Eccentric and charming, she mixed bold colours and bespoke patterns with a wide range of influences, including neoclassicism, Biedermeier and period Russian and English furniture.

The key rooms of the house are dominated by vivid patterns on the walls of the bedroom and study and the main drawing room on the ground floor (*right*). Bronze Chinese fawn sculptures from the 18th century guard the fireplace, and the furniture mixes a leather lounge chair with an ornate and quirky period sofa against the backdrop of a wallpaper chosen by Castaing.

The leopard-print paper used on the walls and ceilings of the study (*opposite*) was a Castaing favourite, and the notice board is preserved as Cocteau left it. A bust of Byron sits on the desk among the artists' materials and notebooks. In the bedroom (*below left*), the canopied bed was placed on a diagonal to face the window while other pieces include a 19th-century ebony and alabaster bust of a child and a low chair made from cowhide and buffalo horns. The mural on the wall (*above right*) is attributed to Jean Marais.

Tony Duquette

Dawnridge / Beverly Hills, Los Angeles, USA, 1949

The flamboyant Hollywood designer Tony Duquette liked to compare himself to the phoenix of legend. For him, the phoenix combined nature and magic, the twin sources of an 'enchanted vision that we carry around in the treasure house of our own minds'. His love for the fabled bird also suggests his talent for constant reinvention in creating fantasies full of life, colour, character and drama. This is certainly true of Duquette's own Beverly Hills home, Dawnridge, which is characterized by a playful exuberance and delightful excess.

Tony Duquette was one of the great originals of the American decorating and design world. He mastered many different media, designing jewelry, hotels and public spaces as well as settings for glamorous parties and events. Yet Duquette is mostly remembered for the homes he created for himself and a number of high-society clients.

These interiors were defined by an instantly recognizable 'Duquette look' that drew inspiration from many different sources – nature, the past, theatre, film and fiction. These elements were assembled in a unique fashion and high style without being elitist: Duquette would happily place a sculpted screen of his own design, made with hubcaps and bearing sunburst motifs, next to a priceless period piece.

Duquette built Dawnridge in 1949, collaborating with the architect Casper Ehmcke. The scale of the house might seem quite generous, but in fact it covers only 84 square metres (900 square feet) and has just one bedroom. In addition to the house Duquette also created a garden, complete with guest house, painting studio and a choice of pavilions and terraces.

The murals on the back of the front door, featuring the figure of an 18th-century footman, were painted by Duquette's wife, Elizabeth (nicknamed 'Beegle'). Architectural elements such as the 17th-century door surround that marks the passage from the sitting room to the entrance hall, are also seamlessly woven into the interiors.

Duquette used mirrors in the sitting room and dining room to create an impression of greater space, more depth and light, and adding to the magical quality of the rooms. In his words, it 'prolongs the real space into dream space and opens new vistas beyond, and ever beyond.'[1]

In the dining room, he used a signature marbled silk in an emerald green to lift the space. 'He thought green was a neutral colour,' says Hutton Wilkinson, Duquette's business partner and now head of Duquette Studio as well as the current owner of Dawnridge. 'He loved clear, bright jewel colours: peridot, amethyst, coral. He also "painted" his rooms using throw pillows and preferred fabric stretched on the walls (no padding, please) because he could get a greater depth of colour that way. And then there was gold, gold, gold, on walls and ceilings and anywhere else he could put it, but in Tony's hands it was never gaudy, just gold.'

Wilkinson bought the house after Duquette's death in 1999, using it as the headquarters of Duquette Studios and as a guest house. Many of the antiques that once adorned the house were sold to settle the Duquette estate, but Wilkinson has filled the gaps with pieces of Duquette's own design and other pieces drawn from the warehouse of treasures that the designer left behind.

The house continues to play a part in showcasing the 'Duquette look', with its theatrical flair and exuberance. The home of the great maximalist remains a powerful production, tinged with kitsch excess, yet all the more intriguing because of it. Dawnridge continues to inspire Duquette disciples with a real sense of individuality and creative spirit.

1 Essay by Tony Duquette in Hutton Wilkinson, *More is More: Tony Duquette*, 2009.

Dawnridge is packed with ideas and exuberance: the main living room (*opposite*) is a hymn to the Duquette style, with theatrical flourishes and bespoke designs throughout. The emerald-green and black secretaire was originally commissioned by Elsie de Wolfe, while the sunburst screens were made with hubcaps; above the door is a Duquette sculptural piece entitled *A Fragment of a Priestess' Robe*.

The seashell screens in the living room by the windows (*overleaf*) were once part of a Duquette-designed grotto, while the chandelier was made using Venetian glass lilies. The stairs lead up to a gallery that accesses the master bedroom, with artworks by Elizabeth and Tony Duquette on the walls.

Biography
Tony Duquette (1914–1999)

Like Oliver Messel and Lorenzo Mongiardino (see page 22), Tony Duquette was a gifted set designer for theatre and film as much as an interiors maestro. He brought a sense of high theatre to his houses and hotels, as well as to the stage, and earned his place in Hollywood as a socialite and multi-talented creative consultant. He was born in Los Angeles and studied at the Chouinard Art Institute, and later worked with Billy Haines before being discovered by Elsie de Wolfe (see page 13) during her sojourn in California. He contributed set designs to many stage productions and Hollywood films, including *Yolanda and the Thief* (1945) with Fred Astaire. Elizabeth Arden, J. Paul Getty and the Brandolini family were among the high-society clients who commissioned interiors from Duquette.

The garden room dining area (*above*) was created from a former terrace that was glassed in, with walls coated in a 'malachite gemstone'-print Thai silk, a Duquette signature design. The white chairs and console table are from a collection of Indian blackwood furniture by Duquette and have been painted white. The sofa (*opposite*) was originally designed for the home of Duquette's client Doris Duke.

Lina Bo Bardi

The Glass House / Morumbi, São Paulo, Brazil, 1951

When Lina Bo Bardi and her husband settled in the Morumbi district of São Paulo, the landscape dominated literally everything. The city had not yet encroached on what was then a forest reserve, which Bardi found full of natural beauty and teeming with wildlife of all kinds: possums, armadillos, deer, snakes, guinea pigs and nighthawks. Bardi once wrote of Brazil as a country 'where everything seemed possible' after the ruins of wartime Italy and Europe, and building in Morumbi must have been like arriving in her own personal Eden.

The house that Bardi created – her first completed building – was, above all, an observatory. It was designed as a lookout station for appreciating the extraordinary landscape and gazing back towards the south-east, across the vibrant city. The aim was to 'come extremely close to nature using all available means'.[1]

Bardi was fascinated by ideas of elevation (which can be seen in a number of her buildings) and the model of Le Corbusier's Villa Savoye of 1931 in particular (see Bradbury/Powers, *The Iconic House*), where living spaces and roof gardens were lifted high above the ground on pillars so that the entire building became a platform. Bardi took this thinking in a new direction with a sensitive, contextual approach and an openness that allowed her to introduce depth of character and individuality to the design, as opposed to the emphasis on purity evident in the Villa Savoye design.

The house is positioned on a sloping site, with the building anchored on the upper slope of the hill and supported by a series of tall, slim columns in front, creating the impression of a home that is floating high above the ground, within the tree canopy. The idea of integrating nature is taken further in the elevated courtyard that pierces the floating house, arranged around a mature tree that grows right through the centre of Bardi's home.

The staircase leads to the master element of the building – a soaring, open atelier framed in glass that opens up to the vista. This dramatic open room boasts a mosaic floor in sky-blue tones and is arranged into a series of spaces for sitting, writing and dining. Much of the furniture, including the dining table and many of the armchairs, was designed by Bardi herself, but she was happy to mix them with antiques and other quirky personal treasures, some of which she and her husband brought from Italy in the hold of the liner *Almirante Jaceguay*. Indeed, some have compared the house

itself to a boat, carrying the Bardis into a new world. Within this sublime space, Bardi used diaphanous curtains for privacy and shade (instead of brises soleil, which she disliked).

Three modest bedrooms and a dressing room are set apart from the generous atelier, while the maid's quarters and service rooms were pushed further back, beyond the rear patio. Throughout the house – in the kitchen, the bathroom and bedrooms – one senses a warmth that comes from a careful use of colour and an intriguing mix of materials that includes coloured mosaics and rich parquet. Add to this the greenery that laps at every window, and the impression is one of a welcoming, well-crafted interior very much at one with its surroundings.

In this sense the structure has more in common with buildings by pioneering Californian modernists such as Schindler, Eames and Neutra than those of Le Corbusier. For Bardi herself, the house was the first great success in a rich life lived by design in Brazil, the adopted country that granted her a place among its greatest talents.

1 Quoted in Olivia de Oliveira, *Subtle Substances: The Architecture of Lina Bo Bardi*, 2006.

Biography
Lina Bo Bardi (1914–1992)

An architect, furniture, jewelry and set designer, writer, journalist and editor, the multi-talented Bardi was born Achillina Bo in Rome and studied architecture at the University of Rome. She went to work with Giò Ponti in Milan and later founded her own architectural practice. Her offices were destroyed by bombs during the war years; at that time she concentrated on journalism and became involved in the Resistance. She married the writer and curator Pietro Maria Bardi after the war and they moved to Brazil in 1946, where he founded the São Paulo Museum of Art (MASP). Bardi's design for a new home for the MASP (1968) became one of her most famous buildings. She worked on many buildings and cultural centres, including the Museum of Modern Art in São Paulo (MAM) in 1982 and the São Paulo City Hall in 1992. She became a naturalized Brazilian citizen in 1951.

Raised among the trees, the Glass House is an intricately conceived observatory, pierced by a floating courtyard (*above*). The large, open living room/atelier (*opposite above*) is the central space in the house, with its mosaic floor and its diaphanous curtains for filtering sunlight. The many Lina Bo Bardi furniture designs in the house include her famous Bowl Chair (*opposite below left*), designed in 1951.

In the living room (*above and right*),
a classical statue and a period bureau
mix with contemporary chairs and
other Bardi-designed elements.
The functional kitchen (*opposite left*)
is enlivened by a strong use of
colour for the storage cupboards
and other elements, complemented
by differently sized tiles for floors
and walls.

The bedroom (*above right*) is modest in scale, also mixing period and modern elements, while the retro packing cases echo the Bardis' own voyage from Italy to Brazil.

Piero Fornasetti

Villa Fornasetti / Milan, Italy, *c.* 1955

The eyes of Lina Cavalieri keep a constant watch over the countless delights of the Villa Fornasetti in Milan: the face of the legendary Italian *fin-de-siècle* opera singer (who was as famous for her beauty as her voice) was an obsession for Piero Fornasetti. In abstract, black-and-white form Cavalieri was reproduced on plates and ceramics hundreds of times over, becoming the key element of the designer's famous Theme & Variations series.

Other motifs reappear constantly in Fornasetti's work and at the villa: birds and butterflies, suns and clouds, and the faces and porticos of classical temples and buildings, all incorporated into surreal trompe l'oeil designs and applied to furniture, ceramics, wallpapers and textiles. The effect, when combined with rich, deep wall colours such as vivid blue and intense emerald green, is startling and intoxicating. It is no surprise that the house has been described as a 'Wunderkammer', a chamber of wonders.

The three-storey villa is located in the Città Studi quarter of Milan and was built at the end of the 19th century by Piero Fornasetti's father, Pietro, who made a living importing German typewriters. Viewed from the entrance courtyard, the exterior of the building seems unremarkable, but on the inside the house reveals the deep inventiveness and rich imagination of one of Italy's most original creative talents, often dubbed the 'designer of dreams'.

Piero Fornasetti adapted and expanded the winding, L-shaped house from the 1950s onwards. It holds countless mid-century Fornasetti pieces, and the yellow hallway alone boasts a complex display of ideas full of wit and originality. A handmade Fornasetti seashell chandelier hangs above a 16th-century portrait, which is juxtaposed with a 1950s bench engraved with drawing instruments and a vintage Architettura cabinet – or trumeau-bar – originally designed by Giò Ponti and modified, hand-printed and lacquered by Fornasetti. A blend of sideboard, bureau and bar, the trumeau-bar is one of the most admired and intriguing furniture types of the prodigious Fornasetti line.

The building occupied a central position in Fornasetti's creative life, and the generous scale of the house allowed space for a design studio and office spaces. Today the studio still contains the Fornasetti archives, and the design business is continued by Piero's son, Barnaba Fornasetti, who preserved and updated the house, continuing the spirit of his father's work.

The bedroom has been reinvented by Barnaba as a guest room: the vibrant blues of ceiling, walls and curtains are complemented by a Fornasetti Nuvole wallpaper on one wall, with a 1950s chest of drawers underneath an 18th-century Italian mirror. One of the most striking rooms in the house is the green sitting room, where one wall is lined with a collection of mirrors of various shapes and sizes, mixing antiques with Fornasetti designs. The rug, tables, blanket box, large centrepiece wardrobe and Biglietti da Visita desk and chair with the playing-card motif all demonstrate the breadth of Fornasetti's work.

Yet the house is clearly not a showroom but a beloved family home that has passed through three generations. It reveals not just the instantly recognizable, idiosyncratic Fornasetti style, but also the mark of an expert with an eye for the art of display and showmanship within the home.

'My father took decorative arts to the same level as the so-called "noble arts"', says Barnaba Fornasetti. 'He was more like a Renaissance artist or artisan, able to move freely between several fields. His position in 20th-century design is unique to such an extent that he cannot even be defined as simply a designer.'

Biography
Piero Fornasetti (1913–1988)

Artist, designer, illustrator and entrepreneur, Piero Fornasetti was one of the most vibrant, original figures of 20th-century Italian design. He studied at the Accademia di Belle Arti di Brera in Milan for two years before coming to the attention of influential architect and designer Giò Ponti and becoming his protégé. Later Fornasetti and Ponti collaborated on a series of interior design and furniture projects. Suffused with a surreal sense of humour, Fornasetti designs became especially popular in the 1950s and 60s, with the familiar motifs gracing a prolific range of ceramics, furniture, textiles and wallpaper. Fornasetti also designed interiors for the San Remo Casino in 1950 and for the ocean liner *Andrea Doria* in 1952.

Rich in invention, the Fornasetti house offers continual design delights from both father and son. The green sitting room includes a dazzling menagerie of mirrors by Piero Fornasetti and others on emerald walls (*opposite*). The coffee table in front of the sofa is actually a Fornasetti blanket chest, wood printed and lacquered by hand, while the wardrobe between the bookshelves (*above*) was custom-made for the room.

The famous Fornasetti butterflies appear throughout (*far left*) while the enigmatic face of Lina Cavalieri is found in the bathroom (*below right*) and on various ceramics. The office and studio (*opposite*) features a giant mural of the *Città ideale* (Ideal city) after a painting by a pupil of Piero della Francesca and a lacquered Architettura cabinet underneath the stairs.

The studio (*overleaf left*) includes a 1940s desk by a pupil of Giò Ponti against a Fornasetti Mediterranea wallpaper, while the guest bedroom (*overleaf right*) is defined by a vibrant red theme that includes even the books on the shelves around the 19th-century Italian walnut bed. The mirror is a vintage Fornasetti design in glass and brass.

E. Stewart Williams

The Kenaston House / Palm Springs, California, USA, 1957

room itself, coating one of the walls. The main living spaces are open plan, and the living room is dominated by a floating fireplace (a favourite Williams device) against a stone wall, while an internal garden planter sits close by, introducing a further note of natural warmth.

Timber is used to great effect in the house, gracing walls in the dining area, the corridor to the bedrooms and the master bedroom, where a wall of irregular timber batons, like a 'topographical sculpture', provides a rich sense of texture.

In 2003, creative director Andrew Mandolene and real estate executive Todd Goddard carefully restored the house, stripping back layers of paint that had obscured the wood finishes and introducing a choice of carefully assembled mid-century pieces. Among their finds was a Williams-designed credenza, bought at auction, that sits to one side of the dining area and helps to divide the space from the rest of the living room.

With its vibrant contrast between cool, reflective finishes and the soothing beauty of timber and stone, the Kenaston House exudes the designer glamour that makes Palm Springs so fascinating. In 2005, the house was used as a backdrop for a landmark *W* magazine photo shoot with Brad Pitt and Angelina Jolie to promote their film *Mr. & Mrs. Smith*.

In the master bedroom (*left*) the walnut panelling has a striking sculptural quality. The corrugated aluminium panelling that coats the exterior walls is continued into the house in the main living room (*opposite above*), behind the 1960s sofa by Paul McCobb. The open fireplace (*opposite below right*) has a more organic stone wall as a backdrop, with integrated planters creating an internal garden. The credenza by the dining table (*opposite below left*) used to be in Williams's own home and was bought at auction.

The city of Palm Springs offers a glorious concentration of mid-century style. In the 1950s and 60s, it was *the* fashionable retreat for Hollywood film stars and the wealthy elite. Frank Sinatra was an early resident there and asked E. Stewart Williams to design a house for him. Famously, Sinatra asked the architect for a mock-Georgian home but Williams only gave him the choice of a period pastiche or something altogether different and more sophisticated. Fortunately for Williams, Sinatra trusted him, and he went on to become one of the most respected practitioners of 'desert modernism'.

An admirer of Mies van der Rohe and Scandinavian masters such as Alvar Aalto (see page 124), Williams responded to the extreme conditions of Palm Springs. His houses were low-slung and single-storey, using banks of glass to open the interiors to the landscape, but also making the most of techniques to protect the house from the summer

sun. He was open to modern materials and new technologies, and favoured the warmth of natural materials such as stone and timber.

This philosophy is very much apparent at Williams's Kenaston House, built on the edge of the city in the fashionable 'Club Circle' district. The house was commissioned by Robert Kenaston and his wife, Billie Dove Kenaston, a movie star from the 1920s who had once won the heart of Howard Hughes, as a wedding gift for their son Roderick. The wealthy Kenastons encouraged their son to enjoy life to the full, and so he and his wife spent much of the year travelling. When they came back to Palm Springs, they often had to shovel the sand away from the front door.

Williams designed a U-shaped house arranged around a central pool and surrounded by terraces. He used corrugated aluminium siding on the exterior of the house to help reflect the heat, and in the living room the siding was incorporated into the

Biography
E. Stewart Williams (1909–2005)

Along with fellow architects Albert Frey and William Cody, E. Stewart Williams helped shape Palm Springs in the mid-century mould. Born in Ohio, he studied at Cornell University and the University of Pennsylvania before touring Scandinavia and Europe. He worked with industrial designer Raymond Loewy and later designed ships for the US Navy during the war, before joining the family architectural practice in Palm Springs. His most famous commission was a house for Frank Sinatra, known as Twin Palms (1947), while other projects include the Edris House (1954), the Palm Springs Aerial Tramway Station (1961) and the Palm Springs Desert Museum (1976).

Robin Boyd

Walsh Street House / Melbourne, Australia, 1958

Architects and designers like to talk about the importance of taking a journey through a building; it should be a modest voyage of discovery, a gradual unfolding of delights rather than grand flamboyant gestures that reveal themselves in a single moment. Robin Boyd's house in suburban South Yarra, Melbourne, offers just such a journey of small pleasures and seductive details.

Seen from the street, the house has a discreet presence. Boyd was concerned about preserving a large pine tree at the front of the long, narrow piece of land that was once the rose garden of a neighbouring house. The new home that Boyd designed for himself, his wife, Patricia, and their children was therefore set back a little from the road, and its rather plain brick façade offers few hints of the interior. One clue lies, perhaps, in an eye-catching series of jarrah timber steps that leads to a front door anchored to the upper level of the building.

Once inside, the house unfolds in a dramatic fashion, with an emphasis on the quality of the interior spaces and links between indoor and outdoor living. 'One of the principal objectives in planning was to create a private indoor-outdoor environment, despite the narrowness of the allotment,' said Boyd. 'The device adopted was to divide the house in two by a garden square, 40 feet deep, two-storey parents' block at the front, single-storey children's block at the back.'[1]

The front entrance sits on the higher storey of the parents' block, with stairs leading down to the lower floor and a combined master bedroom and sitting room, lifted by high clerestory windows facing the street and glass doors leading to a balcony overlooking the internal courtyard. This room is characterized by exposed brick walls painted a soft grey, contrasting with a vibrant red carpet chosen together with interior designer Marion Hall Best. Sofas are by the designer Grant Featherston (for whom Boyd later designed a house) while the bed can be turned into another seating area in the daytime.

Most striking of all is the sinuous form of the slatted timber ceiling, which is partially supported by taut steel cables. The cables carry the roof out on to the balcony, creating a sunshade, and run across the courtyard as bare 'spines' connecting to the children's block at the back of the house, where the ceilings are identical. The undulating curves of the timber slats throughout the house are one of the high points of Boyd's ingenious design.

The lower level of this portion of the house is mostly open plan, with a large white rug on the brick floor marking out seating and dining areas. A painting by Boyd's father – *Winter Triumphant* – once hung above the dining table but has been replaced by an abstract piece by Asher Bilu. A galley kitchen is partially separated off by a long, low, bespoke storage cabinet and the stairs. Boyd also designed other pieces of furniture

specially for this space, including the sofa and coffee table.

Banks of glass create easy connections to the courtyard with all its light and greenery, while a discreet, sheltered walkway to one side of the courtyard allows for a dry passage between the two blocks of the house even in poor weather. The children certainly enjoyed the freedom of having a 'house within a house'; a telephone extension served to call them over for meals.

It seems that Boyd, who died too young, just like his father before him, was disappointed at times that larger architectural commissions seldom came his way. But his influence lives on in his writing and in houses like Walsh Street, which is packed with original ideas on flexible, sociable and enjoyable living, tying together indoor and outdoor spaces.

1 Quoted by Geoffrey Serle in *Robin Boyd: A Life*, 1995.

Biography
Robin Boyd (1919–1971)

As an architect, designer, writer and educator Robin Boyd was one of the most influential modernist architects in post-war Australia. He was the son of the painter Penleigh Boyd, who died when Robin was very young, and was raised by his mother, also a skilled painter. He studied in Melbourne and served an apprenticeship with architect Kingsley Henderson, qualifying after war service. Early on in his career, Boyd focused on the design and promotion of inexpensive but well-designed prefabricated houses, before setting up practice with Frederick Romberg and Roy Grounds in 1953 (shortened by some to 'Gromboyd'). Many of Boyd's commissions were residential, although other projects included the Australian Pavilion at the 1967 Expo in Montreal. He also wrote several books, the most famous one being *The Australian Ugliness* (1960).

From the front door (*left*) visitors get a glimpse of the combined sitting room and master bedroom on the upper level of the house. The main living spaces are positioned on the lower level of the house, leading out to the central courtyard. The bespoke cabinets (*opposite*) are made of mountain ash, and the painting is by Australian artist Asher Bilu.

The open stairs (*above*) connect the entrance and master bedroom/private sitting room with the principal living spaces below. The study (*right*) in the children's part of the house shares a common approach to colour, with grey brick walls mixing with the organic tones of the furniture and accents in red.

The Boyds' private sitting room and bedroom (*opposite above left and opposite below right*) includes a vivid red carpet accompanied by a low sofa and coffee table designed by Robin Boyd, and a R161 Contour settee by Grant Featherston. The bathroom (*opposite above right*) and kitchen (*opposite below left*) are positioned between the stairwell and the front of the house.

Halldor Gunnløgsson

Gunnløgsson House / Rungsted, Denmark, 1958

Biography
Halldor Gunnløgsson (1918–1985)

Born in Frederiksberg, Denmark, Gunnløgsson was the son of a merchant and an actress. He studied at the school of architecture at the Royal Danish Academy of Fine Arts in Copenhagen, graduating in 1942. He spent part of the war in Sweden before returning to Denmark and founding his own architectural practice in partnership with Jørn Nielsen. Key projects include the Tårnby City Hall (1959) and the Ministry of Foreign Affairs in Copenhagen (1980). He also became a professor and later dean of the school of architecture at the Royal Danish Academy.

The house is characterized by organic, warm materials, particularly timber and stone (*far left and left*). The interiors are open and unified by Kolmarden marble floors (*opposite*) and a restrained palette of materials where notes of brighter colour stand out. In the bedroom beyond the dining area, the bespoke bed was painted black to recede into the walls and the dining table and chairs are Poul Kjaerholm designs. The entrance area (*overleaf*) has a Japanese-influenced sense of purity, with integrated storage cupboards and an entrance porch tucked into the linear outline of the house.

A sense of calm pervades the simple but beautifully designed house by the sea that Jakob Halldor Gunnløgsson created for his wife, Lillemor, and himself. Overlooking the Øresund strait, which links the North Sea and the Baltic, the low, single-storey building affords stunning views of the water and the surrounding gardens through its glass walls – so much so that they become an integral part of the experience of being in the house. The materials are organic as well as exquisitely detailed, which results in the building achieving a powerful purity of form in harmony with the sublime setting.

Gunnløgsson and his wife began looking for a site for their house not long after they got married, following a long trip to Japan. They came across a parcel of land just off the coastal road between Copenhagen and Helsingør, an area of large period country houses, where the clean lines of Gunnløgsson's designs would create a welcome contrast.

The architect excavated the waterfront site to create a level surface for the house and planted hedges around the garden boundary. Within this enclosure Gunnløgsson set about designing a house with essentially two rooms: a large, open-plan living room and a bedroom that could be divided off from the main space by a large sliding door. A modest galley kitchen and a bathroom are contained within a narrow service core at the heart of the building, toplit by skylights that form a neat series of

periscopes on the flat roof. A garage and entrance area are positioned to one side, facing the road.

The open aspect of the interior, illuminated by floor-to-ceiling glazing with sliding doors that lead to adjoining timber decks, is lifted by the architect's restrained and adept use of materials. The floors are covered in grey Kolmarden marble (leftovers from Gunnløgsson's Tårnby Town Hall project) and the structural timber beams are exposed and filled in with slats of fir. The brick end walls are faced with timber that is painted black and polished to create a shining, lacquered finish.

Some furniture pieces are bespoke and designed by the architect himself, including the leather couch and the bed. Others are carefully selected designs made by Gunnløgsson's friend and fellow modern master Poul Kjaerholm, who designed the PK25 lounge chairs in the seating area and the table and chairs in the dining zone. Within the limited colour palette the eye is steered repeatedly towards the views, but in this considered context small splashes of colour stand out boldly: the blues of the painting in the bedroom by Arne Haugen Sørensen; the red of the handwoven rugs in the bedroom and near the bespoke bookshelves; the intense lacquered red of the storage units tucked away behind the timber doors in the entrance hall.

The use of natural textures and tones, the sensitivity to the landscape and the mastery of form are all distinctly Scandinavian. Yet there is also a sense of Asian purity that seems to infuse the house,

inspired by Gunnløgsson's travels. The processional quality of the entrance area echoes the Japanese *genkan* (entryway), and the vast sliding doors opening to the bedroom and the kitchen are reminiscent of *shoji* screens. There is evidence of a deep, thoughtful ingenuity at work that offers many subtle but functional pleasures, from the sea-chest storage and dressing cabinet in the bedroom to the wall-mounted folding picnic table on the sea-facing terrace. Simple yet wholly seductive, the Gunnløgsson House is a sophisticated, joyful wonder – 'soft modernism' at its best.

In the light-filled spaces, furniture assumes the character of sculptures in a gallery, including Poul Kjaerholm's PK25 lounge chairs by the fireplace (*opposite above*), a bespoke wall-mounted sofa by Gunnløgsson (*opposite below left*) and paper pendant lights by Esben Klint (*opposite below centre*). The kitchen (*right*) is a modestly proportioned but flexible space that can be divided off from the main living spaces by a sliding door.

Alvar Aalto

Maison Louis Carré / Bazoches-sur-Guyonne, France, 1959

Some extraordinary houses are born of a close and creative partnership between designer and client – very much the case with the Maison Carré, where legendary Finnish architect Alvar Aalto and French modern art dealer Louis Carré created a carefully considered and delightfully detailed house.

Carré was the son of an antiques dealer, who had a successful gallery in Paris as well as a satellite in New York. He exhibited work by Paul Klee, Juan Gris, Picasso and Le Corbusier, whom he knew well. However, when it came to commissioning a house for himself on 4 hectares (10 acres) of land on a gently sloping hillside southwest of Paris, he decided that cement constructions as preferred by Le Corbusier would not be ideal for this rural setting.

Carré and Aalto had friends in common and first met in Venice in 1956, at the Biennale, where they got on famously. Carré asked Aalto to create a house that would be small on the outside, big on the inside and made the most of natural materials.

'I wanted a house built with materials that had lived,' he said. 'This was an unconscious reaction to steel architecture. Consequently, I needed stone, brick – because brick has become nobler through its use – and wood. There again, Aalto was perfect for me. He was extremely sensitive to materials. I think that is related to his poetic talent: he is a poet.'[1]

The house that Aalto went on to design makes the most of these choices. The building was positioned at the top of the site, with the main living spaces looking out onto the gardens and views of the countryside, now partly obscured by mature trees in the grounds. A sloping monopitch roof, coated in blue-black slate from Trélazé, echoes the gradient of the land while the house itself is made of a layer of Chartres limestone topped with white-painted brick and timber detailing.

The entrance hall is one of the greatest spaces in the house, topped with a sinuous free-form ceiling in the form of a vast wave made with strips of Finnish red pine. The textures of the timber are brought out by high clerestory windows above the front door, which also protect the artworks on the walls from direct sunlight.

'The vault is a masterpiece,' Carré said. 'I would have been satisfied with what I thought of as Aalto's signature, that is to say, a kind of exposed framework that holds the ceiling like a hand. But Aalto outdid himself…. Aalto is the only great architect who is a master carpenter. It is a kind of cupola. From the beginnings of architecture a cupola has always been the most difficult thing to

achieve. But this vault is not a copy of something else; it is an endless wave. It is the sign, the value of the house.'[2]

The hallway is the junction of the house, with a small rank of steps leading down to the generous living room, where banks of windows open the space up to the countryside. Another route leads to the dining room and service spaces, while a partial wall of timber cupboards disguises a discreet entry, via a slatted wooden gateway, to the private areas of the house, including the ground-floor bedroom suites of Carré and his wife, Olga. A clear distinction was made between the more public parts of the house, often used for parties and entertaining, and the more restricted and intimate sections, while servant bedrooms were contained in a modest upper level.

Most striking of all is the mesmerizing sense of cohesion that comes with a house where every detail has been carefully considered and created. Carré travelled to Finland to pick out a number of Aalto's Artek furniture designs for the house, but many elements are bespoke Aalto creations, from the sculpted door handles in brass and leather to the tailored multi-directional pendant lights in the dining room that illuminate the table and the artworks on the walls. Other specially created pieces include desks, tables and armchairs, which were all designed with the same care and passion for materials, beauty and functionality.

Maison Carré continued to bring pleasure to its owner until his death in 1977, and later to his widow. A monument now open to the public, Aalto's only house in France and one of his most accomplished projects, it continues to seduce and surprise his disciples.

1 Interview with Irmelin Lebeer, in Esa Laaksonen and Ásdís Ólafsdóttir (eds), *Alvar Aalto Architect: Maison Louis Carré, 1956–63*, 2008.
2 Ibid.

The entrance hall of the house (*left and opposite*) offers a dramatic introduction to the interiors, with an undulating ceiling in Finnish red pine and natural light streaming in from the clerestory windows. The steps lead to the main living area, while a bespoke bank of cupboards to one side doubles as a boundary, with a slatted door beyond leading to the kitchen and bedrooms.

Biography
Alvar Aalto (1898–1976)

One of the most widely admired Scandinavian architects of the mid-century period, Aalto developed a version of 'soft modernism' that emphasized natural materials and a love of nature. He grew up in a rural part of Finland and studied in Helsinki, before establishing his own practice in 1923 and marrying architect Aino Marsio the following year. Initially influenced by neoclassicism, Aalto was increasingly drawn to modernism and developed his own unique style within an ergonomic, humanist approach to architecture. Famously, his talents as a designer were applied to furniture and many other areas beyond architecture. Key buildings include the Paimio Tuberculosis Sanatorium (1933) and Villa Mairea (1939), both in Finland.

The main salon (*above, opposite above left and opposite below right*) features generous windows with a view across the sloping grounds and countryside. Nearly all of the lighting and furniture, including the nest of tables in the corner, was designed by Alvar Aalto, while the sofa is by his wife, Aino. The dining room (*opposite above right and opposite below left*) is positioned to one side of the entrance hall and includes a bespoke dining table by Aalto and multi-directional suspended lights that illuminate the table and the artworks on the walls.

Russel Wright

Dragon Rock / Garrison, New York, USA, 1961

The ideas that lie behind the creation of Dragon Rock seem particularly relevant today, despite dating back to the late 1950s. Wright aimed for a new natural home, one that would celebrate and respect the extraordinary rural landscape, while integrating inside and outside living, and combining natural and man-made materials in seamless harmony. Wright worked out exactly how he wanted to live at Dragon Rock and designed accordingly, even developing a strong sense of the way in which he wanted the interiors of the house to change and evolve from summer to winter.

Wright's eye for original and innovative detailing was extraordinary, and he was also highly articulate in expressing his ideas about design and modern ways of living. Dragon Rock is set within 30 hectares (75 acres) of rugged former logging country in the Hudson Valley known as Manitoga, a few hours north of New York City. Here, Wright set out precisely how he wanted the house to function and look, passing his ideas on to his collaborator, the architect David Leavitt.

'The house should complement this tiny part of the world,' he said. 'We should all try to preserve its beauty and be careful not to injure or desecrate it. More than this, we wish to demonstrate and enhance its natural beauty and charm. Expression of the particular use to which the house shall be put is important. The house is to be occupied by me and my daughter, both of whom have a great love of nature. While in it, we want to express our love of this land.' [1]

Wright had bought the site back in 1942 together with his wife, Mary. The land included a small cabin and Wright began looking at ways to subtly landscape the site, turning quarries into water pools and creating a series of woodland paths. When Mary died in 1952, their daughter, Annie, was only two years old but Wright decided to press on with his plans for a house at Manitoga (which in Algonquin means 'place of the great spirit') as a retreat for them both away from the pressures of New York City.

Together with Leavitt, Wright designed Dragon Rock on an extraordinary hillside spot overlooking a quarry pool and surrounded by woodland, where the only sounds are the wind, the birds and the sound of the waterfall feeding the old quarry below. The house is pushed into the hillside and set over eleven interconnected levels, with large pieces of granite worked into the fabric of the house. The upper levels included bedrooms for Wright's daughter and her nanny, while the kitchen was situated on the bottom level. Between them were generous living spaces opening out on to terraces and partly arranged around a fireplace fashioned from stone boulders.

Wright also created a separate single-storey, green-roofed studio at a short distance from the house, connected to the main building by a pergola. This was Wright's personal retreat to sleep and work, with a desk overlooking the woods and water. The studio in particular suggests the strong influence of organic Japanese design, which fascinated both Wright and Leavitt.

Wright introduced many of his own furniture designs to the house, and created many bespoke and experimental elements. At times it seems as though nature itself has crept into the house in the form of tree-trunk pillars or pebble-stone door handles. Elsewhere, Wright pioneered the use of plastics, largely supplied by DuPont, creating laminated panels emblazoned with flowers and plant life.

Saved from the elements by a sensitive restoration programme, and now open to the public, Dragon Rock proves itself to be well ahead of its time in many respects. Full of life, character and exquisite details inspired by the natural world, it is a hymn to a sensitive, contextual way of living that embraces the landscape.

1 Essay by Russel Wright printed in *Russel Wright: Good Design Is for Everyone*, 2001.

The house and studio (*below left*) overlook the quarry pool and are separated by a short walk. The main house is built into the cliff itself, with a spiral stair curving around a cedar tree trunk to connect the kitchen and dining area on the lower level with the main living room above (*opposite*). The chairs are by Charles Eames and the china is from Wright's American Modern range. The bespoke kitchen features a formica and oak counter.

Biography
Russel Wright (1904–1976)

Russel Wright was one of the first American designers to succeed in creating a lifestyle brand around his work, paving the way for contemporary designers such as Karim Rashid, Martha Stewart and Philippe Starck. He was born in Ohio and studied in Cincinnati and at Princeton, before moving into theatre set design in New York. He founded his own design firm in the late 1920s, around the same time that he met his wife, Mary, who helped Wright promote and market his homeware and furniture. They co-wrote the best-selling lifestyle manual *Guide to Easier Living* in 1950. Wright's hugely popular American Modern ceramic dinnerware set was another bestseller, but he also used plastics and other new materials to produce affordable and accessible designs.

The living room (*previous pages, left*) opens up to a terrace. Stone from the cliffs was used to make the corner fireplace, steps and other elements in the room, while the sofa and wall-mounted cupboards are bespoke pieces by Wright. The sunken bath (*previous pages, right*) is lined with blue Murano glass tiles, and the sliding plastic panels, also designed by Wright, are layered with butterflies.

The studio (*above and opposite*) offered a self-contained living and work space removed from the main house. The desk, oak shelves and fitted sofa are all bespoke elements by Wright; the round table, also by Wright, can be raised. Motifs and materials woven into the fabric and decoration of the studio echo the natural world beyond the windows.

John Lautner

Garcia House / Los Angeles, USA, 1962

Perched on the hillside high above the city, the house has a gravity-defying sense of drama (*left*). The terrace and stairway combine into one design statement, creating an outdoor room within the overarching shelter of the sweeping roof (*opposite*). The coffee table is by Eero Saarinen, the chairs are by Janus et Cie, and the artwork on the wall is from Studio 111 in Palm Springs.

John Lautner was *the* great architectural dramatist of his age. His chief partner was geography itself, as Lautner created a series of gravity-defying statement houses in California and beyond. Rather than attempt to tame or temper a site, Lautner would work with nature, anchoring his futuristic sculpted houses to hillsides and clifftops, as with his Elrod House in Palm Springs (1968), the Arango Residence in Acapulco (1973) and the Garcia House on Mulholland Drive.

Here, Lautner created a mesmerizing home for jazz musician Russell Garcia and his wife, Gina, completed in 1962. Garcia, a composer and conductor, worked with many of the big Hollywood studios and also collaborated with Ella Fitzgerald and Louis Armstrong. The house Lautner designed was pitched up in the Hollywood hills, clinging to the steeply sloping terrain while drinking in the epic views of Los Angeles.

V-shaped rugged-steel beams anchor the building to the ground at the front, while concrete supports rest on the flatter ground to the rear. The shape of the house is characteristically bold and vibrant; a vast vaulted roof encloses the entire building, which is mostly on one level, punctured by a semi-transparent core holding the entrance to the rear and a terrace to the front, and overlooking the canyon below. A sweeping spiral staircase within this core leads up to a guest suite on a modest second storey at the apex of the arching roofline.

The Garcia House reinforced the idea that Lautner was not simply adept with architectural statements but also a master in creating theatrical, playful interior spaces. The central living room is a soaring composition with high ceilings and bathed in sunlight from different directions. Much of the furniture is bespoke and built-in, including the L-shaped combined sofa and timber shelving together with the banquette-style cushions. Such pieces lend clarity to the interiors and help, along with subtle shifts in the floor level, to define key zones in the open-plan layout at the heart of the house. Rather than being hidden away in a secret service zone, the fitted kitchen is treated as an integral part of the house and is positioned alongside the sitting area.

Because the site was so rugged and barren in the early 1960s, Lautner decided to punctuate the glass walls of the house at the front and back with panes of coloured glass to give a friendlier, warmer feeling to the place. The generous use of natural materials such as stone and timber also adds a layer of warmth and texture, contrasting with the adventurous quality of the architecture itself. Lautner's gift for dissolving the boundaries between indoors and outdoors is in evidence on the integrated terrace, which has the feel of a futuristic and partly wall-less room that opens up to the panoramic view. With the sweeping central stairwell running alongside, the terrace also has the theatrical feeling of a stage.

However, Russ and Gina Garcia did not stay long in the house. In 1966, at the peak of his fame, Garcia sold up, bought a boat and went sailing around the world. In 2005, new owners acquired the house and commissioned architects Marmol Radziner to sensitively restore and update the house in keeping with Lautner's vision.

'The Garcia House is one of Lautner's most iconic works,' says Radziner. 'Some of that is to do with the simplicity of the expression of the form – the one arched roof that spans the entire living space with that hole through the centre framing the views of the city beyond. It's one of maybe five houses in Los Angeles that really define the city clearly, that are really known as part of Los Angeles.'

Biography
John Lautner (1911–1994)

John Lautner is best known for a series of highly imaginative houses, mostly in California and on the Pacific coast, which open themselves up to the landscape or the ocean within spectacular fluid forms. He was a protégé of Frank Lloyd Wright but established a unique, innovative and extravagant style that was very much his own invention. Buildings such as the Malin House (1960) in Los Angeles – also known as the Chemosphere – and the Elrod House in Palm Springs (1968) helped to define glamorous Californian mid-century modernism.

The main living room (*left*) affords sweeping views of the garden; the chairs by the table are by Hans Wegner. Bonet's famous BKF Butterfly chair, designed with Juan Kurchan and Jorge Ferrari, sits in the walkway that connects the pavilions (*opposite above left*). Blue mosaic tiles brighten the kitchen (*opposite below left*), and in the master bedroom a half-height wall encloses the bespoke bed without interfering with the curves of the vaulted roof (*opposite above right*).

Oscar Niemeyer + Michael Boyd

Strick House / Santa Monica, Los Angeles, USA, 1964

'I have always argued for my favourite architecture: beautiful, light, varied, imaginative and awe-inspiring',[1] Oscar Niemeyer once wrote. It seems an apt description for a house that he designed in the 1960s in Santa Monica, Los Angeles, though never visited. The Strick House was for many years a forgotten gem and one that did not appear on many official lists of Niemeyer's work. He had been unable to visit the site or supervise construction, having been denied entry to the United States because of his Communist sympathies.

The building was commissioned by American film director Joseph Strick, who visited Brasília and Niemeyer's own Canoas House of 1954 (see Bradbury/Powers, *The Iconic House*) following a trip to Argentina. Strick was appalled by the visa restrictions but pleaded with Niemeyer to design the house. Niemeyer came up with two initial schemes, one with a sweeping, sensuous roof that Strick and his wife Anne rejected, and another with subterranean bedrooms under the neighbouring golf course that the local planners ruled out.

'The result is a design that has more in common with his thirties and forties International Style type of approach to residential buildings,' says mid-century specialist and design consultant Michael Boyd, who now owns the house with his wife, Gabrielle, and family. 'His curvilinear signature was left out of the building but appears in the landscape and hardscapes.'

The house was built by subcontractors who had worked on John Entenza's 'Case Study House' Program, leading some to argue that the house is also an unofficial Case Study contender. During construction Strick split from his wife, so she and their two children eventually moved into the finished house without him.

The brick and glass design was essentially for a T-shaped pavilion, with a generous portion of the building holding a soaring, open-plan living, dining and kitchen area, while the bedrooms were contained in the adjoining crossbar. This surprisingly open and loft-like living area was bordered with glass to either side, connecting to the gardens and the landscape, and lightly zoned by a shift in floor level that separated the dining table and kitchen from a large seating space.

As part of their sensitive restoration of the house, the Boyds added a palmwood floor and re-landscaped the garden, taking inspiration from legendary Brazilian landscape architect Roberto Burle Marx. The living room became a sumptuous backdrop for a lovingly assembled collection of mid-century pieces, including leather and aluminium chairs and ottomans designed by Niemeyer for the French Communist Party headquarters in Paris. Other gems include the striking Maison du Mexique wall unit by Perriand, Prouvé and Delaunay, and there is still plenty of room for a grand piano.

The Boyds also transformed a study and basement garage into a two-storey library with a mezzanine gallery to hold some of the rarer pieces from their furniture collection.

'The houses we live in leave some of the most lasting impressions on us',[2] Niemeyer wrote. The Strick house was cherished by Anne Strick and now delights the Boyds. The architect's only completed house in the United States, it is now recognized as a powerful part of the Niemeyer canon.

1 Oscar Niemeyer, *The Curves of Time: The Memoirs of Oscar Niemeyer*, 2000.
2 Ibid.

Biographies
Oscar Niemeyer (1907–)

The most influential Brazilian architect of the 20th century, Niemeyer helped to shape the identity of his country through design, particularly with his work in Brasília, where he designed buildings that include the National Congress (1958) and the Metropolitan Cathedral (1959). Born in Rio de Janeiro, he studied at the city's National Art Academy. From 1934 to 1938 he worked with Lúcio Costa and Le Corbusier on the Ministry of Education and Health building in Rio. In the late 1950s, Niemeyer was appointed chief architect of the capital, Brasília. The changing political situation at the end of the 1960s led Niemeyer to seek exile in France, but he returned in 1982 to continue teaching and practising architecture. While he initially focused on Brazil, later projects took him around the world – he designed the UN Headquarters in New York with Le Corbusier in 1952 – and he won the prestigious Pritzker Prize in 1988.

Michael Boyd (1960–)

Michael Boyd is a designer, writer, consultant and collector of vintage modern design. He is the principal of BoydDesign, which has restored and updated many iconic homes, including the Strick House and homes by Paul Rudolph, John Lautner, Richard Neutra, R.M. Schindler and Craig Ellwood. He is also a furniture designer, and created the PLANEfurniture line.

The matching black leather chairs and ottomans in the living room (*opposite*) are Niemeyer designs from the early 1970s. A Marshmallow sofa by George Nelson for Herman Miller (1956) is placed against the windows that open out on to the terrace and pool. On the other side of the room stands a Maison du Mexique wall unit by Charlotte Perriand, Jean Prouvé and Sonia Delaunay dating from 1953.

In the kitchen (*previous pages, left*), a row of Eero Saarinen Tulip stools for Knoll (1956) is placed at the counter. The clock is a George Nelson design (1956). The dressing room (*previous pages, right*) features a George Nelson chest for Herman Miller (1955) and an oil painting by Nassos Daphnis above. In the living room (*above*), a Visiteur chair by Jean Prouvé sits in front of a painting by John McLaughlin.

In the dining area, a 1950s George Nelson Thin Edge cabinet sits underneath an oil painting by Burgoyne Diller (*opposite right*). The study/library includes a mezzanine reading room at an upper level (*left*), and a Gerrit Rietveld sideboard underneath an artwork by Donald Judd (*above*).

Claude Parent

Maison Bordeaux-Le Pecq / Normandy, France, 1965

In the 1960s, French architect Claude Parent, working together with theorist Paul Virilio, came up with the idea of the *fonction oblique*. At the heart of their manifesto was a call to arms against the right angle and the horizontal plane, and they argued in favour of fluid, sinuous forms that would liberate space and the way we use it. It was a radical reaction to the simplicity of a building seen as a simple, geometric white box and an argument in favour of dynamic design.

It is a philosophy that might not seem very radical today, as we have grown used to the shape-shifting athletics demonstrated by architects such as Frank Gehry and Zaha Hadid. But in its day the *fonction oblique* was a pioneering idea, resulting in buildings that were full of surprises, crafted forms and sloping floors. The church of Sainte-Bernadette in Nevers designed by Parent in 1966 was an extreme expression of the genre, an imposing, provocative presence in sinuous concrete with the monumental mass of a wartime bunker.

But it was at the Maison Bordeaux-Le Pecq in Normandy that Parent's ideas were realized in more sublime and poetic form within perhaps his most famous achievement. Here, the concrete was woven into lighter forms, sculpted into sweeping gull's wings coated in copper and coalescing in the roofline of a powerful pagoda. Within, the barrel-vaulted ceilings were epic, sculpted surfaces that echoed the curves of the walls. It was as though the house had burst from the earth.

'There is a French word, "*surrection*", which describes this exactly,' says Parent. 'The architecture seems no longer to be rooted in the ground, but rather to be erupting out of it – almost as if the ground itself was lifting up to make the form.'[1]

The house was commissioned by art dealer and curator Andrée Bordeaux-Le Pecq, who worked with Christo, Yves Klein and Alexander Calder. Like Parent himself, she was immersed in the world of the avant garde and had once owned a Bubble House by Jacques Couëlle. She also had a strong temperament, and the interiors of the house, with the large central living space and adjoining satellites, evolved through strenuous argument and debate.

The anchor of the living room is a vast Parent-designed fireplace in concrete and brick, with polished brick floors forming a herringbone-pattern parquet. A mezzanine study overlooks the living room, with a metal balcony designed by Bordeaux-Le Pecq herself. Bookcases and other fitted elements in the house are designed around the

swirling forms of the architecture. After Bordeaux-Le Pecq's death in 1980, her son added many pieces of mid-century modern furniture to the house.

For all the heated discussions between architect and client, the house stands as Parent's most lyrical creation, with a lightness of touch and form, while the interiors have the grace and monumental presence of a cathedral. This was *fonction oblique* at its best.

1 Interview with Claude Parent by Irénée Scalbert and Mohsen Mostafavi, included in Jacques Lucan et al., *The Function of the Oblique*, 1996.

Biography
Claude Parent (1923–)

Born in Neuilly-sur-Seine, Claude Parent studied in Toulouse and at the École des Beaux-Arts in Paris. He trained in the office of Le Corbusier for some time in the 1950s and was close to avant-garde artists such as Fernand Léger, Sonia Delaunay and Yves Klein. In 1963, with theorist Paul Virilio (1932–), he formed the Architecture Principe group, promoting ideas of the *fonction oblique*. The partnership lasted until 1968, and key buildings include Maison Drusch in Versailles (1965) and the church of Sainte-Bernadette-du-Banlay at Nevers (1966). Parent continued working on his own after this period, with projects including the French Pavilion at the Venice Biennale (1970) and the Théâtre Silvia-Monfort in Paris (1991).

The roofline of the house (*opposite*) forms a dynamic pagoda. Within, Marcel Breuer Cesca dining chairs surround the circular table in the dining area (*left*), and an armchair by Warren Platner is placed opposite a bespoke bookcase (*above*).

Ray Kappe

Kappe Residence / Los Angeles, USA, 1967

There is a pragmatic sense of beauty to Ray Kappe's home. When the architect found a steep, sloping site in Rustic Canyon, Pacific Palisades, he decided to work with the challenging topography rather than try to tame it. An underground spring made the situation even more complicated, so Kappe came up with the idea of creating six concrete towers that would hold the building in place. Using these towers to anchor the house, Kappe then worked with the shifting levels of the hillside to create an extraordinary post and beam structure that progresses over seven interconnected levels, stepping up the site like a series of climbing boxes woven together.

'The greatest challenge was to get the towers into place while disturbing the underground the least,' explains Kappe, who says he was influenced in part by the work of Paul Rudolph although directed by the contours of the land itself. 'But what really pleases me most about the house now is the way that it relates to the sun and the light during the day, and the moon at night.'

On paper, the floor plan looks relatively simple, with the master bedroom in one corner and the bedrooms of Kappe's three children placed in the opposite corner. Yet the interiors have a rich complexity, with a studio on the lowest level of the house and a progression of living spaces through the house from south to north until one reaches the kitchen. The sense of connection between these different zones gives the house an open and generous feel. Top-lit voids within the six concrete towers are used for bathrooms, sleeping areas, study spaces and stairwells.

Perhaps most striking, given the intricacies of the structure and design, is how naturally the house fits in with the site, with a wealth of natural light from many skylights and windows, as well as numerous connections between inside and outside space. Throughout the house, a variety of vistas provides constant enchantment.

'The house has lots of glass, and the view is of endless trees, so you feel like you're in a forest,' says Kappe. 'The entire site is used as a garden. I prefer the house when it's filled with light and sun. In California, that's most of the year.'[1]

A sense of cohesion is provided by the fact that so much of the furniture was designed and built by Kappe himself, often using redwood, which creates a subtle synergy with the Douglas fir used for the laminated beams that make up the bulk of the skeleton of the building. Many integrated pieces of furniture, such as the blue timber-based sofa in the main living room or the integrated bench and step opposite, cleverly pick up on and tie in with the strong Cubist quality of the house with its bands of horizontal and parallel lines. Built-in seating and sleeping platforms not only enhance the clarity of the interiors but also provide ingenious space-saving solutions.

Part of the drama of the house lies in the way that the interiors create intriguing contrasts between materials such as concrete and timber, as well as balance the linear quality of the building with an organic, natural aesthetic. The continuing appeal and influence of the Kappe Residence also lies in the fact that – unlike many typical Los Angeles homes – the house evolved from a meaningful dialogue with the hillside itself, integrating the building with the land rather than seeking to change the site to suit the house.

1 Interview with Hannah Booth, *Elle Decoration*, March 2010.

Biography
Ray Kappe (1927–)

Born in Minneapolis, Kappe and his family moved to Los Angeles in 1940. He studied at the University of California, Berkeley, when modernist master Erich Mendelsohn was teaching there and later worked as a draftsman on Eichler Homes. He launched his own practice, now known as Kappe+Du, in the 1950s. Early projects included a series of timber houses and in Pacific Palisades alone Kappe went on to design ten houses, including his own house and the Benton House (1990). Kappe also taught at the California State Polytechnic University before co-founding the Southern California Institute of Architecture (SCI-Arc) in 1972. In 2006, he started working with LivingHomes on a range of prefabricated houses.

The multi-layered house works with the steep slope of the site, which in turn softens the form of the building (*above*). The living room (*opposite*) connects with other parts of the house through horizontal openings and fluid transitions in shifting floor level. The blue sofas and chairs were designed by Kappe, as was the glass coffee table.

The main living room (*opposite*) offers a direct sense of connection with the gardens through the glass doors, and the Douglas fir gives an organic flavour to the house that contrasts with the concrete elements. The small table is another Kappe design, with a Charles Eames chair next to it. The master bedroom (*above*) includes a bed designed by Kappe, and a daybed and desk positioned within one of the six concrete towers that support the house.

Dieter Rams

Rams Residence / Frankfurt, Germany, 1971

The designer Dieter Rams is intimately associated with the pioneering work of Braun. Anyone who grew up in the 1960s, 70s or 80s will remember some of the five hundred products that Rams designed for the German electrical appliances company, from coffeemakers and kettles to calculators, hair-dryers and electric irons. They made their way into countless homes, united by key principles of design (as developed by Rams) that made them fine objects to look at but also compact, easy to use and accessible.

Rams articulated his thoughts in ten concise points, arguing that good design should be innovative, make a product useful, be aesthetic, help the consumer understand the product, be unobtrusive, be honest, be long-lasting, be thorough to the last detail, be environmentally friendly and involve as little design work as possible.

The emphasis on purity and simplicity was applied to electronics in particular, with Rams making the most of a new generation of miniature components to create hi-fi systems and music appliances that were compact and often multi-functional. Many were also modular, allowing users to take a flexible approach to the way they configured or presented them. Rams's hi-fi systems could be hung on the wall like works of art, or slipped into the pocket, as was the case with his TP1 range of radios and record players from the late 1950s – designs that paved the way for the Walkman and the iPod.

Rams met his wife, Ingeborg, in 1957 at Braun, where she worked as a photographer. Their house was designed according to Rams's ten principles and his maxim 'less but better'. It was built to his specifications on land acquired by Braun near Frankfurt (overlooking the company headquarters) and was originally intended as part of a large development of houses for company workers. Eventually, Braun sold the land to the city and Rams's plans for the development were somewhat diluted, yet the designer's home remains exactly as he intended it.

The L-shaped building is pushed into a sloping site, with gardens dominated by an outdoor pool, where Rams does his morning lengths, and an ordered garden with a Japanese influence that also feeds into his bonsai collection and elements of the interior. The lower level of the house contains a work studio, where Rams developed many Braun products.

The main living spaces upstairs are pure, crisp and functional, filled with Rams's products. The walls are white, the floors finished in white tiles and artworks carefully positioned. The living room is dominated by an assembly of armchairs created for Vitsoe, facing a vintage Braun television and a neat fireplace. One wall is dedicated to a Rams-designed flexible Universal Shelving System (also for Vitsoe).

There are some carefully selected pieces by other designers: Thonet dining chairs and a pendant light over the dining table by Poul Henningsen. In the office, a Braun hi-fi system is mounted on the wall, with records neatly lined up on matching shelves. Here, too, the ten principles are very much in evidence.

It is tempting to see Rams's home as a showcase for a way of living that his approach to interiors and domestic products made possible. His compact, exquisitely detailed and functional appliances swept away the need for clumsy, space-swallowing machines that resembled period furniture. The development of a modular and easily adaptable approach to furniture and other appliances for the home allowed for a new spectrum of choices for how one might want to live in the same space from day to day. It is a powerful message that has shaped the world of contemporary design.

Biography
Dieter Rams (1932–)

As a product designer, Dieter Rams has been profoundly influential. His emphasis on a considered combination of beauty, logic and function in pared-down, easy-to-use products has been widely imitated and his lessons have perhaps been applied most successfully by Apple designer Jonathan Ive. Rams was born in Wiesbaden in Germany and was influenced by his grandfather, a carpenter, whom he often observed at work. He studied architecture and interior design at Wiesbaden School of Art before joining the architectural office of Otto Appel in Frankfurt. He was first employed by Braun as an architect and interior designer in 1955, initially working on Braun showrooms before moving to product design. He was appointed director of design at Braun in 1962 and held the post until his retirement in 1995.

The ordered and sophisticated approach that Rams applied to modular hi-fi systems and electronic products, such as the wall-mounted Braun music system in his study (*opposite below*), is also applied to his crisp, functional and flexible home (*above*). The main living space (*opposite above*) is populated by a collection of Rams's leather Sesselprogramm 620 armchairs for Vitsoe.

Terence Conran

Barton Court / Berkshire, UK, 1971

Few figures in the design world have left such a deep impression within so many different spheres. Terence Conran has helped to shape the way we think about design itself, applying his unique sense of creativity to restaurants, hotels, furniture and interiors. Through his shops and books he has helped spread the message that good design can be accessible to all, and in doing so he has influenced the look of thousands of homes.

Within the extraordinary empire of design that Conran has created over the years, his own home at Barton Court in Berkshire has been a centre point and an inspiration in itself. Conran bought the 18th-century house, which used to be a boys' school, in 1971 when the building was in a derelict state, with the roof collapsing inwards and the windows smashed.

'As soon as I saw it I fell in love with it, primarily because it's Georgian and I love the symmetry and restraint of the period, as well as the generous proportions,' says Conran. 'I could see how I could make it simple and modern and that the proportions would make a perfect 20th-century home, with contemporary furniture mixed alongside antique finds and my collections.'

Many period details inside the house had long since been destroyed, offering the freedom to treat the interiors as a blank canvas that could be tailored in a simple, modern way, although Conran was anxious to preserve the elements that had remained, including the staircase, flagged floors and ceiling mouldings. A generous living room, 24 metres (80 feet) long, was created at the front of the house by removing two walls, to became a focal point of the house. The open, informal quality of the space sets the tone for the interiors.

'I have always thought that a mixture of old and new works well if it is done tastefully,' Conran says. 'Easy living is what I have tried to achieve at Barton Court. It's this sort of unpretentious informality which makes a comfortable modern home – for me at any rate.'

In the living room, and many other parts of the house, white walls create a plain background that allows Conran's furniture and collections of glass, ceramics and other pieces to stand out all the more. Colour is used in the house but subtly and sparingly. The rear hallway painted in sky tones is particularly striking and forms the setting for a collection of Bugatti pedal-powered racing cars in shiny Oxford blue, hung on the walls like the moths and butterflies that Conran collected as a child.

Here and elsewhere in the house, Conran uses conduits and corridors as key elements of the interior rather than as secondary spaces, treating them as additional seating areas or galleries for displaying his many treasures. The art of display is, in itself, one of Conran's talents, used to great effect not just at Barton Court but throughout his stores and restaurants.

'Displaying the things that I have found, discovered and loved gives me more pleasure than anything else,' Conran says. 'It is an extension of my personality. If it is an undervalued part of interior design then it certainly isn't by me. I also love putting modern furniture and objects in traditional environments and have always mixed antique furniture with the very best of modern design to create a look that I think makes modernism more interesting.'

Barton Court has changed subtly over the years as the collections have grown and new pieces of furniture have been introduced every now and then. Out in the workshops at Barton Court, Conran's own Benchmark Furniture company is another key part of his design empire, producing pieces to his own design as well as furniture by Jens Risom (see page 260) and others. Back in the house, a Benchmark desk anchors Conran's office, which is one of his favourite spaces: a private museum, laboratory, library and study, all combined into one. It offers a calm and crucial space to work and design, and take in inspiration, just like Barton Court itself.

Biography
Terence Conran (1931–)

A designer, retailer, writer and restaurateur, Sir Terence Conran has played a pivotal role in bringing good design, and good food, to a wide and appreciative audience. He studied at the Central School of Arts and Crafts in London before working for architect Dennis Lennon on designs for the Festival of Britain. He created his first company in 1952, producing furniture and working on interior design commissions, and he opened his first eatery a year later. The Conran Design Group was founded in 1956. Conran launched the popular home furnishings store Habitat in 1964 and opened the Conran Shop in 1983. An innovative polymath, Conran is also the author of many books, and the founder of the Design Museum in London.

The open, generously proportioned living room (*opposite above*) occupies the space to either side of the entrance hall, where the dividing walls have been removed. The glass-topped 1930s metal table by the front door is from France, the blue modular sofa was designed by Conran for the Conran Shop, and the glass chair is by Thomas Heatherwick. The kitchen (*opposite below left*) is an open, comfortable space with easy transition from the cooking area to the table. The more formal dining room (*opposite below centre*) sits alongside the kitchen and features a dining table by Eero Saarinen.

A collection of twenty blue Bugatti pedal cars lines the walls of the ground-floor corridor like an art installation (*opposite above*). The master bedroom on the first floor (*left*) retains the original plastered ceiling, and a collection of Indian miniatures has been arranged behind the bed. The master bathroom (*above*) is a favourite retreat, featuring an open fire and a large bathtub. The bath and shower area is lined with rich brown travertine, which is also used for the sinks. Also in the master bathroom, a detail of a miniature Bibendum – or Michelin Man – and vintage shaving brushes (*opposite below*).

Hugh Buhrich

Buhrich House II / Castlecrag, Sydney, Australia, 1972

Emigré architect Hugh Buhrich built two houses for himself and his family in the leafy Sydney suburb of Castlecrag, on the same street at Sugerloaf Point but thirty years apart. Few of Buhrich's buildings survive today, but these houses came to represent the finest part of Buhrich's design legacy and Buhrich House II has been described as one of the best mid-century houses in Australia.

There is no doubting the beauty, cohesion and natural elegance of the house, packed as it is with innovative ideas and self-designed furniture. Most striking is the undulating cedar ceiling; some suggest that the form echoes the waves down in Middle Harbour, while Buhrich himself said that it was a way of getting around planning restrictions on the height of the roof at various points in the building. Either way, it is one of the great delights of the house – achieved by steaming and bending the timber and then nailing the boards into place – reminiscent perhaps of the crafted, curving ceilings of Alvar Aalto's Maison Louis Carré in France (see page 124).

Hugh and Eva Buhrich had first come to Castlecrag in the 1940s, a few years after arriving from Europe, having fled Nazi Germany. Their son, Neil Buhrich, remembers the first house having more of a rectangular, Bauhaus quality with a flat roof and no veranda, but graced by a beautiful spiral timber staircase and a sandstone wall around the fireplace in the living room. Around 1960, Hugh Buhrich bought some land at the very end of the road, with a direct view of the water below, and started building a yacht on the site. By the 1970s, with their two sons growing up fast, the Buhrichs were ready for a more modestly scaled home.

'House II is smaller and much more organic,' says Neil Buhrich. 'There's an understated curve to the sandstone fireplace, which again was made with hand-cut stone on site, and of course the wavy ceiling. The rooms themselves are also less rectangular, but this may have been [done] to fit the house on the triangular plot of land.'

The house has two bedrooms, the larger including a study area with a bespoke, built-in table, and a small deck. A generous proportion of the house is dedicated to a semi-open-plan area holding the living room as well as the dining area and kitchen, partially divided off by changes in floor level and a large timber-faced storage cabinet. The use of timber, as well as the slate floors and the crafted sandstone fireplace wall, give this part of the house a warm, earthy quality, enhanced further by a

wall of glass looking out over the surrounding greenery and the ocean.

Many of Buhrich's early commissions, before he was fully registered as an architect in Australia, were for home interiors, and his mastery of interior space shows in the clarity of the main living space, with its many tailored pieces of furniture and minimalist detailing. The dining table and sofa are built in with a lightness of touch and appear to float in the space. Buhrich disliked fussy detailing, so cupboards are designed with spring-loaded doors to avoid the need for handles and hi-fi speakers are all hidden away behind the walls.

One of the great surprises of the house is the sinuous mandarin red bathroom, made with fibreglass – a choice that Neil Buhrich suggests may have been inspired by his father's interest in boats and boat-building. This is the only splash of artificial colour in the house and stands out all the more because of it, although it is confined within a carefully delineated space.

'When the house was heritage listed, my father was more pleased than he let on,' says Neil Buhrich. 'He may well have considered this house as his best. I remember that he once stepped from the kitchen to the living room, stopped, looked around and out of the blue he said, "Yes, this space works".'

Biography
Hugh Buhrich (1911–2004)

Born in Hamburg, Buhrich studied architecture in Munich and later in Berlin, where his tutor was Hans Poelzig. He also met his future wife, Eva, there, and they moved to Zurich and then Danzig, where Buhrich finished his studies. From there they fled the Nazi regime to Holland and then London. Eventually they decided to leave Europe altogether and emigrated to Australia in 1939. However, they found that their professional qualifications were not immediately recognized, which caused further problems. Eva ultimately became a writer, while Buhrich initially concentrated on furniture and interior design. He mostly worked alone and residential commissions in and around Sydney formed the bulk of his work, although he also designed synagogues and other buildings.

The exterior of the house (*left*) includes a 'floating' concrete-panelled wall with a latticed shutter of interlocking timber. The wavy ceiling in the open-plan living area (*opposite*) is made of cedar, and the dining area is subtly separated from the sitting room by a change in floor level. The built-in leather sofa was designed by Buhrich, along with the glass-topped dining table, and the chairs alongside are by Charles Eames.

The pony-skin chairs in the sitting room (*opposite*) were designed by Buhrich, inspired by a Marcel Breuer design. The compact kitchen (*opposite below*) is a bespoke design with a monolithic storage unit in a silver ash veneer providing partial separation from the living area. The striking bathroom (*above*) stands out with its mandarin-red fibreglass against the more organic materials used in the rest of the house.

Robert Venturi + Denise Scott Brown

Venturi House / Philadelphia, USA, 1972

Bradbury/Powers, *The Iconic House*) that launched his career. He and Scott Brown moved into their own home in 1972, the same year that their Las Vegas book was published. They respected the architecture and structure while painting the walls in playful patterns and the collecting continued: ceramics, chairs, prints and paintings, books, models and more were assembled.

'We began collecting florist's vases and the uglier they were the cheaper they were,' says Scott Brown. 'We buy things while they are cheap and then if they get discovered by collectors we change to something else. But we are not really art collectors. If we really collect anything then it probably is the chairs.'

One end of the library is a chair gallery. The sofa in the living room was salvaged from the legendary Traymore Hotel in Atlantic City, which was demolished by implosion in 1972. The table in the dining room once stood in a library and the dining chairs are also from the Traymore. Around the top of the walls, above a framed sequence of 1898 alphabet prints by William Nicholson, are the painted names of Venturi and Scott Brown's heroes: Beethoven, Le Corbusier, Toscanini, Borromini, Aalto, Loos, Wren, Soane, Adam and Mackintosh among others – a typically eclectic list.

1 Denise Scott Brown writing in *Architecture Today*, August 2008.

Biographies
Robert Venturi (1925–) & Denise Scott Brown (1931–)

Architects, designers, academics, theorists and writers, Venturi and Scott Brown have had a profound influence on the direction of 20th- and 21st-century architecture and design. Their writings, especially *Learning From Las Vegas: The Forgotten Symbolism of Architectural Form* (1972), helped shape the post-modern movement. Robert Venturi was born in Philadelphia and graduated from Princeton before working with Eero Saarinen and Louis Kahn. He also spent time travelling and teaching, and met Denise Scott Brown at the University of Pennsylvania. Together they founded their own architectural practice in the 1960s, now known as Venturi, Scott Brown & Associates. Their buildings include the Sainsbury Wing of the National Gallery (1991) and the Seattle Art Museum (1991).

An old petrol station sign sits on the lawn to one side of the house (*left*). In the dining room (*opposite*), the chairs surrounding the table are from the former Traymore Hotel. A sequence of framed alphabet prints by William Nicholson encircles the room, and some prints are displayed in the integrated Arts and Crafts cabinets.

A philosophy of inclusion is threaded through the home of Robert Venturi and Denise Scott Brown. Step into the generous entrance hall of this Art Nouveau-style building at the end of a quiet cul de sac on the edges of Philadelphia and you are greeted by original touches and flourishes, including a sweeping staircase and Moravian Pottery tiles, mixed in with a large and welcoming McDonald's sign plus a small assembly of plywood chairs to Venturi's own design – part of a series for Knoll that embraced Queen Anne, Art Deco, Sheraton and Chippendale styles in the same line.

Venturi and Scott Brown have famously embraced a wealth of architectural and cultural influences in their work, proclaiming 'less is a bore' and fighting against the bland mediocrity of so much in contemporary urban architecture. Their pivotal book, *Learning from Las Vegas*, argued that 'we learn from the architecture and urbanism of gaming as much as we do from gothic cathedrals.'[1]

One does not expect their home, then, to be a minimalist vision in white, and it certainly does not disappoint: neon signs rub shoulders with Art Nouveau furniture, artwork by Andy Warhol and Ed Ruscha is mixed with model Las Vegas signs encased in Plexiglas boxes. The house is packed with personal collections, curios and mementos from a thousand trips.

'I love the eclectic quality of combining all these things,' Venturi says. 'And we did experiment with certain things in this house, like the patterns on the walls, but that's more about us. We had fun doing all these things.'

The house itself was completed in 1909, commissioned by a German industrialist who had come to Philadelphia to open a new factory. The Art Nouveau design combines German and English influences with touches of Charles Rennie Mackintosh, who was popular in Germany at the time. The gardens feature a Lutyens bench commissioned by Venturi and a large orb that once graced a petrol station.

Venturi and Scott Brown are not far from the famous Vanna Venturi House of 1964 (see

The living room (*opposite and below left*) features a floral stencil on the walls and fireplace buttress; the sofa is another salvage piece from the Traymore Hotel. On the mantelpiece is a photo of the Algiers Hotel in Las Vegas next to a metal Coca Cola sign and a landscape by Xanthus Smith. The library (*above right*) includes comfortable family furniture, an Art Nouveau copper chimney piece and a French standing clock as well as models of Las Vegas signs in Plexiglas cases. The entrance hall (*below right*) features an original floor with tiles from the Moravian Pottery.

Marcos Acayaba

Milan House / São Paulo, Brazil, 1975

For Marcos Acayaba, the Milan House in the suburbs of São Paulo has to be the finest project he has ever done. Completed in 1975, with a sweeping concrete roof enclosing the split-level living spaces within, the house has certainly stood the test of time. Acayaba and his wife, Marlene, a writer and expert on Brazilian modernist design, have made the house their home ever since and little has changed over the years.

The house was first designed as a commission for Marlene Acayaba's sister, the psychoanalyst and writer Betty Milan. She gave the architect almost complete freedom to design a home in what was then a quiet green hillside spot on the outskirts of the city. 'She gave me carte blanche,' says Acayaba. 'She requested four bedrooms and a long swimming pool and her husband asked for a photography studio.'

Partly inspired by the sloping site and influenced by the sinuous curves of some of Oscar Niemeyer's buildings, Acayaba designed the all-encompassing, sculpted concrete roof as a vast shell over the entire house. Inside the shell, Acayaba made use of the shifting ground levels to create three distinct but interconnected platforms, with the open-plan living space at the centre, a dining area, kitchen and service spaces on a lower level, and the bedrooms on the more secluded higher level.

'The design was all about enhancing the relationship between the house and the garden, and creating a balance between the two within the site's generous dimensions,' Acayaba says. 'The solution was the reinforced concrete shell…conceived as a roof, which shelters all the inner spaces and allows them to visually connect to the tropical gardens at either end of the house.'

As the project neared completion, Acayaba's sister-in-law decided to relocate to Paris, so she never lived in the house. Acayaba himself, who was only twenty-eight at the time, decided to move into the building with Marlene, and the two of them made the Milan House their family home in the December of 1975.

The strength and beauty of the house lie in the epic contrast between the linear nature of the living spaces and the sinuous curves of the overarching roof, together with the juxtaposition of the sculpted concrete artistry of the building and the lush gardens surrounding the house that soften and enhance it.

The terraces around the pool and the main living level within are unified by the use of red tiled floors inside and out, while many built-in and

bespoke elements of furniture such as the concrete banquette create a sense of clarity. In the master bedroom, restrained minimalism prevails but is enhanced by the rich quality of natural light and ingenious elements such as the vast internal wooden shutters of the en-suite bathroom. The use of pivoting shutters and doorways adds originality to the house while also helping to control ventilation and light levels naturally.

'The ideas that I explored with the Milan House certainly influenced other architectural projects of mine as well,' says Acayaba. 'They were ideas to do with the integration of nature, the continuity of space and the use of natural light…. We love the simplicity of the house and the lightness and, of course, all those connections with the gardens.'

Biography
Marcos Acayaba (1944–)

Marcos Acayaba is among the most respected architects of his generation and a leading Brazilian modernist pioneer, well known for his use of sinuous forms and the way his interior and exterior spaces complement one another. He was born and grew up in São Paulo. In addition to his many architectural projects, Acayaba teaches at the University of São Paulo, which he also attended as a student. His wife, Marlene Milan Acayaba, is a respected author and critic.

The transparent façades at either end of the building allow the greenery of the gardens to seep in (*far left and left*); the lush gardens have been carefully nurtured by Marlene Acayaba over the years. In the main living room (*opposite*) the integrated concrete sofa was designed by Marcos Acayaba while the two leather Chesterfield sofas add a different flavour to the space. The use of red cement tiles inside and outside helps create a fluid transition between the two areas.

The bedrooms and bathrooms (*opposite, above left and above right*) feature large pivoting shutters and doors made of Brazilian timber, providing access to the terraces and gardens as well as an easy way of controlling the glow of natural light. The bespoke sink units were designed by Marcos Acayaba. The studio office (*below right*) is set apart from the main house, beneath the elevated terrace running parallel to the swimming pool.

Ricardo Bofill

La Fábrica / Barcelona, Spain, 1975

It is one of the most ambitious architectural conversions anywhere in the world. On the western fringes of Barcelona, back in the mid-1970s, architect Ricardo Bofill began the work of converting a vast, derelict cement factory – La Fábrica – into a studio complex containing his architectural offices and his own home. Bofill was not daunted by the vast scale of the fomer industrial site. He thought that at the time few people cared what happened to these extraordinary buildings.

'Our main concern was to decide which elements should be preserved and which had to be destroyed,' says Bofill, whose office, Taller de Arquitectura, is still based at La Fábrica. 'The abandoned and half-ruined factory was a magic box of wonderful, surrealist elements. The biggest challenge was to preserve the complex [which seemed] halfway between a ruin and a cloister.'

It included monumental silos, underground tunnels, machine rooms, a smokestack and administration buildings. The factory had grown over the decades, piece by piece, but it was simply too large to be manageable. Bofill began with the careful demolition of around seventy per cent of the factory, carving out the spaces that he wanted to preserve like a sculptor working on a block of stone. The next phase involved landscaping and planting around the factory, creating an organic framework for the buildings while also softening them and making them more accessible and less imposing. It was as though nature had begun to take hold of the factory again, seeking to reclaim its territory.

Key spaces evolved within La Fábrica, chief among them the Cathedral – a central hall and fulcrum functioning as a meeting place, dominated by a vast table designed by Taller de Arquitectura and surrounded by Charles Eames chairs. A piano sits at one end of this dramatic space, which also features giant hoppers and soaring ceilings, with a Gaudí double-backed chair alongside. The juxtaposition of more formal spaces and informal elements, such as the piano, suggests the rich relationship between the worlds of work and the personal realm at La Fábrica.

'We first occupied the silos as both private and work spaces, but the need for additional space for the studio made me reconsider the convenience of separating my private life and my professional activity,' says Bofill. 'I then decided to move my home to the building at La Fábrica that was clearly detached.'

Here, Bofill has created another powerful composition. The home has the feel of a vast, loft-like space, with raw finishes, old pipes and other echoes of its cement factory days. Different zones within the space are delineated by rugs and the purposeful arrangement of furniture rather than any solid partitions, which would undermine the epic volume of the space. One area is populated by crisp white Taller de Arquitectura sofas and Charles Eames recliners, while a library of books is placed against one wall. Another area is arranged as a study-cum-gallery, with pictures arranged on easels. A simple, graphic white staircase leads up to a high mezzanine, where Bofill has created a dining

room, with a table and chairs by Charles Rennie Mackintosh, opening out to the gardens.

'La Fábrica is a magical place with a strange atmosphere,' says Bofill. 'I like life to be perfectly programmed here, ritualized, in total contrast with my turbulent nomadic life.'

It is certainly an extraordinary and brave achievement. The degree of creativity applied to a building that many, at the time, only thought worthy of demolition has helped to inspire the re-evaluation of many former industrial buildings and encouraged their creative reinvention.

Biography
Ricardo Bofill (1939–)

Ricardo Bofill studied architecture in Barcelona and Geneva. He founded the Taller de Arquitectura in 1963 and was associated with the birth of postmodernism in the 1970s, although Bofill rejected the label in later years. Among his early projects was Walden 7 (1974), a large-scale apartment building close to La Fábrica. Other key commissions in Spain included Barcelona Airport Terminal 2 (1991), the Catalonian National Theatre (1996) and the W Barcelona Hotel (2009). Other projects have taken Bofill and his studio partners Peter Hodgkinson and Jean-Pierre Carniaux to America, Japan and other parts of the world.

The former silos and industrial spaces of La Fábrica (*left*) have been transformed into a vibrant creative hub and home, softened by the greenery of the surrounding gardens. The Cathedral within (*opposite*) is a soaring space that is used as a meeting place and conference room by Bofill's Taller de Arquitectura. The table was designed by Bofill's practice, and the chairs are by Charles Eames.

In the private living quarters (*opposite above and above*), soaring ceilings and open spaces create the impression of a vast, loft-like apartment subtly divided into zones for sitting, entertaining and study. The white sofas and armchairs are by Taller de Arquitectura, and the reclining chairs and ottomans are by Charles Eames. The dining area is positioned on a high mezzanine with furniture by Charles Rennie Mackintosh. The dining chairs in the marble salon (*opposite below centre*) and the double-backed chair by the piano in the Cathedral (*opposite below left*) are Gaudi designs.

Andrée Putman

Putman Apartment / Paris, France, 1976

When Andrée Putman first moved into her Paris apartment in the middle of the 1970s, there was no such thing as 'loft living' in France. There were attics and studios but no lofts. It was too early for such concepts and the interior designer's decision to move into a former printing workshop was viewed with bemusement and suspicion, despite her reputation as a pioneer who was one step ahead of the times.

'At the time I received condolences,' says Putman. "Poor Andrée," people would say, "when do you think you will find a real apartment?" Now lofts are so fashionable in Paris – so "*tendance*" – that if it weren't such a physical effort I think I would move.'

Bathed in flattering light from the banks of windows and skylights, tied together by a poured-concrete and resin floor, lightly divided into zones for dining, relaxing and sleeping, Putman's open-plan apartment is as striking, fresh and elegant today as when it was first conceived. Original semi-industrial hallmarks like the iron pillars and metal window frames have been retained but Putman's home is rich in character and comfort. Like so much of her work, her home was conceived with an eye solely for originality, not fashion.

Putman's interiors are always expertly conceived and constructed, with a strict control of detailing, craftsmanship and composition. In one corner of her open-plan studio a seating area has been lightly delineated by a natural weave rug bordered with sofas and chairs, designed by Putman herself. Her bedroom to one side is siphoned away by sheets of hanging gauze curtains, with spaces for dining and work also sharing this one vast room.

Many pieces of furniture are rich in memories and have their own stories to tell. The extraordinary 18th-century grandfather clock – all the more dramatic against the simple backdrop of white-painted walls and concrete floor – was a piece that Putman had periodically chased around Paris as it moved from dealer to dealer, until one day a grateful client unexpectedly presented it to her as a gift.

The pair of ornate, carved wooden armchairs by the side windows were designed for the famous actress Sarah Bernhardt for her plays. The ornate period chest of drawers in one corner, topped by a golden pot by Jean-Pierre Raynaud and golden orbs by Lucio Fontana, belonged to her grandfather.

Other pieces are classics from the 1930s: the Jacques-Émile Ruhlmann dining chairs, the dining table by Paul Dupré-Lafon, as well as the dramatic black lacquered desk by Jeanne Lanvin. Walls have been kept a uniform white, partly to better present Putman's collection of artwork, including pieces by Max Ernst, Julian Schnabel, Bram van Velde and photographer Peter Lindbergh.

'I actually like the relationship between objects – the mixture of things – even more than the individual pieces themselves,' says Putman. 'I like the way they go together because that's unique, and I have found some incredible things because I like to go looking in unusual places. But also flexibility is one of the things I like, so I can change things and move things around in the apartment quite easily. It doesn't just stay still.'

To one side of the main studio, Putman designed a separate bathroom, all tiled in white, and upstairs, on the roof of the building, she created a glass room to house a kitchen and breakfast area, with the lush roof garden outside offering dramatic views across the rooftops of Paris. A personal, calm and quiet space, Putman's apartment offers a retreat from her working life. It has also inspired countless imitations and variations on sophisticated loft-style living.

Biography
Andrée Putman (1925–)

Encouraged by her mother to enter the world of music, Putman initially thought she might become a composer, but daunted by the prospect of isolated study, she decided on a different path, in design. She began her career in Paris working in magazines and then in product design for the Prisunic stores. She launched herself as an interior designer and founded Ecart – a gallery championing designers such as Eileen Gray and Pierre Chareau – in 1978. In the years that followed, her work involved not only residential schemes but also many cultural projects and hotels, including Morgans in New York and Pershing Hall in Paris, as well as ranges of furniture and products. Putman is widely credited as a key influence by generations of younger designers.

The poured-concrete floors of the apartment are coated in resin to create a reflective surface to circulate light around the space (*above and opposite*). The Art Deco dining table was designed by Paul Dupré-Lafon, and the 1930s dining chairs are by Jacques-Émile Ruhlmann; the black lacquered desk was designed by Jeanne Lanvin. The bedroom (*below*) is divided off by diaphanous gauze curtains.

Nicholas Haslam + John Fowler

Hunting Lodge / Hampshire, UK, 1977

Always looking for something new and never one to repeat himself, Nicholas ('Nicky') Haslam is a true chameleon. He reinvents himself and his look constantly so his design style is almost impossible to pin down. Grounded in tradition and neoclassicism, he draws on references from countless sources. Haslam responds to every project differently, creating a highly tailored result.

'I have no style,' he says. 'The room has a style, the building has a style, the country has a style. Not one of my jobs is the same.'[1]

Haslam's country home in Hampshire offers a glorious, very personal indication of his tastes, but it is also pivotal in the evolution of British interior design. The Hunting Lodge was built for Henry VII, and his oldest son, Arthur, is thought to have first met Catherine of Aragon here. A picture-postcard Jacobean gable was added around 1620.

The house is owned by the National Trust and has been rented by Haslam on a long-term basis since the late 1970s. The previous tenant was the legendary John Fowler, co-founder of Colefax & Fowler (see page 19). Haslam respected Fowler's ideas for the house, preserving and restoring many finishes, fabrics and paint colours, including the oxblood and distemper mix on the sitting room

walls and the wall covering in the master bedroom. Unable to extend or adapt the house, Fowler also built a freestanding summer sitting room in a pavilion in the garden, which is now used by Haslam for entertaining.

Haslam has added many elements of his own that sit well with the tone set by Fowler. The rooms are modest in scale and Haslam has filled them, adding layer upon layer of furniture and artworks to create a comfortable cluttered country-house feel. 'It's certainly casual,' says Haslam. 'But there has to be a kind of built-in structure, otherwise it gets too messy.'[2]

The dining room marks the biggest change since Fowler's time: two small rooms have been turned into a more generous space, with the walls painted in a decorative chinoiserie pattern by trompe l'oeil artist Paul Czainski. To one side of the room, a neoclassical 18th-century French pedestal rises upwards, almost to the ceiling, creating a powerful focal point. An oversized English Gothic cabinet also adds to the sense of drama.

It is not easy to distinguish where Fowler's influence ends and Haslam's begins. It is, ultimately, a collaboration that spans decades, tying together two significant talents of British interior design.

Haslam's respect for Fowler's work says much about Haslam himself, but the Hunting Lodge also has a wider significance, offering a quintessentially English take on country living, full of character and charm.

1 Interview with Lynn Barber, *The Observer*, 26 November 2000.
2 Quoted in *Traditional Home*, November 2003.

Biography
Nicholas Haslam (1939–)

Designer, writer, social commentator and *bon viveur* Nicholas Haslam has a reputation as a larger-than-life character, and his accomplishments in the world of interior design are undisputed. The son of a diplomat, Haslam was educated at Eton, where he gravitated towards art and design. After a short period at art school, he moved to New York, where he worked at American *Vogue* under Diana Vreeland, and later to Arizona. In the early 1970s he went back to London and launched his career in interior design. He founded NH Design in the late 1980s and clients included many society figures. In 1995, Haslam's former business partner Paolo Moschino took ownership of the Nicholas Haslam shop, which sells Haslam's collections of furniture and fabrics.

The colours of the walls in the sitting room (*opposite below left*), originally chosen by John Fowler, were made with oxblood and distemper, and the sepia engravings behind the sofa were picked by Haslam. The walls in the dining room (*opposite below right*) were painted by Paul Czainski; the French column is topped by a fibreglass urn.

Albert Hadley

Hadley Residence / New York, USA, 1978

It was one of the most influential partnerships in the world of interior design: on one side, Mrs Henry Parish II, or Sister Parish, as she was most widely known, a socialite and admirer of sophisticated American country style, influenced by Nancy Lancaster (see page 19) and Colefax & Fowler. Her passion was for rooms of an informal elegance, with layers of pattern, chintz and period furniture. On the other, Albert Hadley, who came from a very different background. A southerner, who had spent time in Europe building airfields during the war, he had studied at the Parsons School of Design and worked at the design firm McMillen. Hadley was open to a range of influences from the United States and Europe, including the work of Manhattan designer William Pahlmann. He also had a strong architectural understanding of the proportions and bones of the spaces with which he was working.

When the two combined forces in 1962, as Parish-Hadley, it was a marriage made in heaven. 'She was a formidable personality, a woman of great style and taste, and with a great eye,' said Hadley. 'We complemented each other. I learned so much from her but I was a bit more adventuresome. By adventuresome I mean investigating new techniques and new materials that we could bring to the pot. Little by little I think I brought a freshness of approach.'

At the time when Parish and Hadley forged their alliance, Sister Parish was just finishing the interiors of the White House for the Kennedys. After John F. Kennedy's death, Hadley helped his widow Jackie with the design of an apartment in New York. The company's client list was extraordinary, including Brooke Astor, Al Gore and Oscar de la Renta.

From the late 1970s, when Parish-Hadley was in its heyday, Hadley based himself in an apartment on the Upper East Side in New York, a location he found highly convenient as he liked to be able to walk to the office and feel at the heart of things. The apartment building dates from the 1920s and the proportions of the apartment are homely. Hadley reconfigured the spaces, adding storage and removing unnecessary elements such as the columns in the entrance hall.

'It has changed over the years,' said Hadley, who also had a country home in Southport. 'I can't stop changing things. Things come and go; there are some things that mean a lot but I'm willing to change if I see something better.'

The most generous room in the apartment was devoted to a large study, with a 1920s desk by the window and bespoke bookcases either side of the fireplace, where a mirror, designed by Hadley for Baker furniture and inspired by a 1930s French design, sits above the mantelpiece. The sense of light in this space, with its eclectic mix of 1930s and 1950s furniture, contrasts with the bright red, textured walls of the entrance hall. Here, the limited volume is lifted dramatically by the intense colour treatment.

In the modestly sized sitting room, a tailored, built-in sofa flanked by discreet closets helps make the most of the available space while a large mirror above it helps maximize the sense of light. A table-top display to one side of the room features a fetching portrait of Elsie de Wolfe (see page 13) and a figurine once owned by Hadley's mentor, Van Day Truex, principal of the Parsons School and the man who introduced him to Sister Parish.

In this carefully considered, delightfully composed and always elegant apartment, Hadley made the very most of every available corner, introducing splashes of colour against a calm canvas of cream and stone. The apartment provides a gentle masterclass in creating sophisticated interiors suited to a sense of well-being, courtesy of one of the most venerated designers in New York.

Biography
Albert Hadley (1920–2012)

Known as 'the dean of American decorating', Albert Hadley influenced generations of younger designers such as David Easton and Bunny Williams. He was born in Springfield, Tennessee, and took a strong interest in design from an early age. He studied architecture before working with A. Herbert Rogers, one of the most respected interior designers in the South. After World War II, when Hadley was involved in building air strips in Europe, he studied and then taught at the Parsons School of Design in New York. He worked with Eleanor Brown at McMillen before joining Sister Parish (1910–1994) to form Parish-Hadley Associates in 1962. Hadley continued the company for a number of years after Parish's death before forming his own practice in 1999.

Hadley's study (*above and opposite*) is the largest of the rooms. The round sculpture is by Cornelia Kavanagh and the painting between the windows is by Mark Schurillo; the leather chair was designed by Antonio Bonet Castellana, while the mirror is a Hadley design for Baker Furniture. The bed in the bedroom (*right*) is a Hadley design underneath a Francis Weinberg painting.

John Stefanidis

Cock Crow / Dorset, UK, 1978

John Stefanidis is the master of refined comfort. His interiors are erudite and thoughtful but they are also luxurious and indulgent, placing emphasis on the essential – yet often undervalued – qualities of comfort and warmth. As a designer, Stefanidis draws on a wide range of influences from around the world but always moulds them into a cohesive and calming entity. Grounded in neoclassicism and tradition, he also brings a contemporary quality to his space as well as a love of texture and colour. He creates his own fabrics and furniture, so houses by Stefanidis usually offer many bespoke elements within a tailored and individual approach.

Stefanidis is something of a chameleon, a designer with a careful, sensitive eye for the context, history and character of a home. His own houses suggest as much, with his home in Patmos, Greece, having, as one might expect, a very different atmosphere from the grand townhouse that Stefanidis kept in London's Cheyne Walk for many years. Then there is Cock Crow in Dorset, the designer's distinctive and enticing reinterpretation of an English country residence.

The subject of Stefanidis's own book *Living by Design*, Cock Crow and its surrounding gardens were created from a disparate collection of farm buildings and barns. When Stefanidis first saw them they were all derelict and coated in ivy. 'I never had a moment's hesitation,' he says. 'I knew when I saw it….No one had ever lived there, but I knew that I could.'[1]

Stefanidis had been looking for a country house for some time, but he did not want a grand home; he was after something informal and relaxed. The cowsheds of Cock Crow, surrounded by an acre of land, offered Stefanidis the perfect opportunity to create exactly what he wanted. Designed around a central courtyard garden that was once the old farmyard, the house has some of the qualities of a Romanesque villa yet is also very much of its place. A choice of private gardens, terraces and green rooms has been created around the house, where the compound nature of the barns allowed Stefanidis to clearly assign particular functions to particular structures, including a large new gallery that connects the master bedroom and sitting room at one side of the house with the guest rooms on the other.

The floors are in red brick, chosen for their rustic character, while the original timber beams were left exposed. The walls are largely painted white, sometimes mixed with a touch of ochre or sienna. Neither furniture nor finishes are overly refined, but have a modesty that suits the nature of the house. 'I wanted maximum luxury in simple surroundings, not grand surroundings with little luxury',[2] he says.

Many elements – from bookcases to cupboards – are bespoke designs, created in sympathy with the character of Cock Crow. Against a largely neutral backdrop, upholstery is used to introduce the key colour notes, such as brown and maroon for the large sitting room, switching to pale sky blues in summer, when covers are placed over the furniture. The Indian sitting room is dominated by sofas and ottomans in a bougainvillea pink, brought alive by the rich quality of natural light.

Cock Crow is a delightful, seductive treatment of English country style. His work can take Stefanidis in many different directions, but this was one of his most influential homes (partly because of the associated book). 'The range is what keeps me interested,' says Stefanidis. 'Otherwise you can become repetitive if you are not careful.'

1 Quoted in John Stefanidis, *Living by Design*, 1997.
2 Ibid.

Biography
John Stefanidis (1937–)

Born in Alexandria and educated in Egypt and Eritrea, John Stefanidis studied at Oxford University, where he nurtured his growing interest in design and art history. He worked for an advertising agency in London and Milan before buying and decorating a house in Patmos, an island that became a second home to him. He established his own design company in Chelsea, London, in 1967 and has concentrated largely on residential commissions for an exclusive and international client base. He has also worked on Le Richemond Hotel, Geneva, designed ranges of fabrics and furniture, and produced a number of books on design.

In the large sitting room (*opposite*) the brick floors are softened by straw matting. A drawing by Matisse sits next to an African head sculpture and a Koran stand on an oak table against the far wall. The library (*above*) includes a carpet, upholstery and ottoman designed by Stefanidis as well as oak bookcases.

The sitting room (*above*) features high ceilings and exposed timber beams, and the gallery (*right*) ties together the two separate wings of the house between the guest quarters and the main part of the house containing the sitting rooms and master bedroom. Above the fitted cabinet with cherry-wood top is a dresser containing Irish Delft blue-and-white plates.

In the corner of the guest bedroom sits a Piedmontese sofa in pink chintz underneath a collection of drawings of Venice by artist Teddy Millington-Drake (*left*). The room contains a four-poster bed designed by Stefanidis with a Yellow Butterfly curtain fabric; the painted cupboard against the wall is French (*above*).

David Hicks

The Grove / Oxfordshire, UK, 1979

The room was dominated by a circular dining table, often set with a pink table cloth, and Hicks kept it deliberately uncluttered. The hallway is wide and generous, with walls coated in a 'watermelon'-colour paper with chocolate banding around the edges.

The library is a more intimate, club-like space, where Hicks emblazoned the chimney breast with red velvet and adorned the windows with vibrant, papal purple curtains. In Hicks's own bedroom a bath was integrated into the room itself, nestling neatly in an alcove. Another bedroom nearby is a radiant yellow and mandarin composition, while purple and gold combine in an attic bedroom. As one might expect from Hicks, there are plenty of startling combinations and colourful tales of the unexpected.

'Like food,' Hicks wrote, 'colour is to be enjoyed. It works on a visceral level, and only by broadening your experience can you begin to assess the impact of a particular shade or the effectiveness of a certain combination.'[2]

The experiments continued, sometimes startling, sometimes more subdued. Hicks lived at The Grove for twenty years and died there in 1998, but his spirit, imagination and creativity clearly live on among all the designers who are willing to experiment and to take risks, and who refuse to take the easiest option.

1 David Hicks, *Style and Design*, 1987.
2 Ibid.

Biography
David Hicks (1928–1998)

One of the most influential interior designers of the 1960s and 70s, David Hicks created not just an international design company but an entire brand around his work, spreading his fame and ideas through countless magazine articles and his own books. Born in Coggeshall, Essex, Hicks was the son of a stockbroker. He studied at the Central School of Art and Design before working in the advertising agency J. Walter Thompson. He developed his own original approach to interiors, and in 1954 *House & Garden* magazine published a feature on Hicks's own London home that launched his career. His glittering client list included Vidal Sassoon, Helena Rubinstein and international royalty. Hicks also launched product ranges, wallpapers and textiles and opened satellite offices around the world. In 1960, he married Lady Pamela Mountbatten. The David Hicks brand is now managed by his son Ashley, who is also a designer in his own right.

Hicks wanted a simple background in the drawing room to display pictures and decorative objects, so the walls of the room were covered in a rose-pink French cotton with matching curtains in an elaborate formation (*left and opposite*). The carpet is one of the designer's trademark geometric designs, adding a more contemporary note to the many period elements. The portraits are by George Romney.

Few designers have had such a profound effect on the way we think about colour and pattern as David Hicks. Through his houses, his commissions, his books and textile designs and the filter-down effect on other designers that followed, Hicks encouraged us to experiment. He laid out his thinking clearly and thoughtfully, yet he also advocated breaking the rules now and then, and became a household name in the process.

'Many of the most successful schemes derive their impact from a startling combination of colours or a novel combination of patterns which fly in the face of accepted practice,' he wrote. 'Rules give structure, but often at the expense of vitality.'[1]

Perhaps the most famous expressions of Hicks's thinking were laid out at his own country homes, Britwell Salome and The Grove, both in Oxfordshire, which were often used as case studies in his own books. Like so many of Hicks's residential commissions, they combined the proportions, scale and architectural detailing of neoclassical architecture with a more radical, original approach to decoration and an often eclectic combination of furniture.

The Grove was essentially a period farmhouse that had been extended in the 1790s, set within parkland and gardens that Hicks redesigned both to show the house at its best from the outside and to create sympathetic vistas from the principal rooms. In the drawing room, Hicks stretched rose-pink cotton on the walls and introduced one of his trademark geometric carpets; he had begun designing his own carpets in the early 1960s when he could not source any interesting ones to suit his projects. A series of portraits by George Romney, inherited by Hicks's wife, Lady Pamela Mountbatten, were hung against the calm, textured pink backdrop.

The dining room, in an *eau de nil* colour scheme, reused painted wall panels brought over from Britwell, where they had graced Lady Pamela's study.

Hicks kept the dining room (*opposite*) deliberately free of clutter, allowing the painted wall panels to become the focus of the room. The library (*above left*) is a more intimate space with the feel of a gentleman's club, but it also offers surprises such as the purple curtains against the windows. The bedrooms (*above*) are more feminine spaces, with a sense of grandeur afforded by the bed hangings – Hicks likened the art of soft furnishing to dressmaking.

Eduardo Longo

Casa Bola / São Paulo, Brazil, 1979

Imagine a vast lattice-like structure many storeys high at the heart of the city. Into this lattice slot a series of spheres large enough to contain a family home, neatly aligned on an ordered grid. The spare spaces around these spheres enable light and air to percolate through the superstructure, while also allowing for privacy and a sense of containment for each apartment within the collective. This was the visionary dream of Brazilian architect Eduardo Longo, who imagined future cities with these spherical apartments stacked one on top of another.

Looking for a way to convey and develop his ideas, Longo decided to build a nearly full-scale prototype of one of these apartments on the roof of his own low-slung home/office in São Paulo, beginning in 1974. 'I became interested in spherical buildings when I was searching for an ideal volume that could become an industrially produced, modular apartment,' says Longo. 'Weight was a very important issue, and no volume is lighter than a sphere.'

Handling much of the work himself, Longo created a steel frame that was coated in layers of moulded concrete. Casa Bola was created with a series of four levels and half-levels gradually stepping upwards through the building, with

bedrooms and storage areas in the lower part of the sphere, the entrance, kitchen and dining spaces at the centre, and the main living spaces up at the top, featuring large windows looking out across the city.

'The living room is my favourite space in the house, for its natural light and peaceful feeling,' Longo says. 'I also like the fact that I hand-built the house, empirically, almost by myself, with no previous experience and no structural engineering calculations.'

Inspired by the compact, rounded hulls of boat and yacht design, Casa Bola treats the interior space as an integral part of the structure and form of the building, rather than as a distinct and separate realm. The living spaces are organic, sculpted and bespoke, with moulded concrete used to create the sensuous curves of the beds, kitchen counters, steps, washbasins, bookshelves and desks that seem to grow from the walls.

Everything is tailored to the house by necessity, given that standard pieces of furniture would not fit in with the curved rooms of Casa Bola. This creates a powerful sense of cohesion, with almost all the elements tied together by a crisp white paint finish. Only the earthy browns of the soft carpet in the living room offer a contrast, while self-designed

banquettes are coated in white leather. There is a playful quality to the house, shown by the spiralling escape slide at the bottom of the sphere.

Longo moved into Casa Bola with his wife and two children, and completed one other spherical house soon after. The idea of great tiers of spherical apartments has not yet been taken up by city developers, but Longo has not lost faith in his concept.

As a home, Casa Bola represents a highly individual approach, its sinuous character reminiscent of a number of other experimental, pioneering buildings of the 1970s and 80s such as Antti Lovag's Palais Bulles (see Bradbury/Powers, *The Iconic House*). The simple, sculpted purity of the interior appears as though carved from a block of stone and the compact and integrated layout has helped to influence the design of many space-saving city centre apartments.

A yellow slide provides an alternative exit to the spherical house (*right*), which stands out all the more against the backdrop of rectangular buildings (*left*). The living room at the top of Casa Bola (*opposite*) includes fitted white leather sofas designed by Longo and a deep pile carpet in a chocolate brown that contrasts with the predominantly white interiors.

Biography
Eduardo Longo (1942–)

Based in São Paulo, Longo was one of a disparate, radical group of utopian architects who began experimenting with new ways of thinking about architecture in the 1970s. They looked for alternative forms, structures and interiors that had little connection with the architectural or design mainstream, but owed more to inspirational thinkers such as Buckminster Fuller. Longo developed more than one hundred projects, some of which have not yet been realized, and has also contributed widely to the ongoing debate about the shape of cities to come. Casa Bola has become his most iconic and distinctive creation.

A whole range of space-saving ideas has been applied to the compact three-bedroom home, which has the feel of a ship, complete with porthole windows (*opposite and above*). Beds, shelves and kitchen counters have been woven into the fabric of the house itself, appearing to grow from the walls organically. A model (*opposite right*) shows what an apartment building composed of Longo's stacked spherical homes might look like.

Anthony Collett

Collett House / London, UK, 1982

There was a time when Anthony Collett was afraid of colour. Not that you would know it now, glancing around his London home. It shines with colours of all kinds: shimmering golds and racing greens, cobalt blues and ruby reds. Collett's sitting room, in particular, is a treat for the senses, with almost every surface covered with a collection of Ruskin, Moorcroft and Bretby pottery set against walls in Dutch gold leaf and a deep, regal crimson below the dado rails.

'Colour is something I came to quite late in life,' says Collett. 'I had always feared colour enormously, and my training in design took me towards a uniform architectural-school grey or black and white because they never looked at how to deal with colour. But what really helped me was collecting the vases. I suddenly realized that if colours are good, like the glaze on these ceramics, they could be put together even if they contrasted with one another. If it's a good colour it can go with virtually anything else.'

This revelation came at a time when, to give his wife a break on a Saturday morning, Collett would take their young children out for a walk down Portobello Road and the street market. The English studio pottery he saw on those weekend trips was affordable so he started collecting, piece by piece, and encouraged by his friends, the artists Gilbert & George, who have one of the largest collections of 19th-century studio pottery in the country.

Slowly, colour began to seep into Collett's home, a high-ceilinged and well-proportioned Victorian house. On the raised ground floor, Collett removed a dividing wall to turn two rooms into one large sitting room, with the pottery collection covering the walls, grouped on a complex formation of sconces. The furniture is a mix of period pieces including a Fortuny standing light and Arts and Crafts dining chairs, with a wealth of bespoke pieces designed by Collett himself, including a sofa, stools and a small dining table. Synthetic velvet curtains, of a kind often used in the theatre, reinforce the drama of the room.

'I do like to think in terms of theatre,' Collett says, 'and I suppose subliminally I was also influenced by Africa and African art, because I was born in Zambia. And so there was the enormous influence of art, music, tribal theatre and things like that.'

Traces of tribal patterns surface in the upholstery and fabrics, and a passion for texture, natural materials and sculptural shapes is evident. The solid foundations of his work, however, are in classical architecture, paying close attention to proportion, symmetry and scale, but applied to a more contemporary look.

Other parts of Collett's house suggest this grounding more clearly, such as the basement that was originally a separate flat and then integrated back into the rest of the house in the form of an open-plan kitchen and dining room. Collett designed the space with oak panelling and a marble surround around the cooking range in the kitchen, painted tongue and groove in the dining area and a salvaged Victorian vestry cabinet along one wall.

'These are the words I use to describe what we do: classical, contemporary, traditional, eclectic,' says Collett. 'But it all depends on where we are. We are chameleons. We will adapt our vocabulary and palette accordingly. It's the same with my house. It's one style, one of many outfits….'

Biography
Anthony Collett (1948–)

Born in Zambia, Anthony Collett went to school and university in South Africa before going to London to study fine art and sculpture at the Hornsey College of Art. He went on to study interior design and attended the Royal College of Art. Collett was mentored by and worked with interior designer John Stefanidis (see page 182) for seven years. A partnership with interior architect John McCloud followed before the formation of Collett Champion, together with David Champion, in the late 1980s. Collett now works in partnership with Andrzej Zarzycki under the name Collett-Zarzycki, focusing on architectural design and furniture design with a range of residential and hotel projects in the UK, Europe and further afield.

The lustrous golden walls of the combined dining room and sitting room (*below and opposite*) provide a powerful backdrop to Collett's colour-coordinated collection of Moorcroft, Bretby and Ruskin pottery, which is arranged on numerous sconces and other surfaces. The chess-board dining table was designed by Collett and is accompanied by Christopher Dresser dining chairs. The sofa in the corner was also designed by Collett.

The kitchen (*opposite*) is positioned
on the lower ground floor and was
entirely designed by Anthony Collett,
including the oak panelling and
the kitchen table. The bathroom
(*right*) has a restrained sense of
simplicity and elegance with its
tongue-and-groove walls and Arts
and Crafts armchairs; the bath
was salvaged from a house that
was being remodelled. The intense
colours of Collett's pottery collection
harmonize with the furniture and
gold-leaf walls (*above*).

Jacques Grange

Grange Apartment / Paris, France, 1984

A step away from the Louvre and the Jardin des Tuileries, Jacques Grange's apartment is at the very heart of Paris. It has an extraordinary pedigree, having once been the home of Colette, the great iconoclastic author and actress. Her favourite spot by the window is now occupied by Grange's own chaise longue and her spirit still lingers about the place: a small bust, capturing her famous riot of frizzy hair, sits on a table and there is a portrait by Irving Penn in a royal red frame. Yet Grange has managed to make the apartment very much his own.

'She lived here until she died in 1954,' says Grange. 'After that, her daughter lived here until she died as well, about thirty years later. Then I arrived and took the flat, empty, just the bust and a portrait. But it was difficult because I respect Colette very much – I care about Colette, I love her books – and I didn't want to destroy her flat. But step by step I had to say it's not my style, it's not my way of life. And step by step I reinterpreted the apartment.'

The flat is richly furnished with pieces by Jean-Michel Frank, Emilio Terry, Paul Iribe, Alexandre Noll and André Arbus. There are ceramics and artworks by Giacometti, Picasso, Christian Bérard and Edward Burne-Jones, as well as photographs by Irving Penn, Cecil Beaton and François-Marie Banier. Grange applies the expert eye of a seasoned collector to his choices. He began buying pieces by Frank in the 1960s when they cost very little and only a handful of people were seeking out his work.

Most of the original architectural detailing in the flat was preserved, including the cornicing, the doorways and the 19th-century skylight in painted glass that forms the dining room ceiling. A fireplace was changed, but the original carefully preserved just in case it might be needed one day. Canvas painted in a sandstone colour inspired by the colour of the stonework of the Palais-Royal itself was placed on the walls, tying the various rooms of the apartment together. Furniture, art and fabrics were combined with a mixture of neoclassical pieces and 20th-century design classics.

'I try to give another manner to presenting the past for today, which is a modern attitude,' says Grange. The sitting room is dominated by a trinity formed by a Grange-designed sofa, a 19th-century neo-Gothic mahogany screen and a 1930s tapestry with an 18th-century look by Ernest Boiceau. There are gondolier chairs in Art Deco style by Iribe and wooden armchairs from the Villa Taylor in

Marrakesh, dating from the 1920s, as well as artwork by Hockney, Bérard and Banier. Every corner has a story, exuberant in detail and composition.

The adjoining library is the apartment's most extraordinary construction, centred around tall bookcases designed by Grange to fit in with a pair of Empire walnut étagères and a large slate and iron desk. Every surface is rich with exquisite gems: a vase by Picasso, white plaster pieces by Giacometti from the 1930s and a Frederic Leighton bronze draped with a coral necklace crowd together on the dark slate. Opposite is a large display rack packed with paintings and photographs, and below a Roman claw foot sits a photograph by Banier of a youthful Grange, looking like a star of the silver screen. The blend is highly individual, considered and seductive.

'I love the end of the 18th century, the end of the Louis XVI period, which I think is the most elegant movement,' Grange says. 'But I also love some artists of the Art Deco period: Frank, Emilio Terry, Pierre Chareau. It is all about mixing objects and furniture from different periods in homes that are comfortable and elegant. I hate the great, official house. You can have great things but in a very low-key presentation.'

Biography
Jacques Grange (1944–)

Born in Saint-Amand-Montrond, France, Jacques Grange studied at the École Boulle and the École Camondo in Paris. He worked with interior designer Henri Samuel and later Alain Demachy and Didier Aaron before founding his own company in 1970. He has designed homes for Yves Saint Laurent, Pierre Bergé, Princess Caroline of Monaco, Isabelle Adjani and many others, and among his hotel projects is The Mark in New York. Key influences include Marie-Laure de Noailles, Jean-Michel Frank and Madeleine Castaing (see page 92), whom Grange first met in the 1970s.

The desk in the library (*opposite*)
dates from the 1950s; sitting on it are
a vase by Picasso and various plaster
pieces by Alberto Giacometti. The
bookcases were designed by Grange,
as was the sofa in the sitting room
(*right*). The tapestry is an Ernest
Boiceau design and dates from the
1930s. By contrast, the bedroom
(*below*) has a simpler aesthetic,
with warmer tones provided by
the wallpaper and fabrics.

Blass Apartment / New York, USA, 1985

'Decorating should be an adventure,' Bill Blass once said, and he was as good as his word. As well as being a fashion designer, Blass had a powerful reputation as a tastemaker. His sense of style flowed through into a passion for collecting and a love of design and interiors. Late in life he launched his own furniture range, which was the result of decades of fascination with interior design. Well known for his talents for layering and editing in the world of fashion, Blass applied the same ethos to the look of his homes, which constantly changed and evolved over the years.

Blass expressed his passion for interior design in both town and country: he had a country home in Connecticut and also an apartment at Sutton Place on 57th Street in New York. Blass was a tenant in this 1927 building, designed by Rosario Candela, for many years. But after buying his spacious penthouse apartment he made many changes, creating a strong, simple architectural backdrop for his extraordinary collections of furniture and art.

Blass collaborated initially with designers Chessy Rayner and Mica Ertegun of Mac II, reordering the apartment in a number of areas. He ruled out many pieces that he had collected in earlier years and enjoyed assembling a fresh gathering of artworks and furnishings. In the 1990s, Blass significantly reinvented the apartment again.

There is a simplicity and purity to the strong and masculine neoclassical nature of the spaces, with the polished timber floors, panelled walls and painted white cornicing. Shutters at the windows dispense with the need for intricate window treatments.

Blass created a spare setting that gave him the space to layer the apartment with his collections. An avid and intelligent buyer, Blass would often travel to Europe with advisers and buy from dealers such as Axel Vervoordt (see page 214), Christopher Gibbs and Geoffrey Bennison. Although he is thought of as an all-American designer, Blass enjoyed mixing pieces from many different sources – France, Scotland and England among them – as well as blending old and new.

Blass's eye for proportion, scale, symmetry and composition was highly trained. He resisted any temptation to overload the apartment with the fruits of his many buying trips, always editing down his finds within spaces that are essentially soothing and uncluttered, creating a quality that is both fresh and timeless.

The bedroom, in particular, is brought to life by the grandeur of its proportions and the luxury of space, with the bed neatly positioned in a corner alcove between the windows and fireplace. The rest of the room becomes a multifaceted gallery, library and study full of interest. A French 19th-century bronze of Napoleon stands by the window, while a 1666 trompe l'oeil artwork by Jacobus Biltius hangs on the opposite wall. In the living room, a period rendering of a warship's hull above the fireplace looks down on a pair of Regency daybeds, with classical busts raised on pillars either side of the fireplace.

These rooms were much photographed and admired; they still are. Blass managed the difficult balancing act of surrounding himself with fine and characterful pieces placed within an environment that was also relaxing, comfortable and homely rather than precious or intimidating. The Blass style has an enduring influence today.

Biography
Bill Blass (1922–2002)

Bill Blass was born in Indiana, the son of a dressmaker and a father who died young. As a young student, Blass filled the margins of his notebooks with fashion sketches and began sewing and selling his clothes in his teens. He moved to New York in 1941, where he studied at the McDowell School followed by the Parsons School of Design. After a period in the army with a camouflage battalion, Blass returned to Manhattan and began designing for Anna Miller and Maurice Rentner. In 1970 he established his own company and the label continued to grow rapidly over the next thirty years. A shrewd businessman as well as a talented tastemaker, Blass is best known for his crisp, impeccably tailored and sophisticated all-American look. His label continued after his death in 2002.

Generous proportions, a love of symmetry, natural light and a neutral backdrop all help to define the large living room in the Blass apartment (*left and opposite*). A pair of Regency daybeds lends a relaxed, luxurious quality, and the classical busts either side of the fireplace add a note of refinement. The white sofa placed in the middle introduces a more contemporary note to this elegant loft-like space.

The extraordinary bedroom (*overleaf*) is a unique blend of a 'sleeping studio', gallery, study and library. With its elaborate cornicing and simple window shutters the room is marked by a strong 18th-century neoclassical influence. A French 19th-century bust of Napoleon stands by the window, while period architectural models are placed on the circular table.

Zeynep Fadillioglu

Fadillioglu House / Istanbul, Turkey, 1987

The fireplace in Zeynep Fadillioglu's living room tells its own, insightful story about the Turkish designer's work. Set against a backdrop of walls marked by the patina of age, with a mantelpiece holding a painting and an ornate clock, the composition seems natural and effortless. The clock is an 18th-century French piece, while the artwork is an abstract painting by contemporary Turkish artist Tayfun Erdogmus, who uses coal, sand and ash in his art. The stone fireplace was salvaged from an Anatolian village, while the walls echo the original colours of the space, which sits within a rebuilt section of an old orangery that collapsed decades ago.

This combination of elements into a seamless whole sums up Fadillioglu's method of blending east and west, old and new into something fresh and enticing. In her living room, collections of ceramics also cover many surfaces – the fruits of years of careful hunting, mixed with pieces inherited from her grandfather – while rugs, textile panels and the rich fabrics on the sofas and chairs introduce deeper, bolder notes. It is a rich and vibrant fusion.

'In my childhood, living with a large family I got used to being bombarded with different ideas, tastes and views,' says Fadillioglu, who studied in both Turkey and Britain. 'In order to catch the rhythms and live in harmony, one must be able to connect all these things together and reach a synthesis. This kind of background gave me the chance and ability to put very different objects together and to be able to create a successful space.'

Fadillioglu began working on the house in 1987 and now shares it with her husband. Not far from the banks of the Bosphorus, it was built in the late 18th century and was once the summer residence of a clockmaker to the sultan, who used to live on the upper storey and store his carriages on the lower level. Fadillioglu was also able to buy the adjoining house and set about combining the two living spaces while preserving a sense of separation to the floors above, which are linked by a terrace. The living room forms the heart of the home.

'After the work was finished I moved into the houses with a lifetime of art, objects and collections, and some antiques from my grandfather,' Fadillioglu says. 'For me the most important qualities in a space are soul, taste and the rhythm between the colours and objects, as well as the lighting that contributes to a sense of harmony in colour and texture. I like the feeling of living in a house with traces of lives left behind, which form the natural elements of the design.'

In addition to the large sitting room in the former orangery, Fadillioglu has created a choice of other living areas in a range of colours, from the crisp celadon walls of the dining room through to the intense ochre of another salon. Great emphasis is placed on small assemblies of seemingly disparate pieces and objects – vessels, urns, candlesticks, curios, keys and framed calligraphy – that combine to create the most pleasing composition.

This studied mélange of different textures, Ottoman textiles, architectural history and more contemporary notes lies at the core of Fadillioglu's work. It has placed the designer firmly at the forefront of a fast-developing Turkish design scene that includes her cousin, the fashion designer Rifat Ozbek, and others, and has an impact far beyond Istanbul.

Biography
Zeynep Fadillioglu (1955–)

Zeynep Fadillioglu was born in Istanbul, where she attended an English school. She moved to the UK to study at Sussex University, followed by a course in Art History and Design at the Inchbald School in London. She began a career as a systems analyst but then moved into designing restaurants and nightclubs in Istanbul and Antalya, working with her husband, the entrepreneur Metin Fadillioglu. She founded her own design practice in 1995, mixing residential commissions with hotels. In 2009, she designed the interior of the Sakirin Mosque in Istanbul, which was the first to be designed by a woman.

In the main sitting room (*opposite*) an abstract artwork by Tayfun Erdogmus sits on the mantelpiece behind an ornate French clock. The low coffee table holds part of a collection of ceramics assembled by Fadillioglu over the past thirty-five years, along with pieces of celadon and blue-and-white china, which she inherited from her grandfather.

Doorways, openings and lintels frame carefully composed views throughout the house. The mix of furniture and fabrics is eclectic, blending East and West, old and new, and family pieces with treasures sourced over the course of countless travels. Colour choices are subtle and considered, with the use of distressed surfaces creating a timeless, evocative atmosphere (*above and opposite*).

Christian Louboutin

Château Louboutin / Vendée, France, 1988

Louboutin wanted a warm, vibrant colour for the grand salon (*opposite*), and the mustard-yellow walls create a strong statement. The chandelier and many of the period chairs were acquired at auction. The doors lead through to the entrance hall, with a sweeping staircase (*left*), and a music room to the other side of the hall.

The attics and hidden storage rooms of Christian Louboutin's country château are stacked with shoe boxes. The teetering towers form a priceless archive of design, including pumps, sandals and stilettos, created for the likes of Nicole Kidman, Gywneth Paltrow and Daphne Guinness, Louboutin's muse. Many of these designs were in fact conceived at his secluded country escape in the Vendée, surrounded by woodland and tumbling greenery.

'I can only work in places that I really know,' says Louboutin. 'I don't understand people who say, "this season I'm going to design my collection in Venezuela" or wherever. I would want tó see the place, to see nature, the monuments. That's why it's important for me to be in a place that I know, a place that is friendly and familiar. It requires a lot of concentration to draw and design a collection.'

Louboutin bought the house with his business partner, Bruno Chambelland, in 1988. Parts of the house date back to the 15th century and were used by the Knights Templar, although the house as it stands owes much to its reinvention in the 18th century. It once belonged to Chambelland's ancestors and his father had tried to buy the château but had failed. Eventually, Bruno Chambelland and Louboutin bought the house together and began restoring it.

The house and garden had been much neglected in the early decades of the 20th century, its parkland used for grazing and the house divided. There was still much restoration work to be done when

Louboutin and Chambelland arrived. A generous L-shaped building, with large rooms of classical proportion and high ceilings, the house was structurally in good shape.

The parquet floors, fireplaces and wooden panelling were mostly intact but it proved a big task to decorate and furnish the space. Louboutin and Chambelland bought much of the furniture at auction in Paris, choosing pieces to complement the period and character of the house, while also adding contemporary touches, pieces from Egypt and flea market discoveries.

From Egypt, Louboutin brought back much of the bed linen for the house as well as a collection of figurines that sits on a French console table in the hallway. A collection of Victorian curios lines the walls of the main bathroom, comprising painted vistas on oval timber palettes originally sold like postcards and once a common sight at Parisian flea markets.

Louboutin has a penchant for vibrant, warming colours, and often retreats from the large formal room downstairs to the Chinese-inspired sitting room upstairs, where the walls are painted a vivid bull's-blood red with chinoiserie panels, and leather club chairs from the 1950s create a more relaxed and informal atmosphere. The walls of Louboutin's bedroom are lined with framed specimens from a French herbarium, assembled during World War I.

The house is not usually a place for great gatherings – Louboutin suggests that he does not

often entertain guests formally – but a place for close friends. Despite its apparent grandeur, he says the house is very relaxed.

'We had just one big weekend here. I wanted to plant a maze and for that you need a lot of people. So we had a maze weekend with 7,000 holes to be dug. So a bunch of friends dug the holes and that explains why the maze will never be straight.'

Biography
Christian Louboutin (1964–)

Christian Louboutin was born in Paris and was fascinated by design from an early age, especially the sketches of shoes he saw in a local museum. He was influenced by the work of fashion and shoe designer Roger Vivier, as well as by the glamour of Parisian showgirls. After a period spent working as a landscape gardener, he embraced fashion and opened his first shoe shop in Paris in 1992. The red lacquered soles of his shoes became a Louboutin trademark and his stiletto heels in particular became extremely popular. Since the early 1990s, the Louboutin brand has grown steadily, with stores opening all over the world. Louboutin has collaborated with many fashion designers including Yves Saint Laurent, Roland Mouret, Jean Paul Gaultier and Viktor & Rolf.

Louboutin describes the style of the dining room (*opposite*) as neo-Gothic; the original colours on the panelled walls were restored. The view from the music room leads back to the hallway (*above left*), while a collection of traditional French painted vignettes from the early 19th century decorates the bathroom walls (*above right*). The walls in Louboutin's bedroom (*left*) are decorated with a collection of dried and mounted herbs dating from the early 19th century, and the bed is from the Directoire period.

Axel Vervoordt

Kasteel van 's-Gravenwezel / Belgium, 1988

The most striking aspect of Axel Vervoordt's work, apart from his highly individual and eclectic approach to design, is the breathtaking scale of his ambition. One section of his wide-ranging empire, which includes interiors, restoration projects, furniture design and home furnishings, is based at Kanaal, an old maltings plant, which forms a vast complex of buildings that Vervoordt and his family are slowly transforming into a new cultural quarter, mixing workshops, showrooms and living spaces.

The other centre point of Vervoordt's work is equally dramatic: the castle of 's-Gravenwezel, where Vervoordt moved with his company in 1988, after four years of restoration work. Parts of the brick and stone castle date back to the 12th century, but the building, which includes a moat and two circular towers, was reinvented in the 18th century by sculptor and architect Jan Pieter van Baurscheit.

From the beginning, Vervoordt used settings and living spaces to present collections of antiques, art, curiosities and salvage, as well as his own designs. At Gravenwezel, Vervoordt was able to take this idea further within an epic structure that is very much a home but also an extraordinary showroom. Within the many varied spaces Vervoordt had the freedom to create interiors lifted by a historic and characterful backdrop, bringing together disparate pieces of furniture and art in the unexpected, surprising and sublime manner for which he has attracted international acclaim and attention.

Vervoordt's tastes span many centuries and continents but he pinpoints three key influences: 'The first is that of contemporary and Oriental art and *arte povera*, which to me represents the importance of empty space and nature, and a deep respect for human existence,' says Vervoordt. 'The second is classical architecture, which represents proportion, balance and harmony. The third strand is Baroque, which I love because of its effect, craftsmanship and sheer exuberance.'[1]

At Gravenwezel, Vervoordt has the space to explore these themes as well as his appreciation of *wabi-sabi*, a philosophy that he encountered on his trips to the Far East in the 1970s, which encompasses the idea that beauty can be found in imperfection and in objects that appear rustic and simple. In Vervoordt's world, such pieces sit easily alongside finer creations of more traditional provenance.

Certain parts of the castle, including the kitchen and service quarters, have a simplicity created by natural, organic materials such as stone, timber and bare plaster. Others call for a more refined treatment and spaces such as the tea room offer a fresher, more feminine atmosphere, with a collection of Ming porcelain displayed on numerous sconces arranged around the walls.

What binds the many varied spaces at Gravenwezel together is the way every corner, surface and wall offers a striking composition worthy of a photograph. Repetition is one delightful aspect of this – the way in which similar pieces, from ceramics to woodwork curios, are grouped together for visual effect. Vervoordt has the eye of an expert curator, as well as the instinctive understanding of space that comes from his work as an interior architect. This combination of elements results in interiors that always contain something unique to discover, but within spaces that are never overbearing or crowded. Vervoordt allows his work the space it needs to breathe.

1 Interview with Michael Paul, *Belle* magazine, 4 May 2010.

Biography
Axel Vervoordt (1947–)

Born in Antwerp, Vervoordt was encouraged on the path to design by his parents, who pioneered conservation projects in the historic Vlaeykensgang quarter of the city. He began browsing salesrooms as a teenager, shrewdly buying pieces that were out of fashion but would later become highly collectable. He studied economics at university, but continued to trade in art and antiques, scoring particular success with a painting by Magritte at just twenty-one years old. Like his mother, he began restoring historic homes in Antwerp, also establishing a home and showroom, and was commissioned to create homes for clients. As well as dealing in antiques, Vervoordt also began to design his own lines of furniture.

The fifty-odd rooms offered Vervoordt the opportunity to create a whole array of spaces of varying styles united by common themes and threads. One of the more feminine spaces is the tea room with its high ceilings and fresh colour palette creating a backdrop for a collection of blue-and-white Ming china arranged on a sequence of wall-mounted sconces (*opposite*).

The different spaces represent an eclectic range of interests all within one extraordinary home. In some rooms the inspiration comes chiefly from the Far East, while in others the focus is on cabinets of curiosities and *objets trouvés*. Pieces are combined according to common colours, textures and patterns, so that each room works as an ordered and cohesive entity (*left and opposite*).

Bart Prince

Joe + Etsuko Price Residence / Corona del Mar, USA, 1989

For architect Bart Prince, each project is completely individual. There is no architectural 'bag of tricks' that he pulls out every time he accepts a commission. Prince begins anew every time, arguing that each building must be a specific creative response to the site itself as well as to the needs of the client. It is a philosophy that is in evidence throughout the home that he designed for Joe and Etsuko Price, a sinuous timber sculpture that combines Prince's organic approach and an interest in Japanese art and design that he shares with his clients. The corporeal, shingle-clad elements of the house appear as though they emerged from the ground itself.

The house was commissioned by Joe Price and his Japanese-born wife, Etsuko. Price has long been interested in architecture and encouraged his father to commission Frank Lloyd Wright (see page 50) to design a tower for the family's oil firm, H. C. Price Company in Bartlesville, Oklahoma. The Price Tower (1956) was to be Wright's only completed skyscraper. Wright also introduced Joe Price to Japanese art when he was young, encouraging a lifelong passion for collecting, which led to many trips to Japan, where Price met his wife. The Prices also commissioned a house from the late Bruce Goff, a close friend and mentor figure to Bart Prince in the 1960s and 70s.

The house that Prince designed for his clients at Corona del Mar, California, took full advantage of the striking location with its views across the Pacific Ocean. The house seems to be woven into the land itself, with the upper level containing Joe Price's office, bedrooms, and television and entertainment dens. The upper storey appears to partially envelop the lower section of the house, arranged around a semi-enclosed entry courtyard and holding the main living and dining space as well as the master bedroom. Decks are integrated into both storeys and a Japanese tea room is contained in a basement area.

In the courtyard especially, complete with a gravel garden, it seems as though exteriors and interiors have fused together. 'Sometimes you can't tell which is which,' says Prince. 'My ideas grow from an "inside-out" response. The form of this building results from the materials and construction methods that made it. They were not forced in order to achieve some preconception of form but became that shape as a result of the spaces within and without.'

Deep inside the house different kinds of timber create a sequence of subtle contrasts between the grain of the laminated fir used for structural pillars and beams, the teak floors and the rosewood cabinets as well as many other kinds of wood, each choice matched to its purpose. The timber contrasts with softer surfaces and coverings – deep pile carpets, sheepskin coatings and thick, fur-textured walls. Copper-coated partitions add another dimension altogether, and Prince also designed a series of elaborate stained-glass windows – bespoke artworks that introduce both colour and light. 'These glass designs "morph" from one side of the building over the ceiling to the other side,' says Prince. 'They bring colour and detail while providing privacy from the outside.'

The Price House is a unique creation – it combines the organic approach favoured by Prince, Goff and others with a handcrafted quality that echoes the work of Wharton Esherick and other 20th-century designers who moved freely between sculpture, furniture and interiors. At the same time, this ambitious home also has touches of cinematic futurism and a vibrant, otherworldly quality.

Biography
Bart Prince (1947–)

Bart Prince was born in Albuquerque, New Mexico, and studied architecture at Arizona State University. In the late 1960s he met Bruce Goff, a pioneering architect who advocated organic design and had worked with Frank Lloyd Wright. Prince worked intermittently with Goff and accompanied him on a number of lecture tours. After his mentor's death, he completed Goff's work on the Shin'en Kan Pavilion of Japanese Art at the Los Angeles County Museum of Art (1988). Prince founded his own practice in 1973, in Albuquerque, and much of his work has been focused on California and the southern states of America. Key projects include his own self-designed home (1984) and the Brad & June Prince Residence (1988), both in Albuquerque.

The partially sheltered courtyard (*opposite*), complete with gravel garden, has the feel of both an indoor and an outdoor space. It is a fitting introduction to a house of timber and shingles that appears to have grown from the earth itself.

Inside the house, the structural, laminated fir beams contrast with the teak floors and rosewood cabinets (*opposite and right*). Much of the furniture was integrated into the fabric of the house itself, while the stained glass was specially designed by Bart Prince to introduce pattern and jewel-like colours to the space.

Rose Tarlow

Tarlow Residence / Los Angeles, California, USA, 1989

Rose Tarlow likes to think of herself as a collector. Her passion for design stems from a love of hunting for and collecting furniture. Her work as a furniture designer has evolved from the experience of running her first store in Los Angeles back in the late 1970s, trading in antiques, particularly pieces from France and Ireland, and from England where she has kept an apartment for many years.

'My success in architecture and building houses comes from building furniture,' says Tarlow. 'It all comes from the antiques, making furniture and then architecture. You really learn to understand balance and proportion.

'I would say that my strong point is that I am not a decorator but a collector. Any time I have taken on a house project it's because of my passion for collecting and needing to have an outlet. It's like John Steinbeck said, you always have to have something to look for in life, and it's the searching that's the fun of it.'

Tarlow's own home in Los Angeles offers sumptuous evidence of her talent for finding the most delightful pieces and weaving them together in a seductive combination. The house

is a calming, fascinating retreat in the hills of Bel Air, hidden among the trees, with echoes of an escapist Italianate villa. The house feels entirely natural in its setting and gives the impression that it has been there for centuries, yet it only began life in 1989.

Partly inspired by the work of Californian architect Wallace Neff from the 1920s and 30s, Tarlow designed the house and the interiors using countless pieces of architectural salvage, particularly from Europe, which were threaded into the fabric of the house – staircases, fireplaces, wood panelling and even timber beams and oak doors.

'It's a puzzle – I love to think of it that way,' says Tarlow. 'I like puzzles and playing with plans. I find things and use them. They inspire me and then I start looking for other things. Just one or two pieces inspire a room for me but until I find them it doesn't really come together.'

The heart of the house is a dramatic double-height sitting room and library, anchored by 17th-century French stone fireplaces at either end, plastered walls and ranks of tall French windows to either side. The sheer scale of the room is

exhilarating, suggesting Tarlow's taste for large-scale and masculine spaces.

The master bedroom sits alongside this pivotal living area, with walls coated in 18th-century timber panelling from France. The dining room and kitchen have a period English country house feel to them, with stone-flag floors and antique chairs, while pieces such as the plate rack in the kitchen were integrated into the architecture of the room. The more intimate spaces of Tarlow's study and guest rooms are positioned on the upper level.

Also much in evidence is Tarlow's love of display as she sets out her finds and collections in carefully conceived tableaux, but always with a sense of informality rather than curatorial precision. A place of art, books, furniture and surprises, Tarlow's house is a natural setting for an avid collector but remains very much a warm retreat rather than a museum.

Vines push through the windows and along the walls of the sitting room (*below and opposite*), lending the room a timeless, fairytale quality. The stone fireplaces at either end are French and date from the 17th century, and a picture by Jean Cocteau sits on the mantelpiece. The sitting room also functions as a library and gallery, with pieces by Richard Serra and others mixed among the antiques and the more contemporary seating.

The dining room (*overleaf left*) has the atmosphere of a 16th- or 17th-century English country house, while the master bedroom (*overleaf right*) is lined with 18th-century French panelling.

Biography
Rose Tarlow (1946–)

Rose Tarlow was born in Shanghai and grew up in New Jersey and New York. As a child at school she was influenced by the beauty of her surroundings at Monmouth College and Tuxedo Park School, as well as of her parents' turn-of-the century ocean-front house. Tarlow studied design in New York and opened a shop there, as well as taking on her first interior design commissions. She then moved to California and opened an antiques shop in 1976. She founded Rose Tarlow – Melrose House three years later, producing furniture as well as fabrics and accessories. Tarlow has also accepted a select number of residential commissions. Influences include Billy Baldwin and Michael Taylor.

Sills Huniford

Bedford Residence / Bedford, New York, USA, 1991

There is a refreshing sense of openness to the work of Sills Huniford. The two designers are open to a wide range of influences, from both Europe and the United States, and from past centuries of design as well as today. Bearing this in mind, what is most striking about their work is its sense of clarity, precision and cohesion. They are able to weave seemingly disparate and varied elements together with a focus on common colour and tone, and within the context of rooms that have a strong architectural sense of proportion and scale.

'There's not really anything that I dislike,' says Stephen Sills. 'Every period has its dogs and its great things. The great secret in decorating is selecting the objects and how they harmonize with other objects – that's really what decoration is about. We are not really fabric people, and the focus is not on the fabrics. Our point of view is focused more on the volumes of the rooms and the objects that live in the room. There's always a thread.'

The living room of Sills and Huniford's country home in Bedford is just such a harmonious composition full of interesting elements, texture and idiosyncratic touches, united by a soothing colour palette and strong bones. Against a rigorous backdrop, Sills Huniford mix Egyptian marble columns, an English globe once owned by Rudolf Nureyev, apothecary vases, a Spanish monk's table and 20th-century art by Robert Rauschenberg and Cy Twombly.

Sills and Hunniford bought the 1920s house in 1991 and shared the residence for many years. It had previously been owned by gardener and writer Helen Morgenthau Fox, who wrote a book about the house and the gardens that she designed here. But by the time the designers acquired the property both were in a poor state: the gardens were in need of significant and careful restoration and the house also demanded a vast amount of work. A crumbling garage was rebuilt as a guest house and in all they spent five years working on the property.

'We kept some of the architectural detailing, some of the original mouldings, the casings on the doors, but that was about all,' says Sills. 'We put the stone floors in, the fire surrounds are new, and the plasterwork in the living room is all our creation. But we worked hard at trying to keep a natural feeling. Then we also designed sofas and some upholstered pieces for the house.'

The library, with its sequence of bespoke built-in bookcases, overlooks the rear garden and functions as an alternative, more intimate retreat alongside the main living room; it features a mirror above the fireplace that once belonged to Cecil Beaton.

The master bedroom is a particular surprise, with walls lacquered in a shining 'pond green' colour, offering a contrast with the more neutral tones of many other walls in the house, as well as providing a suitable background for a night-time retreat. Above the fireplace, a congregation of thirteen 18th-century Dutch mirrors forms an intriguing tableau.

A love of European period design is evident but the mix of elements is complex, imaginative and richly eclectic. 'It's European design but with an American eye – edited and cleaned up,' says Huniford. 'There's an American sensibility to do with function, form and practicality. And we always find strong architectural elements. I don't think a room can be successful if the background isn't strong.'

Biographies
Stephen Sills

Stephen Sills was obsessed with painting and design from a very early age. Born in a small town in southern Oklahoma, he was encouraged by his artist parents and grandparents. He studied design in Texas and lived in Europe, working as an assistant to Renzo Mongiardino (see page 22). Sills began working as an interior designer in Dallas, before moving to New York and co-founding Sills Huniford Associates. Clients include Nan Swid, Anna Wintour and Vera Wang. In 2008, Sills founded his own practice, Stephen Sills Associates.

James Huniford

James Huniford has always been deeply fascinated with design, with an eclectic line of influences including Eileen Gray, Karl Friedrich Schinkel and Karl Lagerfeld. He was born in New York state, north of Syracuse, and co-founded Sills Huniford in 1984. He is a furniture designer as well as an interior designer and co-founded the Dwellings collection with Stephen Sills in 2003. He launched the Huniford Design Studio in 2008.

The guest house echoes the look of the main building within a simpler, more rustic shell. It was rebuilt from the remnants of a derelict garage and has a large, open living space at the centre (*opposite*) with stone pavers and striking round windows. The fireplace between the windows acts as a focal point, and the chairs are Regency.

In the living room of the main house (*above*), a slate-topped Spanish monk's table sits to one side with an array of apothecary vases and a Robert Rauschenberg painting on the wall. The library (*right*) is dominated by an 18th-century French wine-tasting table topped by a lobster carapace in a display case. The walls of the master bedroom (*opposite*) are painted green and decorated with a collection of 18th-century Dutch mirrors.

Jacques Garcia

Château du Champ de Bataille / Normandy, France, 1992

One day, as a child, Jacques Garcia went on a trip with his father to visit a grand château out in the flat, tamed countryside of Normandy. His parents were shopkeepers, and their own home back in the Paris suburbs was some 100 kilometres (60 miles) away. But Garcia took in the Château du Champ de Bataille – a monument to 17th-century splendour, once the home of counts and dukes – then looked up at his father, telling him that some day the place would belong to him. Now it does.

In Garcia's hands the château has become a vast laboratory of ideas. He bought the house in 1992 and has been bringing it back to life gradually ever since, including the gardens, careful to balance sympathetic restoration with the creation of a living home.

'The building was used as a hospital before I bought it and had been for forty-five years,' says Garcia. 'There were just three rooms that were more or less original, so I had the paint removed to find the original colours and the woodwork cleaned as well – everything was redone as it would have been. Then when those three rooms were back to their original state I began working on the rest of the house, designing each room in a similar style, which gave the house a sense of cohesion.'

The grandest, most formal rooms in the house are on the piano nobile, a sequence of opulent spaces in expansive Grand Siècle style. The dining room, with windows overlooking the formal gardens and parterres below, offers one of the many optical illusions in the house, with walls painted in a faux-marble effect. The twelve dining chairs once belonged to Louis XIV. The 'marble salon' next door, a room for entertaining, features an assembly of precious stone, including ancient onyx columns from Egypt, a porphyry table on a pedestal commissioned by Napoleon, and a glimmering collection of crystals and minerals.

Garcia is an inveterate and talented collector, and the château is filled not just with an astonishing collection of period furniture, but also with all sorts of displays, from the brass telescopes and scientific instruments in Garcia's study to old hunting trophies and ancient stuffed birds.

'I have been attracted by houses from the 17th and 18th centuries, because it's easier to display the pieces that I have collected in the right surroundings,' says Garcia. 'But I'm not a specialist in any one period. My work has led me to reflect on the style and philosophy of many different eras: the 19th century, the 1940s, modernism. And for me, it's in the past that one discovers the future.'

The eclectic nature of Garcia's approach becomes apparent in the more informal parts of the château. While a number of the formal spaces in the house are now open to the public, many others remain private and out of sight. Here, imagination and fantasy are allowed free rein, with an exotic swimming pool in the depths of the house, and a Moroccan-themed hammam, which adds a note of contemporary luxury.

Other rooms across the ground floor fuse old and new, and play with references from across the centuries. A second dining room has been designed around the theme of the natural world, the panelled walls covered in framed images of flora and fauna, with stuffed birds perched on the chandelier and staring down from the mantelpiece.

Nothing stays still, with Garcia endlessly moving and reordering his collections. The house slowly evolves and shifts to accommodate whims and ideas. The château is a lifetime's work and the work continues.

Biography
Jacques Garcia (1947–)

Early on, Jacques Garcia showed a talent for drawing and a strong interest in antiques and design. He studied at the Met de Pennighen and the École des Métiers d'Art but also began trading in antiques and dealing in modern art from a young age. In the early 1970s, he began working as an interior designer, creating hotels and private homes with an emphasis on layers of fantasy, drama and comfort laid over solid architectural foundations within a blend of neoclassicism, orientalism and period references. Commissions now take Garcia around the world, and his hotel and restaurant projects include the Hôtel Costes in Paris, La Mamounia in Marrakech and L'Hôtel Metropole in Monte Carlo. He is a recipient of the Légion d'Honneur.

The marble salon (*opposite*) is situated on the piano nobile of the château and designed in the Grand Siècle style. The replica floor in period marble is modelled on a room at the Château de Clagny. The alabaster columns surrounding the fireplace are Egyptian; other pieces in the collection once belonged to Napoleon and Louis XIV.
(Photographs by Eric Sander)

The salon de compagnie (*opposite and above right*) is rich in 18th-century detailing; many of the original colours have been restored. The 17th-century bureau is by André Charles Boulle and the statue placed on top is by Jacques Buirette, also dating from the 17th century.

The formal dining room (*above*)
on the piano nobile overlooks the
parterre and gardens below; the
walls and cornices have been painted
with a marble effect. The Duchess'
Bedroom (*opposite above*) was
inspired by the 17th century, and the
stairway (*opposite below left*) makes
use of internal windows to create
vistas through the piano nobile.

William Yeoward

The School House / Cotswolds, UK, 1992

William Yeoward's work is often described as quintessentially English. He borrows ideas from many periods of design and reworks them into something fresh and unique with a good sense of humour and a passion for colour and pattern. There are neoclassical notes, Victorian flourishes, Edwardian flavours and also a certain sophisticated bohemian quality that recalls the work of the Bloomsbury set and the beauty of their country seat, Charleston (see page 42).

The result is distinctive, hugely popular and very much 'Yeoward'. His designs for furniture, textiles and wallpapers are as popular with other designers as they are with the public, partly because his work is so malleable, integrating as easily with a contemporary home as a Victorian terrace. Above all, Yeoward's style is never dull, as he refuses to put like with like and places an English emphasis on comfort, detailing and craftsmanship.

The most enticing setting for Yeoward's work is provided by the country house in the Cotswolds that he shares with his partner, interior designer Colin Orchard. The Victorian Gothic stone building is a picturesque amalgam of a former school and an adjoining cottage that once belonged to the school mistress, joined together by an entrance hall that was crafted from a passageway formerly used to divide these two neighbours.

The house once belonged to Yeoward's aunt and he bought it after her death. It had been adapted before, but poorly, in the 1970s and Yeoward and Orchard thoroughly remodelled the interiors in two phases, creating interiors with sympathetic architectural detailing, layered with warm colours and an eclectic mix of antiques and pieces designed by Yeoward himself, in a style that is bold but also intelligent and warm.

The heart of the house is the generous drawing room that takes up a good section of the old

schoolroom with its dramatic high ceilings, walls in a textured turquoise and Gothic-style cornicing picked out in white. The large windows are dressed with curtains in a Yeoward pattern to an arrangement originally designed by John Fowler. The tongue-in-cheek papier mâché chandelier is a 1960s design, hanging above Italian mirrors, period portraits and a glazed cabinet, also designed by Yeoward.

The spacious kitchen, sitting within the remaining section of the schoolroom, is a warm and welcoming reinterpretation of the classic English farmhouse kitchen, dominated by a vast dresser topped by urns and a wooden crest. A Dutch portrait and two coats-of-arms flank the Aga, lending it a certain ironic solemnity.

The nature of the house makes it quite bottom heavy, with just two bedrooms upstairs; the master bedroom is dominated by a vibrant floral wallpaper and an Edwardian sofa positioned at the end of the bed. As someone with a particular love of entertaining, Yeoward found an answer to the lack of bedrooms at the School House in the form of a guest cottage nearby, transformed into a welcoming private retreat for friends and family.

Bound together by common colour tones and imagination, the rooms combine many delights within spaces that are optimistic and playful but also accomplished and elegant. Yeoward offers a refreshed, forward-looking take on English style, and the School House shows this at its best.

The entrance hallway (*below*) features Gothic detailing and includes a hallway table with a Regency clock, lamps designed by Yeoward and stone fragments from architectural salvage. The glazed cabinet against the far wall in the sitting room (*opposite above*) was also designed by Yeoward, the chandelier is from the 1960s and the mirror is an Italian design. In the kitchen (*opposite below left*) a Dutch portrait from the 19th century keeps watch above the range. A Designers Guild wallpaper lifts the space in the master bedroom (*opposite below right*), which also includes an Edwardian sofa.

Biography
William Yeoward (1957–)

Drawing on inspiration from many centuries of design history, William Yeoward is a designer who has revitalized many different aspects of design, from furniture and textiles to wallpaper, crystal and lamps. He studied art history, literature and theatre design before starting work as an interior designer and opening his first store on London's King's Road in 1985, where he sold a mix of antiques and self-designed pieces. Yeoward later dropped private interiors commissions in favour of expanding his own home product ranges and business abroad, particularly in America. William Yeoward Crystal was founded with Timothy Jenkins in 1995, and Yeoward also works with Designers Guild. He has written a number of books about design and entertaining.

Vicente Wolf

Wolf Apartment / New York, USA, 1993

Designer Vicente Wolf sees his Manhattan loft as a stage. His home constantly shifts in a slow but steady process of evolution, as Wolf brings back pieces from his travels and edits and adjusts the eclectic compositions within the space. He is helped by the fact that the loft is spacious, with strong light, powerful proportions and wonderful views across the Manhattan skyline from its position on the eleventh floor.

'The first time I entered the space it just felt so New York,' says Wolf. 'I wanted a loft because I didn't want to live in a conventional apartment. Even empty, I wanted it to be a space that would satisfy me.'

Wolf first moved into the 1920s building in the early 1990s, and a few years later he was also able to buy the apartment next door, creating a broader canvas of 150 square metres (1,600 square feet) for his collections of furniture, photography and art. Determined to respect the raw quality and intensity of the space, Wolf avoided partitioning or changing the nature of the loft, leaving the windows uncovered, painting the walls white and coating the floors in reflective deck paint. A large and luxurious bathroom was sectioned off with a frosted glass wall that still allows natural light to filter through, while walls and floors here are coated in limestone. An emphasis throughout on natural materials and organic tones helps tie many disparate pieces of furniture together.

'There are always things that are coming and going,' says Wolf. 'There's a new favourite and so I fall in love with it, and then on my next trip there's something else. My work has been described as sybaritic – it's elegant but relaxed, working in very mercurial colours, with a blending of different periods and elements. But the result is always a modern environment.'

The open spaces of the living room have been subtly zoned into a series of areas for sitting, relaxing and dining. In one corner by the windows, a sofa and a club chair designed by Wolf are placed around a Giacometti-inspired circular table. A painted Swedish 18th-century folding table is a particular favourite and is positioned alongside a Louis XVI bench, while a small assembly of chairs is lined up against a nearby wall, featuring various pictures and photographs, including a portrait by Richard Avedon.

As both a photographer and a sharp-eyed collector himself, Wolf has a particular passion for 20th-century photographs. The loft holds images by Edward Weston, Martin Munkácsi, Robert Mapplethorpe, Diane Arbus and Edward Steichen. The master bedroom contains a small gallery of shelves neatly displaying part of this collection, while the bed itself floats freely in the space at an angle, which helps to dissolve the linear nature of the space.

Wolf's apartment – and perhaps his work as a whole – is sophisticated but neither elitist nor overly fashion-conscious. Wolf follows his own dictates in creating spaces with a timeless quality, selecting pieces not simply for their origin but for their intrinsic beauty.

'I like things that are unique,' says Wolf. 'I'm always looking for things that have a twist to them. But I'm not a designer who ponders. There's always a sense of spontaneity because I'm working from instinct.'

Biography
Vicente Wolf (1946–)

Vicente Wolf's parents were involved in the construction business in Cuba, so as a child the designer became familiar with architects and building sites. When he was fifteen, the family moved to Miami, and he lived there for three years before moving to New York, where he felt immediately at home. He took short-term jobs in advertising, modelling, acting and fashion before settling into design. Wolf began collaborating with designer Bob Patino and founded his own studio after Patino's death. Also a photographer, Wolf made the most of editorial opportunities to publicize his work. As well as many private homes, Wolf has also designed hotels, restaurants and stores as well as furniture, accessories and products for Baccarat, Ralph Pucci and others. David Hicks and Jean-Michel Frank were formative influences.

Art and photography collections and chairs are arranged in the corners of the apartment (*left and opposite above right*), while floors throughout are coated in a reflective deck paint, matching the white walls and ceilings. In the guest area (*opposite below right*) the steel-framed daybed was designed by Wolf, as were the sofa and club chair in the corner seating area. In the bedroom (*opposite above left*), the bed was designed by Wolf and is anchored by a three-quarter monolith, while part of Wolf's photography collection is placed on shelves nearby.

Frédéric Méchiche

Méchiche Apartment / Paris, France, 1996

Frédéric Méchiche pronounces the word 'decoration' like a curse. For him 'decoration' implies contrivance and falsehood, whereas he constantly labours for interiors that feel natural, comfortable and warm – spaces where every piece of furniture or art has been given a place because it encourages an instinctive, positive response.

'To feel comfortable in a house or an apartment, you need to have this impression of naturalness, of simplicity,' says Méchiche. 'For example, in my own apartment in Paris there are some extraordinary pieces of art but they are not placed as though they were in a gallery – they are part of my life. If people know what they are, then perfect. If they don't, it's not a problem. All the things that are here are not for decoration but because they speak to me and to my way of life.'

Indulging his love of the vibrancy of the city and its constant sense of motion, Méchiche found three adjoining apartments in Paris – stripped of detail and character – at the heart of the compact, busy lattice that is the Marais. He reorganized the architecture of these spaces, spread over two floors, to form one harmonious home with the atmosphere of a small Directoire townhouse, updated for contemporary living. He brought together an extraordinary collection of wooden panelling from an 18th-century postal staging inn, cornicing and mouldings, mirrors and fireplaces, and began to weave these pieces of salvage together.

'I wanted to give the impression that I had just arrived here and really found it like this,' he says. 'I just added my books, my sculptures, and my paintings. Even if it's a calculated look, that's the feeling I wanted – arriving in an 18th-century apartment, painted very simply with white walls, and no curtains, no carpets. Very few of the things that people often call "decoration".'

Méchiche planned his home around the library, which became the heart of the apartment – a space that one has to repeatedly pass through to reach the sweeping staircase or cross from one room to another. A Florence Knoll sofa and chairs, and a Marcel Breuer glass table mix easily with the wooden panelling and floors and the Directoire fireplace. The dining room sits to one side, with four individual granite-topped tables, designed by Méchiche, that give the space the atmosphere of a sophisticated, intimate bistro (they can be combined to form a larger dining table).

Upstairs is largely devoted to a generous, loft-like sitting room. The cohesion of the space,

bound together by white walls and wooden floors, belies the radically different origins of the individual elements of the blend. There are period pieces – such as the Louis XVI daybed or the 18th-century Italian console table – which rub shoulders with 20th-century classics by Eames and Mies van der Rohe, as well as sculptures and paintings by Jean Dubuffet, César and Jean Arp, photographs by Nan Goldin and Cindy Sherman, and pieces of African art. 'People think it's enough just to mix anything up,' says Méchiche, 'but I'm sorry, it's not. It's about composition, perspective.'

The master bedroom and bathroom on the lower level have been designed with a more restrained approach, offering a sense of contrasting atmospheres within different spaces in the apartment. The ivory bedroom is sparse and dominated by a splash of bright red from a painting by Jean-Pierre Raynaud.

'While I am happy to have a minimal bedroom I couldn't imagine living in a whole apartment like that,' says Méchiche. 'You need to have different

kinds of rooms, a different ambience, so you feel more comfortable as you pass from one atmosphere to another. I like to have opposition between rooms in a house.'

Biography
Frédéric Méchiche

Parisian-based interior architect Frédéric Méchiche was born in Algeria, where began his studies. The son of a doctor, he realized at a young age that he wanted to work in the world of design. He moved to Paris at the age of seventeen to study at the École Camondo. Soon after completing his studies he was given his first commission, a triplex apartment with roof gardens and a swimming pool. Since then, Méchiche has worked mostly alone, with projects in France and abroad including residences, yachts, restaurants and hotels such as Joël Robuchon's The Astor.

The living room (*left*) contains a black and white sculpture by Jean Dubuffet and chairs by Mies van der Rohe and Eames; the daybed is French and dates from the Louis XVI period. The library (*opposite above and opposite below left*) is the heart of the duplex, arranged around the stairs and the Directoire fireplace with a glass table by Marcel Breuer. The dining room (*opposite below right*) is arranged almost like a bistro with a collection of Méchiche-designed granite-topped tables, which can be combined or used separately. The black-and-white photograph on the wall is by Robert Mapplethorpe.

The bathroom (*overleaf left*) features Directoire panelling and a painting by Jean-Charles Blais. The bedroom (*overleaf right*) has a lighter, simpler character; the picture is by Jean-Pierre Raynaud and the lamp is Italian from the 1960s.

Agnès Emery

Maison Emery / Brussels, Belgium, 1996

Even as a child, Agnès Emery was fascinated by colour. When she began to study architecture in Brussels, her love of the whole colour spectrum seemed at odds with the vogue for white-walled architectural purity. Yet her passion survived and flourished, gradually leading her away from architecture and to a new company – Emery & Cie – that would develop tempting ranges of paints, ceramics and textiles in collaboration with artisans in Europe, Morocco, India and elsewhere.

The Emery & Cie collections suggest a love not only of colour but of craft, with Emery's Moroccan-made tiles, for instance, characterized by a delicate irregularity that makes them all the more special. Her interior design projects and commissions make the most of this combination of colour, craft and individuality. Above all, the instantly recognizable Emery aesthetic revels in a layering of associated colours that offer the most subtle of contrasts as well as a soothing sense of unity.

One can see this layering at its best in the kitchen of Emery's townhouse in Brussels, where the wall colours, the tiles and the finish on the kitchen cabinets mark a modest but delightful journey across a colour palette of soft and tempting greens, culminating in a tiled splashback behind the cooker in a modest rectangle of sea-blue tilework. This is 'pure Emery'.

'I find that the effect of colours that contrast too much is tiring,' says Emery. 'So in general I keep to a palette of close tones and limit myself to a few small touches, which offer more of a sense of contrast and add value to key points. I had lived in the countryside for twenty years when I moved to the house, and it was more of a practical decision than heartfelt. So I chose colours of the countryside that made the walls come alive. The lower floors are in green and then as you go upstairs you move towards the colours of the sky.'

In the dining room, Emery has drawn together a collection of mirrors for the moss-green walls, which create a sense of drama and also have the practical purpose of helping to reflect light around the space. 'The multiplication of mirrors of very different shapes and forms helps deconstruct the room,' says Emery. 'The walls seem to disperse, and you have a sensation that's rather like being underwater.'

No major changes had been made to the 19th-century building since the 1950s, meaning that many original period features, from the stairway to the cornicing, had been retained, and were woven

into Emery's treatment of the house. The middle floor of the house is dedicated to a combined sitting room and library, where the books have been arranged according to the colours of their spines to create a calming visual quality.

In the master bedroom on the top floor, Emery wanted to position the bed facing the window, almost at the heart of the room. Adding a half-height wall at the end of the bed created a headboard that gave it a natural anchor while also providing a subtle partition that still allowed the proportions of the room as a whole to be read as one. It is a technique for lightly dividing space that Emery has also used elsewhere, particularly in her Emery & Cie stores.

Just like Emery's home in Marrakech, the house is most striking for a distinctive use of colour that is both rich and calming. Emery suggests that contemporary design is ready for a more adventurous approach to colour in the home, although learning how to apply it is always going to be more demanding than working with white walls. Emery's house offers the perfect case study.

Biography
Agnès Emery (1943–)

Agnès Emery's parents worked with ceramics and her grandfather was a mirror maker, so Emery developed a love of drawing and design at a young age. She studied architecture at the La Cambre school of the University of Brussels, graduating in 1971, after which she taught architecture for a number of years. She then began restoring Art Nouveau interiors in the city and also received commissions for murals for private homes. In 1993, she opened her first shop in Brussels, specializing in Belgian-made paints, Moroccan-crafted ceramics and tiles, and later pieces from Nepal, India and Vietnam. In the years that followed, Emery & Cie expanded with stores in other countries and added a wallpaper and textile collection. Influences include the Arts and Crafts movement, Belgian architect and designer Victor Horta and William Morris.

In the kitchen (*opposite*) tiles and paintwork in a range of tones are used to great effect. Emery & Cie 'Vert Bleu' paint is used on the walls and 'Vert Russe' on the kitchen units; the chandelier is Moroccan. The tiled and painted hallway (*above*) ties in with the colours of the kitchen and dining room.

A collage of mirrors is used to create a wall of light in the dining room (*opposite*). The curtain fabric and paint colour ('Vert Pale') are by Emery & Cie. In the library (*left*) the books are arranged by colour. In the blue master bedroom (*above*), Emery positioned the bed to face the window, with a monolithic partial wall, enabling a sense of the overall proportions of the space to be maintained.

Todd Oldham

Oldham House / Pennsylvania, USA, 1997

Todd Oldham's country home in rural Pennsylvania was quirky even before he started work on it. At the heart of the modest building sits a soaring double-height living room, drawing in light from large banks of windows, but many other spaces in the house are more unusual: the dining room and kitchen spur out from the sitting room at a strange angle, while areas such as the den in the lower section of the house and the master bedroom at the top of the house have quite low ceilings. The site surrounding the house had hardly any trees at the time Oldham bought it, as it had been landscaped as a three-hole golf course. Oldham and his partner, Tony Longoria, spent years planting new trees and reinventing the grounds.

On the inside, Oldham managed to turn a simple white-painted interior into a highly individual home full of character, vibrant colour and pattern. The living room is the natural focus of the house: Oldham created murals around the gaps between many of the windows and above the fireplace, and a large self-designed La-Z-Boy sofa anchors the room. One wall is dedicated to a sequence of framed bird prints by modernist artist Charley Harper, the subject of a monograph written by Oldham. Stacked above each other, these pictures combine to form a delightful tableau. The floor tiles were laid at an angle to diffuse the linear quality of the room and to soften the irregular shift into the dining area and kitchen off to one side.

In the kitchen, chairs by Russel Wright (see page 128) are placed around the dining table, and Oldham enlivened the space by adorning the walls with pieces of Japanese silk screens. Perhaps most striking of all are the bold broad stripes of wall pattern used here and in other sections of the house, particularly where the different living zones intersect. It is a technique repeated in areas such as the master bedroom. 'I use bold stripe to create a sense of pace and flow through each area, but you have to be strict to make this work,' says Oldham. 'I never have an odd number of stripes and I never cut into one – hard to achieve but a really successful way of creating the illusion of a very large, light and airy space. The house looks and feels gigantic but it's not, it's tiny.'[1]

Oldham follows self-imposed rules for his choice of pattern, using shared colours and similar scales to help tie together different elements in the same space. What stands out in Oldham's home is the emphasis on individuality without any feeling of constraint. Self-made pieces are mixed with

mid-century designs and favourite artworks, including the Harper prints, photographs by Hiroshi Sugimoto and a scattering of abstract wooden diamonds by chainsaw artist Jim Shaw.

The gardens, too, are a canvas for self-expression. There is a deck with an outdoor cinema screen, a lounge area by a pool and a gazebo with half a roof that offers a choice of sunlight and shade in the same space, not to mention a fully-fitted and functioning tree house out in the woods. This is an escapist retreat full of wonderful ideas.

1 Interview with Amanda Talbot, *Elle Decoration*, October 2007.

In the double-height living room (*opposite*) of the house, which is pushed into the sloping rural site, there is a strong emphasis on pattern and colour, with a bespoke mural above the fireplace, geometric carpet tiles and a collage of framed prints by Charley Harper. The sofa is an Oldham design for La-Z-Boy.

Biography
Todd Oldham (1961–)

Todd Oldham initially found success as a fashion designer before expanding into many other areas of creativity, including interior and furniture design, photography, writing and television presenting. He was born in Texas, studied in Dallas and took his first job in the alterations department at Polo Ralph Lauren. He launched his own fashion label in 1989 and later moved to New York. In 1999, he designed The Hotel on Miami's South Beach, followed by the Fairfax Hotel in 2007. Oldham also designs furniture for La-Z-Boy and Target.

The exposed wooden beams and panes of glass lend the dining room overlooking the garden an organic flavour (*opposite*). Elsewhere, Oldham uses strong colours and bold pattern to create vibrant spaces; the vertical stripes create an impression of more generously proportioned rooms.

Ministero del Gusto

Maison Ministero del Gusto / Marrakech, Morocco, 1998

There is nothing quite like it in Marrakech. In a country so rich in exotic sights and images, contrasts and extremes, Ministero del Gusto still manages to stand out as something extraordinary. Suffused with originality and imagination, this house turned gallery and showroom is the vision of two Italian designers, Alessandra Lippini and Fabrizio Bizzarri, who settled independently in Morocco in the mid-1990s before co-founding the Ministero del Gusto (Ministry of Taste).

Stepping over the threshold of the house from an anonymous winding walkway in the heart of the medina is like entering another world. Furniture designers, inventors and interior architects, Lippini and Bizzarri have turned the Ministero headquarters into a spectacular fusion of ideas borrowed from around the globe. The bones of the house are Moroccan, yet the sinuous, organic feel of the building also pays homage to the sun-baked earthen architecture of Mali and Mexico.

The sculpted windows are reminiscent of the work of Gaudí, and the house holds a collection of masks and other treasures from sub-Saharan Africa and vintage mid-century pieces from Europe and America, as well as Ministero furniture designs. The result is striking and also contemporary.

'We do travel a lot, picking up ideas from around the world,' says Bizzarri. 'You have to, because in a sense everything has been done before, so you need to develop and reinterpret ideas to make something new.'

As the business grew they decided that they needed a dedicated base that could serve not just as a house, but as an office and a showcase for their work – a multi-functional laboratory of ideas. They decided to convert a crumbling structure with a warren of rooms that had been built in traditional *pisé*, a mix of mud and straw.

'We began to replan and remodel, taking out some of the walls to create a more open space,' says Bizzarri. 'But then after two months of work the house just collapsed so we had to start again.'

Faced with an unexpected blank canvas, the designers began thinking about the organic, sinuous towers of Mali mosques, and stirred up the melting pot of ideas that became the Ministero. They wanted to extend the structure upwards to create more space and include roof terraces, but retained the central courtyard, complete with plunge pool, that is common to traditional Moroccan city homes.

'The fact that we did keep the patio is certainly Moroccan but also Romanesque,' Bizzarri says. 'The indented ceilings often remind people of the earth basins used by the artisans as vats in the dyers' souk in Fes.'

As well as the pitted *pisé* ceilings, a series of sculpted fireplaces – some as sensual and seductive as a Georgia O'Keeffe floral painting – form centre points in the key living spaces. Bizzarri mixed up many of the colours for the house himself to paint the walls and ceilings in hot spice tones of cinnamon, paprika, cumin, turmeric and saffron.

An exuberant, playful and flamboyant portfolio piece, the Ministero offers both simplicity and complexity. Blending sophistication with organic, sinuous forms, it is a house with a singular charm.

Biographies
Alessandra Lippini (1956–)

Born in Bologna, Lippini studied psychology before moving into the fashion industry as a stylist. She settled in Morocco in 1994 and founded Ministero del Gusto with Fabrizio Bizzarri a year later. Del Gusto projects include own-label furniture and residential commissions, including houses in Marrakech for creative consultant Franz Ankoné and fashion designers Imelda and Stefano Cavalleri.

Fabrizio Bizzarri (1959–)

Bizzarri studied art and literature at the University of Bologna before moving into design and filmmaking. He settled in Marrakech in 1995, where he co-founded Ministero del Gusto the same year. Bizzarri and Lippini work closely with Moroccan craftsmen, making all their furniture in and around Marrakech.

The roof terrace (*below*) echoes the mud mosques of Mali, and the table is designed by Hassan Hajjaj. The ground floor salon (*opposite*) is arranged around an open courtyard and features a wooden hanging sculpture of termite-eaten timber by François Lellange. The metal balustrades are Ministero del Gusto designs and the rugs are Moroccan.

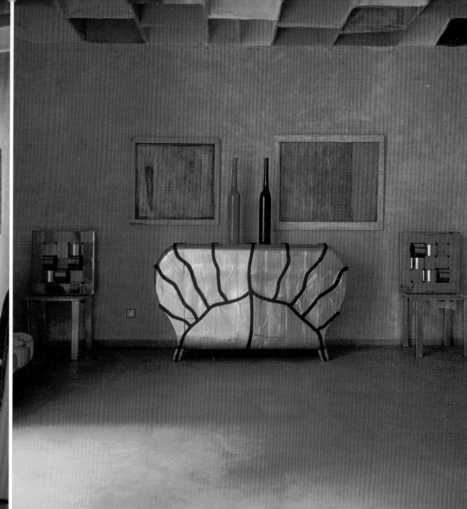

On the first floor (*left and opposite*), the indented ceilings in the two salons are reminiscent of the earth basins used at the dyers' souk in Fes, while the windows were inspired by Gaudí. The furniture includes a vintage chair by Joe Colombo alongside a 1970s table from Italy (*above left*), a golden cabinet by Ministero del Gusto (*above right*) and a 1930s leopard-print chair mixed with an Eames reclining chair, a 1950s Herman Miller lamp and a low table by Ministero del Gusto (*opposite*).

John Pawson

Pawson House / London, UK, 1999

Minimalism involves a sensitive, intelligent process of reduction, a gradual stripping away of all extraneous elements. What remains is an emphasis on proportion, scale, line, light, materials, detail and texture. The result should be a space that is pure, calm and natural, where the intrinsic beauty of carefully crafted surfaces and finishes stands out.

The master of this approach is architect John Pawson, who has built an international reputation with his considered buildings and interiors that are studies in light and purity. His work has inspired the look of countless reductionist homes and stores.

'It's very complex to make something simple,' says Pawson. 'If you make it simple, visually clear and unornamented, without decoration, then all the lines have to be straighter. Primarily, I want to provide spaces in which people feel good.'[1]

Pawson's own family home in London has drawn particular attention for its minimalist interiors and the way in which the architect clearly lives the kind of life advocated by his design philosophy. There have been barn conversions, country houses and even a monastery, but Pawson's own house still provokes endless fascination.

The façade of Pawson's mid-19th century terraced home, which overlooks communal gardens, has been preserved, but behind it lies what is essentially a new four-storey house. Pawson stripped away the internal structure to liberate the plan of the building and remove all remaining ornament.

A narrow new staircase was positioned at one side of the house, toplit by a skylight above the stairwell, freeing up the rest of the internal spaces, and services were hidden away in slots carved into the supporting walls. The basement level is dedicated to a combined kitchen and dining area, with Italian limestone floors and a central wooden table and dining chairs. To one side is a procession of floor-to-ceiling storage cupboards to hide the clutter of everyday life. To the other side runs a long kitchen worktop that pierces the glass wall at the rear of the house and pushes its way into the back garden, which is designed as an outdoor room and alternative space for dining and entertaining.

The sitting room on the floor above is a soothing, simple space painted in a 'quiet white'. The fireplace is a central feature but forms an unornamented slot above a stone shelf that can be used for display or extra seating. The restrained nature of the space allows the furniture, including a Hans Wegner rocking chair, to assume the status of artworks. The children's bedrooms are situated on the next floor, with the master bedroom at the top, and a bathroom with a retractable glass roof offering views of open skies and chimney pots.

'What I'm trying to achieve is a series of private and calm spaces,' Pawson says. 'I want an empty room, with just a bed in it. I want to be able to walk into a room that is only a shell....But living in a loft in one big room with everything in it is not necessarily the answer. The advantage of having all the levels in the house is that, in a sense, you don't need a wall, because the floor does the job for you.'[2]

1 Interview with Sheryl Garratt, *Saturday Telegraph Magazine*, 4 September 2010.
2 Quoted in Deyan Sudjic, *John Pawson: Works*, 2005.

Biography
John Pawson (1949–)

Born in Yorkshire, John Pawson worked in the family textile business before travelling and teaching in Japan for a number of years. He studied at the Architectural Association in London and founded his own practice in 1981. Early projects included an apartment for the writer Bruce Chatwin in 1982. Pawson formed a brief partnership with Claudio Silvestrin from 1987 to 1989, collaborating on the Neuendorf House in Majorca (1989). Other key projects include the Tilty Barn in Essex, UK (1995) and the Novy Dvur Monastery in the Czech Republic (2004). Pawson has also designed a series of Calvin Klein stores around the world and created furniture and cookware ranges.

On the lower ground floor, a long kitchen worktop with bespoke units runs the length of the room (*opposite*), tying together the indoor and outdoor spaces (*left*). The dining table was designed by John Pawson and is complemented by JH 501 round chairs by Hans Wegner.

The theme of sophisticated simplicity is carried through the house, with an emphasis on unadorned finishes and exquisite detailing. In the sitting room (*opposite above*), which overlooks an elevated terrace, the fireplace is also reduced to a minimum. The two chairs are by Hans Wegner and include a JH 512 folding chair design for Johannes Hansen.

Jens Risom

Risom House / New Canaan, Connecticut, USA, 1999

Furniture designer Jens Risom has lived in New Canaan, Connecticut, since the late 1940s. The town offered easy access by train or car to New York, where his company, Jens Risom Design, had its showrooms and it was also close to the factory that Risom had set up to manufacture his furniture. The schools were convenient for his children, and the area pleasant and leafy. Risom was one of the first of what became a vibrant enclave of designers and architects that included Philip Johnson, who built his famous Glass House close by.

The 1940s and 50s were a particularly busy time for Risom. Coming from a Scandinavian design background, he was passionate about natural materials and organic forms, and also showed a talent for marketing, advertising and promotion. Having worked with Hans Knoll in the early 1940s on a classic line of Risom pieces, including a number of timber and webbing chairs from the 600 series, Risom started out on his own, after serving with General Patton's army in Europe, and launched his own furniture empire. Jens Risom Design established satellite offices around the world, spreading a message of mid-century design that spoke of quality, craftsmanship, detail and an appreciation of ergonomics as well as beauty.

'Wood is my favourite material,' says Risom. 'I like walnut very much – it has a richness and a grain characteristic which lends itself to all kinds

of things. We did very little metalwork. That Bauhaus style didn't appeal to me and I thought metalwork was unattractive and not the way to do it. Working in wood was totally different.'

It is no wonder then that the natural, timber tones of Risom's own designs tend to stand out in his own house, which he shares with his wife, Henny. This is Risom's third home in New Canaan; it was built in the 1970s, and he described it as a 'nothing house' when he first discovered the place. But Risom managed to reinvent the one-storey building, blessed with generous gardens backing on to a nature reserve, in his own particular way and create something truly original.

Risom reordered the internal living spaces and converted one of the three bedrooms into a work studio and study, while another became a small office for Henny. The living room at the heart of the house is the focal point, graced with a series of Risom designs and two chairs by Arne Jacobsen and Risom's classmate Hans Wegner. Particularly striking among his pieces is a wall-mounted timber cabinet that combines display niches, bookshelves, drawers and storage for music and papers.

Among the chairs in the room are a Risom-designed C275 chair with a red seat, one of Risom's famous webbing and timber 654W lounge chairs for Knoll as well as a Risom Rocker rocking chair produced by Design Within Reach. Another Risom chair model, with a padded yellow seat, is a Design Within Reach re-issue of a piece originally designed in 1949 for the Caribe Hilton Hotel in San Juan, Puerto Rico.

'The most interesting piece of design is a chair,' says Risom. 'I have several chairs that I do feel pleased with – we would take them into our home and get to like them. But the chair is also the hardest piece of furniture to design. There's no doubt about it.'

In the dining room, another wall-mounted console unit by Risom shows his eye for detail, with cutlery drawers neatly holding the family dining set. The crafted metal handles of the cabinet contrast with the warm grain of the timber in a variation on a standard cabinet design. Such touches have made Risom a master of mid-century style and lie behind interiors lifted by texture, character and warmth.

Biography
Jens Risom (1916–)

The son of an architect, Jens Risom was born in Copenhagen, where he studied design at the Copenhagen School of Industrial Arts and Design under Kaare Klint, together with Hans Wegner. He went on to work in the architectural offices of Ernst Kuhn, designing interiors and furniture, and moved from Denmark to the United States in 1939. Two years later, Risom met furniture manufacturer Hans Knoll and designed a fifteen-piece collection for his company. In 1946, Risom founded his own design and manufacturing company, which was eventually sold in 1970. Risom designs continue to be sold by Design Within Reach, Ralph Pucci and Rocket, as well as by Knoll.

The sitting room (*opposite*) serves as a showcase for many of Risom's designs, including his famous 654W webbed lounge chair from 1941. Other Risom pieces include the rocking chair in the corner for Design Within Reach. The small painting of the doors above the fireplace is by Vilhelm Hammershøi and is a particular favourite.

Models of Risom's 654W chair sit on a Risom side table in his study (*above*). The dining room (*right and opposite left*) includes a wall-mounted unit designed by Risom with dedicated cutlery drawers and moulded metal handles. The dining chairs and table are also Risom designs. The bench by the back door in the sitting room (*opposite right*) is a Risom piece for Design Within Reach.

Robin + Lucienne Day

Day House / Chichester, Sussex, UK, 1999

Robin and Lucienne Day passionately believed that good design can make a real difference to the quality of people's lives and they wanted to make their work affordable and available to a wide audience. They knew how to present their image in the media and came up with their own marketing ideas: when Robin Day's famous Polyprop chair was launched in the 1960s, he had the inspired idea of sending an actual chair to the offices of various architects, journalists and tastemakers.

Although the Days set up an office together and worked side by side for decades, they seldom collaborated directly. One exception was the 1951 Festival of Britain, when Robin asked his wife to provide textiles to sit alongside his steel and ply furniture in the Homes and Gardens Pavilion, and another was the canvas of their own home.

For many years they lived on Cheyne Walk in Chelsea, where they moved into a Victorian house in 1952 and decorated the interiors in mid-century style. But in 1999 they decided to move to Chichester, where they could be much closer to their country cottage. They settled on a 16th-century house with a Georgian façade, close to Chichester Cathedral, and brought with them much of the furniture and artworks that had graced the house on Cheyne Walk.

Naturally, many of the pieces in the house are their own designs, which, in the main living spaces at least, stand out against the white carpets and walls. The dining room is dominated by a silk mosaic by Lucienne, overlooking a dining table surrounded by Robin's famous Polyprop chairs. The sitting room features a brick fireplace painted white as well as one of Robin Day's black Forum sofas from 1964, while a portrait of Lucienne, painted by a fellow student from the Royal College of Art, hangs above a Robin Day sideboard.

Rather like the New Canaan home of Jens Risom (see page 260), the house is a retrospective of a lifetime in design, as well as a home. The kitchen holds other Robin Day-designed chairs as well as a bespoke elm table, also to his design. While Lucienne Day reduced her design work when the couple moved to Chichester, Robin continued working and created a studio in the garden. A panoramic image of the Alps graces one wall – Day was an enthusiastic walker, climber and skier – while drawing boards, models, and cabinets full of sketches and drawings populate the space. There is room throughout for occasional surprises and curiosities.

'People might expect these pioneers of modernism to have constructed rather purist interiors but, in fact, their taste was eclectic',[1] says their daughter, Paula Day. 'They appreciated excellence, whether old or new. They made space for things, not because they fitted into some pre-conceived aesthetic, but because they liked them. This made for a warm and lively atmosphere.'

1 Writing in *The World of Interiors*, 'All in the Day's Work', June 2011.

Biographies
Robin Day (1915–2010)

Born in High Wycombe in Buckinghamshire, Robin Day studied at the Royal College of Art, where he also met his future wife, with whom he later founded a design office in 1948. He focused primarily on furniture as a freelance designer, working with Hille International and others. Day's most famous chair design was the injection-moulded Polyprop stacking chair (1963), made by Hille, which sold in the millions and still appears in countless schools and village halls. His Hillestak chair (1950) is another key design, made from moulded plywood. Day also designed furniture for the Royal Festival Hall (1951) and the Barbican Centre (1973).

Lucienne Day (1917–2010)

Lucienne Day's distinctive, colourful and optimistic textiles helped to define mid-century design. Born Lucienne Conradi in Surrey, she studied at the Croydon School of Art and the Royal College of Art in London. Influenced by abstract contemporary painting, as well as by a passion for natural forms, she channelled her creativity into textile design, and her famous Calyx print was shown at the Festival of Britain in 1951. She designed textile ranges for Heal's furniture stores as well as carpets and wallpapers.

Robin Day's Polyprop chairs are used in the dining room (*below*), while the sitting room (*opposite above right and opposite below right*) includes a portrait of Lucienne Day and a 1964 black leather sofa by Robin Day. Models, filing cabinets and chairs of his own design populate Robin's studio (*opposite above left*).

David Mlinaric + Hugh Henry

Fighine / Tuscany, Italy, 1999

When Max and Joy Ulfane decided to look for a home in Italy, they could not have imagined that it would lead them to a project spanning a dozen years. When they found the partially derelict hilltop castello at Fighine in Tuscany after four years of searching, the Ulfanes thought that they might restore the building while living in one of the stone houses in the hamlet. In actual fact, the work at Fighine continued for a long time, under designers David Mlinaric and Hugh Henry, while the Ulfanes went on to restore the hamlet, including houses for rent and a restaurant, church and theatre.

The Ulfanes' private home in the castello took three years of work in itself. The fortified castle dates back to the 11th century and had been remodelled on a grander scale in the 16th century, while some of the ceilings in the principal rooms had been painted in the 19th century. By the time the Ulfanes bought the property, ivy was covering the building and the decor was crumbling away.

For Mlinaric, one of the greatest challenges when taking on the project was working out how the rooms in the castello, spread over four storeys, should be ordered. A master of architectural space as well as of interior design, Mlinaric took his time to look at the history of the castello as he established the function of each room. Rustic service areas at ground level such as the olive press room were simply restored and whitewashed. Going up, the grand salon on the piano nobile was turned into a comfortable drawing room, with a central hall and music room alongside. Mlinaric was careful to avoid splitting up any of the rooms or compromising the proportions of the spaces, preferring to work with the structure of the castle in creating a choice of many intimate spaces rather than trying to create more formal rooms on a grander scale.

'Both David Mlinaric and Hugh Henry had a huge input,' says Joy Ulfane. 'There are a lot of rooms in the castle and instead of having lots of bedrooms, they gave guests their own bedroom, bathroom and sitting room, which works incredibly well. David was more architectural, and Hugh was marvellous with colours and putting the right furniture in the right place.'

In a process of careful restoration and updating, Mlinaric and Henry brought in experts from across Italy to work on the house. They reused materials wherever they could, while also working with local stone, tiles and timber. The painted vaulted ceilings were restored, and Henry designed a new library, complete with bespoke bookcases and furniture.

The furniture was sourced specially for the castello and much of it came from Italy, while English sofas and armchairs were introduced in the drawing room and guest sitting rooms to create a welcoming atmosphere of comfort.

'We tried to find furniture that was appropriate for the building,' says Henry, 'realizing that some parts were early while other parts had painted decoration from the Risorgimento. It now feels like a very friendly, comfortable and agreeable place to live.'

While the castello is, in many ways, 'quintessentially Italian', the elements of English comfort create a welcoming, fully cohesive and natural fusion of styles. 'When people come here, they can see that it has been done by English people,' says Joy Ulfane. 'There is a lot of Italian furniture and paintings, but somehow there is an English feel. It is comfortable but also very sympathetic. Nothing jars.'

Biographies

David Mlinaric (1939–)

Greatly respected for his scholarly, sensitive and erudite approach to architectural space and interiors, David Mlinaric has worked on many country houses, the interiors of the Royal Opera House in Covent Garden and the British Galleries of the Victoria & Albert Museum in London, as well as on private commissions for well-known clients. He studied at the Bartlett School of Architecture in London, having shown a strong interest in design from an early age. Mlinaric founded his own practice in 1964, which became Mlinaric, Henry & Zervudachi in 1989.

Hugh Henry (1946–)

Having studied at the Glasgow School of Art, Hugh Henry joined David Mlinaric Limited in 1969. After establishing the partnership Mlinaric, Henry & Zervudachi, they opened two sister companies in New York and Paris. Since David Mlinaric retired the company has continued working under the guidance of Henry and Zervudachi. Henry is particularly regarded for his approach to colour, pattern and texture. Projects include historic country houses, residences, museums, galleries and restaurants.

In the sitting room (*opposite*), comfortable English-style seating mixes with Italianate-style, 19th-century ceiling decoration. The large ebony cabinet is Flemish and the painting above the fireplace dates from the 17th century. The formal gardens (*left*) were designed by Federico Forquet.

This more intimate sitting room (*above*) offers a private retreat removed from the communal spaces. The decorative paintwork has been restored and the fresh colours are complemented by a collage of bird prints. The high, vaulted ceilings lend the rooms a sense of drama, including the former olive press rooms on the ground floor (*opposite above left*), where the walls were simply painted white. In the master bedroom (*opposite below right*), the original colour scheme was restored; the bed hangings are by Rubelli.

Jonathan Adler

Adler/Doonan Apartment / New York, USA, 2001

A designer with an instantly recognizable, distinctive and playful style, Jonathan Adler has rapidly become one of the most influential East Coast style-makers. He began his design career as a potter but soon expanded into designing homes and hotels, furniture, fabrics, lighting and stationery, and opened his eponymous stores, selling furniture and decorative home accessories. The Adler style draws heavily on retro influences, but combines these with vibrant colours, geometric patterns, eccentric flourishes and touches of kitsch.

Adler cites David Hicks (see page 186) as a key influence but suggests that textile designer Alexander Girard, fashion innovator Bonnie Cashin and Danish artist Bjørn Wiinblad are his 'holy trinity' of design heroes. At the peak of their powers, in the 1950s, their individuality and drive in carving out an individual approach proved a great inspiration for him.

'All of their designs were eccentric and odd but incredibly chic at the same time, which is what I aspire to achieve with my own work,' says Adler. 'But the other thing that I love is that their work is really about enjoying design. You can tell that they loved what they made and followed their own path.'

This excitement about design is very much in evidence at Adler's New York apartment, where the designer is constantly adding his own pieces of furniture and pottery to see how they work together. The apartment, which he shares with writer and creative director Simon Doonan, is very much a laboratory for Adler, a constantly shifting and evolving space.

'We both like things to be bright, poppy and graphic, as well as personal and eccentric,' says Adler, who also has homes in Palm Beach and Shelter Island. 'Home should be very ebullient and pattern should be everywhere, because why not?'

Doonan first bought an apartment here back in 1994 and when Adler acquired the flat next door, seven years later, the two spaces were combined. At the heart of the home are two dramatic, high-ceilinged, barrel-vaulted rooms with unusually tall windows. As with the rest of the main living spaces, Adler painted these rooms in an 'optimistic white' that acts as a canvas for experiments with colour, pattern and layered composition.

The dining room is dominated by a George Nelson dining table (rumoured to have belonged to Nelson himself), sitting on an eye-catching rug of blue concentric circles designed by Adler. The formal living room tended to be neglected in favour of the nearby sitting room, so Adler added a ping-pong table made from two Eero Saarinen table bases and a surface covered in a bold Cole & Son wallpaper. He also hung two paintings near the full-height window, creating a surreal illusion of floating images.

The sitting room blends Adler designs such as the geometric rug, the sofa and the striped slipper chairs with other elements, including a Joe Colombo armchair and a Gae Aulenti coffee table. Smaller spaces such as the narrow stairs to the master bedroom on the upper level are brought alive with bright bursts of pattern, provided by bespoke wallpaper and a David Hicks carpet design.

Adler tends to treat bedrooms differently: the master bedroom is more of an 'evening space' with walls of 'choccy brown' contrasting with a vibrant orange damask for the niche behind the bed and repeated in occasional flourishes elsewhere. Here, as elsewhere in the house, the look is unmistakably Adler.

The vibrant colours and patterns of the artworks, furnishings and various treasures stand out even more against the backdrop of crisp white walls. In the dining room (*opposite*) a George Nelson dining table sits on an eye-catching Adler rug, while some of Adler's own ceramics are placed on the table itself. In the ping-pong room (*overleaf left*), the table tennis surface sits on Eero Saarinen table bases. In the stairs leading up to the bedroom (*overleaf right*), a geometric Adler wall coating complements a David Hicks carpet.

Biography
Jonathan Adler (1966–)

Born in New Jersey, Adler took up pottery at twelve years old and it remained a passion for him when he studied semiotics and art history at Brown University. He worked briefly with a talent agency serving the film industry but launched his own ceramics business after Barneys department store showed an interest in his work. Adler still calls himself a potter, although his design work has now branched out to include many different spheres. Adler has a string of stores and an online retail business, and as interior designer he has worked on a number of homes for private clients as well as hotels, including the Parker Palm Springs.

In the hallway (*opposite far left*) the orange table and golden vase are by Adler; pieces of Adler's pottery are placed on the dining table (*opposite above right*). The master bedroom (*opposite below right*) makes use of orange damask to highlight the niche behind the bed against a backdrop of 'choccy brown' walls. In the sitting room (*right*), the green chair is by Joe Colombo and the marble coffee table by Gae Aulenti; the rug, sofa and greyhounds are by Adler.

Marcio Kogan

Gama Issa House / São Paulo, Brazil, 2001

São Paulo is a city of high energy and chaos. It is a metropolis that is fascinating and exhausting at the same time – the kind of city where an escapist retreat is more than welcome. The Gama Issa House is certainly a haven, tucked away behind high walls on a leafy boulevard, offering a sense of calm and order. At the heart of the building is a dramatic double-height living space with a sequence of vast sliding windows that offer an instant connection with the terrace, gardens and swimming pool.

The house is a glorious box shape, a form favoured by Brazilian architect Marcio Kogan for its simplicity and purity. It was commissioned by graphic designer Claudia Issa and advertising director Alexandre Gama for themselves and their young family. The couple had stumbled upon an eye-catching contemporary house one morning on their way to work and decided to build a new home for themselves. After buying the site for their dream house, Gama and Issa went to meet Kogan, who proceeded to show them a picture of a building he had once designed – it turned out to be the very same house that they had seen that fated morning.

The couple had a list of references and ideas that fed into Kogan's design for the house, most importantly the concept of a great, open living space: the ceilings are 6 metres (20 feet) high and a rear wall forms a great library of books, with a mezzanine gallery, protected by a glass balustrade, for access to books on higher shelves. A narrow pair of staircases behind the shelves, top lit by a skylight, offer access to the gallery and the upper level of the house.

'The owners have a beautiful library of art books, so we took advantage of the double-height ceiling to expose that,' says Kogan. 'But the design was driven by the desire to explore the relationship between inside and outside living. The integration of the interiors and exteriors, and the way that the owners occupy the space and keep it alive and interesting – these are the things that please me most about the house.'

The living room became a generously spaced, high loft with a degree of organic warmth offered by the timber hardwood floors. On this gleaming timber surface rugs are used to lightly delineate two distinct zones for sitting and dining, featuring

sculptural furniture and lighting by modernist masters such as Eero Saarinen, the Castiglioni brothers and Eero Aarnio as well as contemporary pieces by Jasper Morrison and others.

A large, abstract artwork by Brazilian artist Marcus Vinicius between the stairs and bookcases stands out for its bold blues that contrast with the other, more muted tones of the room. The sparing but individual use of colour also enlivens other spaces in the house, such as the kitchen, where an orange Corian worktop on the central island brings the room to life, helped by sliding glass doors that offer easy access to the terraces.

Yet there is a sense of restraint that threads through the interiors, matching the simple but elegant form of the house itself. This was key to the idea of creating a calming family retreat and escape from the world of work and the big city outside.

It is also a building that shows the vibrancy of the contemporary design scene in Brazil and São Paulo, as architects such as Arthur Casas, Isay Weinfeld and Marcio Kogan himself build on and develop the powerful modernist legacy established here in the second half of the 20th century.

Biography
Marcio Kogan (1952–)

Influenced by the great Brazilian modernists such as Lúcio Costa, Oscar Niemeyer and Rino Levi, Marcio Kogan was also inspired by his father, who worked in the construction business and built a high-tech house for the family in the 1950s. Kogan grew up in São Paulo and studied at the Mackenzie Presbyterian University. He founded his own practice, Studio MK27, in the early 1980s and largely concentrated on the design of private houses in Brazil and beyond, including the Paraty House (2009) and the BR House (2005) in Rio de Janeiro (see Bradbury/Powers, *New Natural Home*). Recent projects also include a hotel in Portugal as well as furniture designs.

The double-height living area opens up to the terrace, gardens and pool in a dramatic fashion (*left*). The long white sofa is by Jasper Morrison, and the ottoman positioned at an angle is upholstered in a black-and-white fabric (*opposite and overleaf*). The dining table and chairs at the far end of the room are by Eero Saarinen, and the picture next to the bookshelves is by Brazilian artist Marcus Vinicius.

The Eero Aarnio ball chair in the
sitting room (*above*) is an original
from the 1960s, upholstered in
leather. The kitchen (*right*) includes a
worktop in red Corian that stands out
against a more neutral backdrop; the
stools were designed by Harry Bertoia.

The bathroom (*left*) was designed by Kogan and features local Brazilian marble. The bed in the master bedroom (*above*) was designed by Claudia Issa using a native Brazilian timber. The recliner on the terrace is by Le Corbusier.

Kengo Kuma

Great (Bamboo) Wall / Beijing, China, 2002

Japanese architect Kengo Kuma deliberately avoids the word 'house' when describing his building by the Great Wall of China. He calls the residence a 'wall' in itself – a wall of bamboo and light, rather than brick and stone. Like the Great Wall, the bamboo pavilion works with the landscape, following the contours of the land and forming a low, linear presence rather than seeking to impose itself upon the countryside in the form of a startling architectural object.

Kuma has long argued for a new kind of architecture that seeks to respond to nature and honours the natural surroundings. The Bamboo Wall building is another stage in this ongoing dialogue. 'If we want to get back to the spirit of respect for nature, we are going to have to discover new materials that can replace concrete and use them to construct buildings, create cities and improve people's sensibility,' Kuma says.[1]

The Bamboo residence is one of eleven houses in a residential development by the Great Wall, all designed by Asian architects, among them Kuma and Shigeru Ban (see page 318). Kuma's house is folded into the terrain of the site, with the appearance of a long pavilion. Most of the living spaces, along with four bedrooms, are positioned on the upper level, while additional bedrooms and service areas are hidden away within the substantial basement.

The house makes use of a steel structure and quite a lot of glass, but the emphasis is of course on natural materials, and the bamboo used throughout the house is locally sourced. Kuma had experimented with bamboo in earlier projects in Japan but here the bamboo canes serve many different purposes: they coat the house, forming a natural skin that ties the building to the landscape, and on the inside gently undulating bamboo ceilings contrast with slate floors. The canes are also used to form screens of various kinds, lightly dividing the house into zones for daytime and night, and forming brises soleil that filter the sunlight, creating an animated rhythm of light and shade that shifts as the sun moves across the sky.

Bamboo and water pools surround a courtyard with a tea room at the heart of the building, which functions as a space for relaxing and appreciating the landscape. The dining room and sitting room seem more western in character, but there is no sense of disconnection between any of these spaces, as they are bound together by shared materials and a contemporary approach to natural living.

These are fresh and enticing spaces defined by the warmth of the materials as much as the minimal furnishings. The furniture throughout ties in with the character of the house, using organic materials and sympathetic textures. The kitchen is dominated by a large counter top that seems to float in the space, and the bedrooms too have a lightness and simplicity of touch.

The interiors are lifted by spaces that flow easily and gently into one another – glowing with light and the earthy tones of the bamboo – but they are also brought to life by the way in which they connect with the landscape beyond. This is a house that blends aspects of China and Japan, of east and west, within a new design approach that respects nature and offers a version of multi-cultural luxury living.

1 Writing in *Kengo Kuma: Works & Projects* by Luigi Alini, 2005.

Biography
Kengo Kuma (1954–)

Much of Kengo Kuma's work revolves around his ambition to reinterpret architecture, moving away from the 'outward expression' of buildings and towards designs that frame the natural world. At the same time Kuma seeks to build on and update ideas from traditional Japanese architecture. Born in Kanagawa, Japan, Kuma studied at the University of Tokyo and at Columbia University in the United States. He founded Kengo Kuma & Associates in Tokyo in 1990. Projects include the Water/Glass House in Atami, Japan (1995), the Kiro-San Observatory in Ehime, Japan (1994), and the Opposite House Hotel in Beijing (2008). Kuma is also working on an outpost for the Victoria & Albert Museum in Dundee, Scotland.

The house is halfway between a solid object set in the landscape and a more ephemeral, organic and partially transparent building (*above*). Within the house, light is used as an 'architectural material' in itself, moderated by layers of glass and bamboo screens, which form a brise soleil as well as structural elements. The interior furnishings mix western influences with an Asian emphasis on minimalism and simplicity (*opposite*).

Rashid House / Scarborough, New York , USA, 2004

Karim Rashid's country kit house was ordered from a catalogue a few years before he was born. Constructed in just three days, the 1956 Techbuilt house provides an ideal setting for Rashid's instantly recognizable style and eye-catching assembly of his own countless home and furniture products. The post-and-beam house fits in neatly with Rashid's design philosophy and the importance he places on the idea of making good design easily accessible.

'The house had only had two owners and its condition was almost perfect,' says Rashid. 'The spirit seemed right and to me a sign of success is that everything works seamlessly together, all the elements fuse, and the result is one harmonious, strong piece of design. When I first discovered the house, I thought of it of course as this kind of blank canvas, but the goal was always to evolve the space into something of my own and to make it home.'

Rashid bought the house on the internet in 2004. Again, the story seems to fit with Rashid's digital age approach and his reliance on computers as his key design tool ('my loom is my laptop,' he says) in designing organic, moulded creations in vibrant candy colours. The one detail that the computer did not reveal was a large shopping mall just behind the trees in the garden that was only disclosed when the leaves started falling the following autumn. Rashid took the news in his stride and embraced the convenience of the mall for easy shopping.

Rashid made few changes to the fabric of the house, although he did add a sinuous pool area to his own design. Similar to his New York apartment, the interiors of the two-storey house became a space for embracing layers of colour and pattern that sit alongside many self-designed pieces. It is a style that Rashid describes as 'simple, full and rich' and dubs 'voluntary simplicity'.

'That's what comes to mind when I think of the fusion of my style and my country home,' he says. 'I believe in accessible and easy design, and casual luxury that is intuitive, joyful, playful, intellectual – organic and modern but sensual.'

Much of the main living space on the ground floor is open plan, with bright bursts of colour from the walls painted in a symphony of blues and yellows, offset by calmer tones for ceilings and carpets. Self-designed furniture includes a moulded white sofa with a built-in storage compartment and Butterfly stacking chairs in pink and white surrounding the dining table. A combination of pop colours works within carefully delineated zones in the house, with key tones tying in with one another.

Upstairs, there is enough space for a study area as well as the master bedroom, which functions as a retreat for Rashid away from the city and his intense work and travel schedule. 'My favourite space in the house is actually my bed,' Rashid says. 'It's the Kalm bed by Bonaldo, and I love to work and sketch there.'

The house shows Rashid's talents for combining powerful futurism with a love of fun, inspired by the Memphis Group, which Rashid cites as a key influence. Given that Rashid is such a driven, productive and highly ambitious designer, there is little doubt that his aesthetic will continue to spread its influence around the world.

Biography
Karim Rashid (1960–)

One of the most prolific and distinctive designers working in the United States today, Rashid is a true polymath who has worked across many different media and designed thousands of products including furniture, perfume bottles, baths, pens, postboxes and newspaper vending machines. He was born in Cairo, to an Egyptian father and an English mother. The family moved to London and then to Canada, where Rashid went on to study industrial design in Ottawa. Rashid also studied under the influential architect and designer Ettore Sottsass in Italy, and the Memphis master proved a powerful formative influence. He worked as an industrial designer in Toronto for eight years, before moving to New York and founding his own design studio there in 1993. Interior and architectural projects include many restaurants and hotels around the world.

Nearly all the furniture in the house is by Rashid and colour choices are characteristically flamboyant. The walls are picked out in bold blues and yellows, although the texture of the exposed brickwork is allowed to shine through in places, and the ceiling and floors are in muted tones (*opposite*).

Bold colours and dynamic furniture define the dining area downstairs (*opposite far left*) and the study (*opposite below right*) and master bedroom upstairs. The bedroom (*right*) benefits from floor-to-ceiling windows overlooking the gardens and is largely defined by warm shades of red and yellow. The Kalm Bed was designed by Rashid for Bonaldo.

Donna Karan

Karan Apartment / New York, USA, 2004

Donna Karan understands how to get the exact results she wants from the design process. As a fashion designer she is known for the way in which she experiments directly with fabrics and prototypes rather than working from abstract ideas. The same is true of her homes: Karan prefers to see full-scale models of dining tables and sofas before committing to a choice, which leads to tailored, fitted pieces that suit her and fit with her distinct aesthetic. In her Manhattan apartment, this process was taken one step further, with the architects rigging up mock walls with fabric panels so she could make a decision on the exact floor plan of her home.

'I am a very visceral person,' says Karan. 'I need to try everything on, to touch it, test it, really see it. The apartment is about views and vistas, and the flow of light and space. I didn't want little separate rooms to block myself in, and I didn't want that "now let's go through to the dining room" sort of a place. So it is open – there are no real internal doors.'[1]

Karan and the architects Bonetti/Kozerski Studio have developed a collaborative way of working over a whole series of projects that includes residences in the Hamptons and the Turks and Caicos Islands, and a number of Donna Karan and DKNY stores around the world. After a long search Karan finally settled on a large space in Manhattan at the top of a 1920s Art Deco building and turned to Bonetti/Kozerski to transform two apartments into a unified, one-bedroom home spread over 725 square metres (7,800 square feet).

'Donna wanted a serene refuge from the city below and creating open spaces, maximizing the views of Central Park and careful lighting were all very important in realizing this,' says Dominic Kozerski. 'On the practical side, the apartment needed to include areas for entertaining, private areas – including a spa bathroom and meditation room – and services areas.'

The apartment has the feel of a serene retreat, set above and apart from the city, with an easy free flow between the interconnected living spaces. A sense of separation from the world outside is partly achieved by a long travertine platform that runs along the exterior wall, forming an integrated bench and display unit, and morphing into stone steps that lead to the terrace.

Karan decided to have just one bedroom so as to enjoy a generously proportioned living space, although the lounge can easily transform into an extra sleeping area when her children and

grandchildren come to visit. The bathroom has the look of a crisp home spa, while another portion of the apartment has been set aside as a yoga and meditation room.

Exquisitely detailed with a soothing black-and-white colour palette, the apartment uses sumptuous materials such as travertine for the floors and Italian ivory plaster on the walls. 'To me, texture is a way to add an almost sculptural dimension to a room,' says Karan, 'whether with a tactile fabric – like cashmere or linen – or via a wall or floor surface, like bamboo or limestone.'[2]

At the same time comfort is also a priority, with a range of soft and tempting areas for relaxing and entertaining. Looking at the lines of her own-label creations in Karan's wardrobe it is hard not to draw parallels between her fashion and her interiors, as they share a trademark attention to detail, line and comfort in a crisp and perfectly tailored approach.

1 Interview with Vinny Lee, *The Times Magazine*, 25 September 2004.
2 Interview with Amanda Talbot, *Elle Decoration*, November 2007.

Biography
Donna Karan (1948–)

Karan's mother, father and stepfather were all involved in the fashion industry, so it seemed only natural when Karan developed her first collection in high school. She studied at Parsons School of Design in New York and then began work at Anne Klein, where she spent ten years before launching Donna Karan Collection in 1985 with the support of her late husband, Stephan Weiss. Karan added the DKNY brand to her business in 1989, followed by menswear, a beauty division and a home collection. The company, which was acquired by LVMH in 2001, has more than one hundred stores around the world and Karan continues as chief designer.

The travertine platform running down one side of the apartment in the living area (*left* and *opposite*) leads to the terrace; a series of moleskin cushions serves to transform the platform into a bench as well as a display area. The dining area beyond also includes fitted benches by Bonetti/Kozerski.

A bespoke travertine bath is positioned by the window in the combined bathroom and dressing room (*opposite*). Much of the furniture in the bedroom (*below right*) and dining area (*below left*) is also bespoke and designed by Bonetti/Kozerski. In the entrance hall (*above left*), a flash of colour is provided by a painting by Francis Bacon, while the walls behind are covered in Italian linen.

John Minshaw

Minshaw House / London, UK, 2004

'Primarily we are designers and architects rather than decorators,' says John Minshaw, who is a dedicated neoclassicist, but one with a love and appreciation of new technology and innovation. 'I like to deal with the bones of a house and then bring everything else in on top of that. Our style is to buy very good antiques, design bespoke cabinet work and put them into pared-down interiors.'

Although he has worked in the countryside and abroad, Minshaw is perhaps best known for a series of London houses in a fresh neoclassical spirit that he has designed for himself and a number of clients. Among them is the six-storey 1780s Marylebone townhouse that is now a home for Minshaw and his wife, Susie, and houses his offices in the basement.

The house was initially in a very poor state and had been sectioned into dental surgeries with residential space on the top two floors, although parts of the building had not been used for fifteen years. The only internal period features that Minshaw was able to retain during the two-year programme of works were the stairs, which needed to be sandblasted to remove layers of paint.

'None of the fireplaces were original and there was little else left,' Minshaw says. 'But because the building had been so neglected we were allowed a slightly freer hand than we might have had otherwise.'

The house was totally redesigned on the inside, from the ground floor up. An Edwardian addition at the rear was replaced with a courtyard garden and a newly designed pavilion beyond the courtyard, which includes an elegant and spacious library illuminated by a vast skylight and featuring bespoke bookcases and a large 19th-century desk.

The ground floor of the main building was reconfigured with a limestone-floor entrance hall and a new windbreak doorway. To one side is a generously sized kitchen with double doors leading to a panelled dining room in the shape of a perfect cube, with a bespoke Macassar ebony dining table.

Here one begins to appreciate – as Minshaw did when he first saw the house – not just the scale of the building with its high ceilings and soaring proportions, but also the quality of the light flooding through the triptychs of windows at the front and back.

'That was the real attraction,' says Minshaw. 'The house does have an overall sense of calm, which I love. I like to confine any fuss and business to one area, like the bookshelves in the library or the dining table, but have very little else in a room so that you maintain that sense of subtlety.'

Upstairs, three former dentist's consulting rooms have been turned into one large, L-shaped drawing room which allows the sunlight to cross uninterrupted through the house. This sense of spatial generosity is continued on the floor above, which is given over to a master bedroom suite. In the bedroom itself, one wall is covered in glazed linen for texture, while floor-to-ceiling Irish linen curtains – used in many other rooms in the house – create a spare but warm window treatment.

The overall impression is one of refined luxury, a theme continued through the more functional spaces such as the indulgently sized master bathroom. However, luxury here does not mean excess. Minshaw's rooms have a calm purity and sense of restraint about them that allows the proportions, detailing and furnishings to be fully appreciated. It is a philosophy of 'less is more' within a neoclassical framework.

Biography
John Minshaw (1943–)

Born in Amersham, England, Minshaw studied fine art at the Camberwell School of Art, but later switched to ceramics and was taught by Hans Coper and Lucie Rie. He also taught at Camberwell for a number of years after graduating and became involved in interior design in the mid-1960s, designing his first house for fashion designer Caroline Charles. For many years Minshaw also designed and manufactured furniture before deciding to concentrate solely on interiors in the UK and abroad. Minshaw places a strong emphasis on bespoke designs for his projects and enjoys playing with scale and unexpected elements. Travels in Italy and Egypt are a particular source of inspiration.

The drawing room on the first floor (*opposite*) includes a sofa and ottoman by John Minshaw, and a large picture frame with mirrored glass dating from the late 19th or early 20th century. The floors are in dyed oak and the table by the window is French, from the 18th century. In the master bedroom (*above*), the headboard is bespoke, while the mirrors are Italian designs from the 1960s; the curtains are Irish linen. The bathroom (*right*) features a John Minshaw-designed vanity unit and a floor in a grid of French limestone, Portland stone and brown marble.

Studio KO

Villa D / Marrakech, Morocco, 2004

It is hard not to be seduced by the warm, gentle beauty of Villa D. This is a house of many delights that manages to be both minimal and warm and characterful. It is full of ideas, contemporary and innovative, but Villa D also feels 'essentially Moroccan' and tied to the land and its setting, positioned within a walled compound in sight of the Atlas mountains.

The house was commissioned by a family who wanted a Moroccan retreat that would be both contextual and modern. They turned to architects Olivier Marty and Karl Fournier of Studio KO, who are much respected for their reinterpretations of traditional materials and sensitive approach to the landscape and environment.

'They wanted a house that was elementary, meaning something that was very close to nature, using earth and water,' says Marty. 'But they also wanted the house to be sincere, and because the client didn't like large windows, we hid the windows as much as we could and designed them as a series of lines scored in the building.'

Made with sun-baked earthen bricks, the main house was designed as a two-storey structure, with a linear sequence of living spaces on the lower floor and a generous master bedroom suite above. The living spaces form a procession, one leading to the other, with the option to lightly divide them using sliding glass doors.

Two salons with dramatic high ceilings contrast with the more subdued and intimate spaces of the dining room – complete with bespoke timber tables and leather-cushioned banquettes to either side of the room – the library and an abstract cloakroom, where a sculpted box at the centre provides storage for coats and shoes. The earthen walls are bare but rich in texture and shifting in tone according to the careful manipulations of light. Carefully chosen bespoke pieces of furniture, including integrated elements such as the fireplaces, assume the importance of curated sculptures within the minimal, gallery-like quality of the living rooms.

The master suite is reached via a soaring, narrow staircase. This bedroom zone is a peaceful retreat, set apart from the rest of the house and conceived as a long rectangular space leading to a roof terrace at one end. Zones for sleeping, bathing and showering are lightly separated by partial dividers, one of them containing a fireplace. A freestanding, cocoon-like Villeroy & Boch bath is carefully positioned in the sightline of a modest window that opens up views across the grounds and palm trees

to the mountains beyond. The bed itself has been designed as a bespoke platform in the middle of the room, holding both the mattress and, at the other side of the headboard, a low banquette facing the roof terrace.

Spaces for the four children of the family are contained in a single-storey wing adjoining the main body of the house. Four identically proportioned bedrooms sit to one side of a long hallway, and a neatly fitted washbasin has been placed outside each of the four doorways. Guests are guaranteed privacy in two satellite buildings set slightly apart from the main house, with courtyards and linear water channels punctuating the spaces between them.

The carefully controlled quality of natural light within the house makes for highly atmospheric interiors, while the minimalist approach allows the focus to be placed on the beauty of the earth and straw walls, and the proportions of the spaces themselves, which provide ordered contrasts as one walks through the house. Villa D has become a key reference point in the creation of a more refined, modern form of North African design that seeks to both respect and respond to the countryside.

Biography
Studio KO

Studio KO was founded by Karl Fournier (1970–) and Olivier Marty (1975–) in 2000, and has offices in Paris and Marrakech. Work in Morocco began when they were asked to design a house near Tangiers for a member of the Hermès family. Their country houses in Morocco and France have gained particular attention for their sensitive and considered approach to the landscape and materials. They include House G (2008) in the Luberon, France, set in a landscape of rolling hills and woodland (see Bradbury/Powers, *New Natural Home*, Thames & Hudson, 2011).

The modern villa (*above*) sits within the enclosure of a farmstead a few kilometres from Marrakech. A small complex of interlinked buildings includes the main house, a spa/hammam building, a guest house and a pool. Within, the main living spaces form a procession of interlinked areas from the library to the sitting room and the dining area and lounge beyond (*opposite*).

A Minotti sofa in the sitting room (*opposite far left*) is complemented by bespoke pieces by Studio KO such as the coffee table, while the softer textures of the Moroccan rug contrast with the *pisé* walls. The hanging lamps are by Artemide. The library (*opposite above right and above*) features bespoke desks, chairs and shelves. The master bathroom upstairs (*opposite below right*) offers views across the countryside and includes a sculpted Villeroy & Boch bath. The dining room (*right*) features fitted leather banquettes and bespoke lighting.

John Saladino

Saladino Villa / Santa Barbara, California, USA, 2005

John Saladino is part Italian, part American, and the two influences come together in the most striking way in the project that Saladino calls his 'opus' – an Italianate villa in Montecito, California, overlooking the ocean. Perhaps more than any other of Saladino's projects, this villa has captured people's attention, showing how natural, comfortable and enticing a combination of classical and contemporary elements can be.

Saladino first spotted the house in the early 1980s, when it was slowly crumbling. He resisted the challenge at first but the house remained in his mind and twenty years later it became his. The sandstone villa and the gardens were built by architect Wallace Frost in 1930, but both the building and the gardens had been badly neglected and were close to ruin. Redesigning and rebuilding the house, as well as re-landscaping the surrounding gardens, would take four years.

Saladino sought to respect the original floor plan as much as possible but in parts of the house, such as the kitchen/breakfast rooms, smaller spaces were combined to create more open and flexible living areas with an improved quality of natural light. Here, as in other parts of the house, the stone walls and timber ceiling beams were exposed,

creating a suitably rustic note. Galley-style kitchen cabinets are topped with thick marble and faced with stainless steel, showing the blend of old and new, the natural and technical in one harmonious space.

The drawing room is particularly generous in size, at around 12 metres (40 feet) long, especially in comparison to the modest scale of the entrance hall nearby. Here, Saladino aimed for a space that was grand in terms of proportion and scale but also welcoming, with a large stone fireplace at one end. An Oriental carpet was used to form a self-contained 'island' with more secluded seating around the fireplace. A 16th-century chest, 18th-century Italian side chairs and other period pieces rub shoulders with a 1970s Cy Twombly painting in considered, unexpected compositions.

'I don't like to walk into a room and instantly fully comprehend it,' says Saladino, who describes himself as a romantic. 'I like a space that intrigues me because it means that I'm experiencing something that I can't immediately grasp; it makes me want to keep exploring….It is why I don't like graphic solutions, such as strongly geometric carpets, or simple colours like canary yellow or grass green. I like colours that are dichromatic or metamorphic, that pose a question or change

with the light….I seek that kind of ambivalent complexity in every aspect of my work.'[1]

The dining room is an intentionally darker, more atmospheric room, designed for the evening and mostly lit by candles. Distressed timber panelling around the fireplace works well with the exposed beams and stonework. Saladino's own bedroom was given a more dramatic treatment, with the Napoleonic bed placed at an angle in the middle of the room, looking out into the gardens.

Saladino's villa is a fully realized, ambitious vision that includes the landscaping and the stone terraces, with their seating areas and quiet, contemplative corners. It is a modern home, full of practical convenience and contemporary comforts, but it is also a lyrical environment where one might easily forget what century it is, which is certainly part of its power and its charm.

1 John Saladino, *Villa*, 2009.

Biography
John Saladino (1939–)

John Saladino was born in Kansas City, Missouri, to an Italian father and American mother and studied at the Yale School of Art and Architecture. After graduating in 1963, he travelled to Europe and worked with architect Piero Sartogo in Rome for two years. He founded his own architectural and interior design practice in New York in the early 1970s (now known as the Saladino Group) and launched his own furniture company in 1986 after designing ranges for a number of retailers. Saladino has become well known for his unique combinations of old and new, classical and modern, with projects across the United States and around the world. Key influences include Palladio, William Kent and John Soane. Saladino is also the author of a number of influential books on design.

The Italianate courtyard formation of the house, with its central garden and loggia alongside (*left*), allows the light to percolate through the living spaces. In the drawing room (*opposite*), the furniture around the fireplace is arranged on a 19th-century Oriental carpet. The sofas were designed by Saladino, and the candlesticks on the 17th-century octagonal Italian table are made from seashells and coral.

(Photographs by Alexandre Bailhache)

The walls of the dining room (*above*)
are lined with 18th-century creamware
plates, and the white cloth on the
table is a 19th-century Marseilles
bedcover. The Italian chest by the
stairs (*right*) dates from the 17th
century, with an Italian painting
of Saint Barbara placed above it.

In the kitchen (*left*), stainless steel drawers are topped by a counter and end pieces in white marble. A Napoleonic bed sits at an angle in the master bedroom (*above*), while the bedside table was designed by Saladino.
(Photographs by Alexandre Bailhache)

Michael S. Smith

Smith House / Bel Air, Los Angeles, California, USA, 2006

Designer Michael S. Smith knows how to make an entrance. For him, the entry hall establishes the narrative of a home. In Smith's own home in Bel Air, the hallway is among his favourite spaces in the house, with its double-height, domed ceiling, welcoming fireplace topped with a painting by Beatrice Caracciolo, and gentle, soothing cream and blush colour scheme, with terracotta dust mixed into the plaster finishes of the walls. Just as Smith intended, the hallway also offers the kind of welcome that you might expect from an English country house.

The English tradition was very much in Smith's mind when he planned the hillside house, overlooking the ocean. 'It's my vision of a dower house, something the great English architect Sir Edwin Lutyens might have designed, if he had been born in Los Angeles instead of London in 1869,' says Smith. 'It's built of old brick, with a slate roof and Georgian details….It's pure Lutyens, gorgeous and theatrical.'[1]

The house was first built in the 1950s as a ranch-style building with a large private garden. Smith lived in the house for a year while he worked out what he wanted to do, and ultimately decided that the design was so flawed that nothing less than a radical rebuild would do. Working with architect Oscar Shamamian, Smith largely kept the original design of the house but extended it in a number of directions. From the outside, the house appears to be on two levels, but it is actually single storey, with a series of high ceilings in the key living spaces. Points of inspiration were William Kent, Robert Adam and the interiors of Colefax & Fowler.

The living room is a dramatic central space, with seating arranged around a fireplace, including a sofa in a self-designed fabric and another one positioned against a wall coated in Venetian plaster. A contemporary abstract painting by Christine Marie Taber adds a different note. The breakfast room is in the form of an octagonal pavilion opening out to the garden, with chequered wallpaper by Smith and curtains in a Moghul-style pattern.

The master bedroom and one of the guest rooms are dominated by four-poster beds – a recurring Smith favourite – that lend the rooms an elegant atmosphere of indulgent comfort. 'If you're going to spend a third of your life in bed, it might as well have a sense of ceremony,' says Smith. 'There's something special about a four-poster bed.'[2]

It is perhaps this focus on sophisticated comfort that makes Smith so appealing to clients in the

The hallway (*left*) is designed as a room in its own right with a carefully defined, welcoming atmosphere and an open fireplace. Smith uses many different shades of white, including the limestone floor; the chair is in Egyptian Revival style. In the living room (*opposite*), the centre table is Japanese and the sofa is covered in the Smith-designed 'Bentley Rose' hemp fabric.

United States and other parts of the world (including Britain), but Smith is by no means completely focused on the past. There are contemporary elements included in the mix, and his interiors are both practical and adaptable.

At the same time one senses a romantic, pastoral quality that permeates Smith's house and work – a nostalgia for open fires, floral patterns, comfortable armchairs and sumptuous, fairytale beds. However, Smith presents his take on romance within a serious framework of symmetry, proportion and scale, and there is no doubt that his elegant reinterpretations of the past are much in demand.

1 Michael S. Smith, *Houses*, 2008.
2 Ibid.

Biography
Michael S. Smith (1964–)

Born and raised in Newport Beach, California, Michael S. Smith attended the Otis College of Art and Design in Los Angeles. This was followed by a period in London, where he completed the Victoria & Albert Museum's decorative arts programme and immersed himself in English-style interiors, with Nancy Lancaster and Colefax & Fowler (see page 19) as particular influences. Smith went on to work with John Saladino (see page 298) in New York before founding his own design company in Los Angeles in 1990. He also designs his own lines of furniture and fabrics, sold through his Jasper label and stores. Key clients include President Barack Obama and his wife, Michelle Obama, for whom Smith created interiors at the White House.

In the sitting room (*opposite*), a
second seating area has been created
at the far end, with a painting by Joan
Mitchell with sconces to either side.
The breakfast room (*above*), sits
alongside the kitchen, with French
doors opening to the garden; the
curtains are made from Smith's
'Moghul Panel' fabric and the
English rosewood table dates from
the William IV period. In the guest
room (*below*), the bed is a copy of a
piece owned by the painter Balthus.

24H Architecture

Dragspelhuset / Lake Övre, Sweden, 2006

Tucked away in a Swedish nature reserve, Dragspelhuset (Accordion House), has the flavour of a fairytale house in the woods. It appears like something out of a Tim Burton retelling of Hansel and Gretel, yet there is nothing scary about this place. The cabin has the look of an unusual cocoon, sitting in the middle of the woods and waiting to surprise viewers with its beauty.

The cabin is owned and designed by Dutch architects Boris Zeisser and Maartje Lammers, of 24H Architecture, who wanted a summer retreat in Sweden for themselves and their daughter. They came across a 19th-century fishing shack by a stream in the Glaskogen nature reserve not far from the banks of Lake Övre. Planning restrictions prohibited any new construction by the lake, so the hut offered a golden opportunity to create a new kind of haven.

The hut did come with certain conditions, however. The structure could be extended only by around 28 square metres (300 square feet), while another stipulation meant that they could not build close to the property line or the stream. But Zeisser was inspired by the model of Frank Lloyd Wright's Fallingwater structure, which cantilevers out over a creek (see Bradbury/Powers, *The Iconic House*) and wanted to push the cabin as close to the water as he could.

The answer lay in a extendable house that could unfold like an accordion when in use and then retract in the winter months. The extension sits on wheels and rolls out along two steel rails via a pulley system. The main body of the original hut became a bedroom, while the new section of the cabin, complete with the accordion element, became an open-plan living area with seating at one end, and a compact kitchen and dining area at the other.

Red cedar shingles form the organic, moulded carapace that envelops the cabin, with socket-like windows and the flue of the wood-burning stove pushing outwards like a rhinoceros horn. The interiors are just as startling, if not more so, and embrace the notion of a crafted, sinuous cabin, where the timber ceilings and supporting beams, as well as many of the windows, abandon right angles and geometry in favour of hand-made and more imaginative lines.

The walls and the curving ceiling are made from silver birch in the form of timber strands slotted together in horizontal strips. They echo the timber floors and wooden beams, and the fairytale quality of the space is enhanced further

by a collection of reindeer skins that line sections of the ceiling for extra insulation.

Solar panels are used to provide lighting and heating comes from the wood-burning stove. Cooking is done with propane gas, and the lavatory facilities are contained in small hut nearby, making the cabin self-sufficient.

For such a modest project, built by the architects themselves and their friends over four summers, Dragspelhuset has gathered an extraordinary level of international attention. It is one of those eccentric buildings that really capture people's imagination. Like Wharton Esherick's handmade home and studio (see page 54), or the organic forms of Bart Prince (see page 218), Dragspelhuset captures the eye and stays with you. It is light, fresh and contemporary but it is also a powerful, sculptural presence.

Biographies
**Boris Zeisser (1968–) &
Maartje Lammers (1963–)**

Dutch architects Boris Zeisser and Maartje Lammers both studied at the Delft University of Technology. After graduating they worked in various architectural offices including Mecanoo, OMA/Rem Koolhaas and Erick van Egeraat. In 2001, they co-founded 24H Architecture in Rotterdam. Projects include residential buildings, schools, hotel projects and an eco-holiday resort in Thailand.

The outward form of the house has a surreal biomorphic quality, resembling the figure of a scaled animal emerging from the trees. On the inside, the walls and ceiling are silver birch with beams forming Art Nouveau-inspired organic shapes reminiscent of the work of Gaudí (*opposite*). Reindeer skins are used to coat the ceilings around the fireplace in the living room (*opposite above right*), creating a fairytale atmosphere. The bedroom (*opposite below left*) has a very different feel to it; it features an integrated wood-burning stove.

Matthew Williamson

Williamson House / London, UK, 2007

The sitting room offers a different approach, with a more neutral backdrop of white walls and a shiny vinyl-coated floor. Colour and pattern are provided in the form of vibrant highlights: a vivid blue sofa with an array of cushions, crimson side tables and fluorescent orange paint on the window frames on either side of the fireplace.

'Whenever I go into a room I know exactly what colour it has to be,' says Williamson. 'I never sit for hours with four swatches of green, or spend weeks wondering about which shade of fuchsia. I kind of log colours I've seen…but it can also be groups of colours…I am drawn to using hot and cold together, like shocking pink with cool turquoise. And I guess another constant in my work is the use of the synthetic or contemporary with the aged. I guess I just live in a bubble of my own ideas.'[1]

In the kitchen and master bedroom, as in the dining room, Williamson experiments with picking out one or two walls or surfaces with a contrasting colour or pattern, such as the bespoke wallpaper around the fireplace in the bedroom. It is one of many devices, used across a number of houses over the years, that have made Williamson a tastemaker for interiors as well as a successful fashion designer.

1 Interview with Toni Rodgers, *Elle Decoration*, January 2009.

Biography
Matthew Williamson (1971–)

British fashion designer Matthew Williamson has established an international reputation with his bright and intricately detailed collections that were partly inspired by his travels to India, Mexico and other destinations. Born in Chorlton, Manchester, Williamson studied fashion at Central Saint Martins College of Art and Design in London, graduating in 1994. He worked with Monsoon and Marni before founding his own label with Joseph Velosa in 1997. Williamson's London flagship store opened in 2004, followed by a New York store in 2009. A year later, he expanded from womenswear into menswear. From 2005 to 2008, Williamson was also creative director at the iconic Italian fashion house Emilio Pucci.

Even as a child, Matthew Williamson had a passion for design and colour, not only experimenting with fashion but also also playing with interiors, painting the walls of his bedroom lilac and the radiator silver at the age of eleven. As a student at Central Saint Martins College of Art and Design in London he lived in halls of residence for a time and again transformed his quarters into an unexpectedly exotic space.

Williamson started travelling during his student years, journeying around Asia, Latin America and India. The latter in particular became a formative influence, driving his interest in bright colours, vivid patterns and exotic detailing. He began working with embroiderers in India and brought back treasures from his trips that fed directly into the spaces around him.

Williamson's homes and studios became part of his image as he embraced the need to market his name as widely as possible as a brand. His studio was featured in *The World of Interiors* and his home in Primrose Hill, north London (particularly in

its 'Bollywood' incarnation), appeared in many other magazines.

That home was followed some years later by a larger one in Hampstead, north London, where the interiors again became an integral part of the vibrant aesthetic. Williamson bought the house from an architect, so the proportions were strong, leaving Williamson free to decorate the house with his trademark exuberance.

The interiors are a contemporary mélange, with vivid colours and patterns, mid-20th-century classic furniture, newer designs and eclectic treasures and artworks sourced from London and abroad. The dining room, which opens to the rear garden, sums up Williamson's design philosophy most succinctly. One wall is brought alive by a flamboyant wallpaper, while the others are in a duck-egg blue, with French-window frames in a fuchsia pink. Chairs by Charles and Ray Eames are placed around a Saarinen table with a Mexican doll, while a 'peacock' wicker chair is placed in one corner.

A neutral backdrop provides a canvas for colour and contrast in the sitting room (*above and opposite*). Mirrored mosaics bring the fireplace to life, while the furniture includes a mirrored armchair and a vintage sofa covered in a Williamson fabric; the wheatsheaf table is from Liberty.

Throughout the house, walls and surfaces are picked out with flamboyant wallpaper and vivid colours, lending interest to the interiors without becoming overwhelming. The dining room (*above*) features a wall in a Designers Guild 'Durbar Hall' paper, and green Charles Eames chairs are placed around a Saarinen dining table.

In the bedroom and powder room, splashes of pattern also bring the spaces to life. The fireplace buttress in the bedroom (*above*) is picked out in a bespoke wallpaper from Rodnik. The sculpted fire bowl is complemented by white Buddhas from Tann Rokka.

David Pocknell

Saling Barn / Braintree, Essex, UK, 2007

Barn conversions are always a balancing act – the soaring, vibrant and open vibrant spaces (an agricultural version of the loft) are full of character and drama that demand to be respected and preserved. Yet doing so, at the same time as introducing elements of contemporary living and standard home comforts, is a challenge.

Designer David Pocknell has established himself as a master of barn conversions, having converted a whole series for both himself and his clients over the years. Most dramatic and unusual of them is Saling Barn – a vast, oak-framed building in the Essex countryside. The grand scale called for a fresh and different approach and so Pocknell slotted in a three-storey home at one end of the barn and a two-storey glass-fronted office at the other. Between the two lies a generous open space from which you can instantly appreciate the sheer scale and beauty of the original structure, with its great sense of space and the skeletal outline of the timbers, as well as the brick of the threshing floor and the great cart doors to either side.

'Barns are such friendly spaces and give you wonderful opportunities,' says Pocknell. 'If you are sensitive to them, they are great buildings to work with. We lived in this great big space, some of which we expressed and some of which we almost denied.'

Simply restoring the fabric of the barn was a daunting task, with 55,000 reclaimed tiles required for the roof and a fifth of the timbers throughout in need of repair or replacement. Windows were limited by the planning authorities to the existing openings in the building, which were more numerous in the section of the barn where Pocknell chose to position his house, which is surprisingly light and airy.

The house itself is largely self-contained, and has its own identity, as though 'hosted' by the barn. There is a large, flexible ground floor, with a semi-open-plan kitchen and dining area, using natural and reflective materials and colours to keep the light circulating through the space. A gleaming Bulthaup kitchen mixes with 20th-century design classics by Breuer and Le Corbusier as well as antique finds and vintage posters. Bedrooms and a studio are positioned on the two floors above. Throughout the house, storage units and other elements such as the bathrooms work as standalone units, and large, monolithic pieces of furniture help to divide the living spaces while leaving the exposed frame of the barn untouched.

'That way you remain aware of the fact that you are living in this big space,' says Pocknell, who has since moved on to another barn conversion. 'We didn't want to hang anything off the barn walls or to make anything sit on the frame.'

The zone between the house and office offers the sheer luxury of open space as well as a flexible area for meetings, gatherings, parties and exhibitions. Two intriguing Monopoly-style miniature houses the size of a garden shed were designed by Pocknell as prefabricated units that could slot easily into two empty bays in this open section of the barn, neatly enclosing services and technology for the office and house.

With views across open farmland and the shortest of commutes between home and office, Saling Barn offers an idyllic living/work space under one cathedral-like roof. As a way of preserving this landmark building, it is a perfect design solution.

Biography
David Pocknell (1943–)

Born in Romford, Greater London, architectural and graphic designer David Pocknell had little formal training. He left school at sixteen and much of his early education was in the form of night classes in drawing and typography. Pocknell worked with industrial and graphic designers Roger and Robert Nicholson before going freelance at the age of twenty-two and starting his own multi-disciplinary design studio in 1965, which continues as Pocknell Studio. He was also a partner at the design consultancy Pentagram in the early 1990s. Pocknell's work comprises buildings, interiors, brand identity projects, graphics and book design.

The vast proportions of the barn (*above and opposite*) allow for enough space to contain an entire house at one end as well as a two-storey glass-fronted office at the other. The space in between, which includes the old threshing floor, provides a multi-functional space for parties and gatherings, and allows the true splendour of the wooden frame to be fully appreciated.

The three-storey house at the end of the barn (*left*) draws in light and uses a semi-open-plan layout and fresh, white colours and surfaces to keep the light circulating. In the living area (*below left*), the sofa is from the Conran Shop and the Gran Confort armchairs are by Le Corbusier. The London North Eastern Railway poster in the dining area (*below right*) is an original period print.

The kitchen units (*right*) are by Bulthaup, while the dining table and chairs were sourced at the Aram Store. The dining and kitchen area is separated from the main lounge by a shift in floor level and half-height counters and cupboards; the threshold between the two zones is marked by black-and-white paintings by Avi Eisenstein. The master bedroom (*below*) features lights by Flos and bedside tables by Marcel Breuer.

Boyarsky Murphy

Christ Church Tower / London, UK, 2007

It is not every day that one sees a building by Sir Christopher Wren in an estate agent's window. It is all the more startling to learn that it attracted little interest at first. Only after a drawn-out adventure was Christ Church Tower finally restored and reinvented as an extraordinary family home right in the heart of the City of London.

Often dubbed England's greatest architect, Wren designed just one private house whose origins have been proven beyond doubt – Marlborough House in London, which dates from the early 1700s and now houses the headquarters of the Commonwealth. But at last another 'true Wren' construction serves as a home, close to the architect's masterpiece, St Paul's Cathedral.

Christ Church, Newgate Street, was one of fifty-one churches that Wren designed or radically rebuilt after the Great Fire of London of 1666, and it was completed in 1678. Centuries later, it was bombed in the Blitz of December 1940. The remaining stone walls of Christ Church's nave were retained as a memorial to the Blitz and the bell tower was repaired and rebuilt in the 1950s by ecclesiastical architects Seely & Paget.

Despite its central City location, Christ Church Tower was a brooding presence on the skyline. It had last been adopted as an office, spread out over six levels, but only the lower half of the building had been in use since the 1960s.

For architects Boyarsky Murphy, who were commissioned by the brave buyer of the Tower, the building presented some serious architectural challenges as they had to find ways to create a contemporary home within the shell of a solid stone monument with a myriad of heritage building restrictions.

'We were intrigued by it, and as we went on it intrigued us more and more,' says Nicholas Boyarsky. 'We knew we could do something but we weren't quite sure where it would take us. It had to be something different.'

They had a number of big issues to address: the domical vault, which now holds the kitchen on the first floor, had to be preserved as much as possible while also making space for a staircase and services within the shell. An elevator was also needed, given that the Tower is 45 metres (150 feet) high.

Light was another big challenge, given that only one small new window was allowed for the whole Tower. The architects had to work with the existing openings, but the existing six levels of the Tower were reworked with ten floors: a ground-floor

reception area and dining room, followed by the kitchen, reception room and a block of three bedrooms and bathrooms, plus a grand living room at the top, complete with a mezzanine gallery, used as a study.

'We really tried to think about how the owner would live in this house,' says Boyarsky, 'and what would be the combination of spaces. In the end, our objective was to make it very simple, because otherwise the spaces could soon end up looking very cluttered.'

Every inch of space needed to be maximized. Nearly all of the furniture is bespoke and anything not built on site needed to be compact enough to fit into the modestly sized lift. Space-saving measures and inventions characterize every room; for instance, there are built-in cupboards hidden in the stairs of two of the double-height bedrooms. Boyarsky compares the Tower to a ship or space rocket, with cabins and communal areas.

The house clearly works, with a procession of spaces that lead up to the large space of the main living room, which feels unexpectedly grand with its triple-height bell tower roofline, complete with the wonderful views one might expect.

The unusual proportions and space restrictions of the tower house required bespoke designs for many elements in the building. The compact kitchen (*opposite above*) includes a fitted oak breakfast table by the windows and a spiral staircase in glass and steel with acrylic treads. An Arne Jacobsen chair sits by the window in the reception room on the third level (*opposite below left*), while the stairs to the mezzanine in the bedroom (*opposite below right*) contain integrated cupboards.

Biographies
Nicholas Boyarsky (1958–)

After completing his training at the Architectural Association in London, Nicholas Boyarsky worked for Zaha Hadid and Michael Hopkins, before co-founding Boyarsky Murphy Architects in 1994 with his partner, Nicola Murphy. He has also taught widely, holding courses at the Bartlett School of Architecture in London. Residential commissions have included projects in London and Sydney, and across the UK.

Nicola Murphy (1964–)

Nicola Murphy also trained at the Architectural Association and graduated in 1989. She worked with OMA/Rem Koolhaas and Stefano de Martino before co-founding Boyarsky Murphy. She has taught interior design at the Chelsea College of Art & Design in London.

Sagaponac Furniture House / Long Island, USA, 2007

Japanese architect Shigeru Ban is famous for challenging conventions in his designs. He has created an eye-catching series of open-plan homes with few solid divisions and retractable glass walls that reach out into the landscape (among them the Wall-Less House, 1997). In the Paper House (1995) in Yamanashi, Ban used rolled cardboard as part of the structure of the building, and his Naked House (2000) combined the theme of openness with experimental materials, including semi-transparent walls that look like rice paper and turn the house into a giant glowing lantern at night.

Out in the Hamptons, the ever-fashionable Long Island holiday enclave for New Yorkers, Ban has designed a pioneering Furniture House. He started these Furniture Houses in Japan in the mid-90s, using cabinets, book cases and cupboards as part of the fabric of the building itself.

These heavy-duty furniture units serve as dividing walls and partitions while also largely supporting the roof. The house in Sagaponac (created with American associate Dean Maltz) forms part of Ban's ongoing experiment with the theme, and he used a total of eighty cabinets to create the outline of the house and separate the different rooms. 'Each project is really related to another one,' says Ban. 'Ideas get developed further and further.'

Surrounded by trees, with only the sound of the birds and an occasional whistle from the railway, the U-shaped single-storey house is wrapped around a large swimming pool. The sleek, sophisticated building has the feel of a classic mid-century home, yet the execution is contemporary, with brick limited to a corner fireplace in the living room.

There was still work to be done to finish the house after it was sold by the developers, so New York designer Shamir Shah was commissioned to complete the interiors. 'I was overwhelmed by the beauty and simplicity of the house,' says Shah. 'It is in an idyllic spot, it works well and the plan is brilliant. But the immediate reaction was that we had to do something to house the art and mitigate the sea of maple, which was expansive.'

While respecting the Ban vision as much as possible, Shah made some careful adjustments to the interiors, especially in the hallway, that preserved the open and fluid layout but also created space for artworks and installations, including a large butterfly installation in the living room. Vintage Moroccan carpets fit perfectly with the soothing colour scheme, with subtle shifts in tone and texture and an emphasis on natural materials helping to tie the elements together.

Furnishings mix classics by Arne Jacobsen, Hans Wegner, Eero Saarinen and others with bespoke pieces by Shamir Shah, such as the dining table. One of the four bedrooms was transformed into a comfortable media room while another doubles up as a study. The result of this unique collaboration between architect and designer is a soothing house of natural warmth and light.

Designed around a series of strong cabinets and cupboards, the house makes use of these furniture elements as structural supports and partitions (*below*). The natural tones of the furniture and fabrics tie in with the timber joinery. The living area (*opposite*) includes vintage Moroccan rugs, bespoke teak coffee tables and furniture by Hans Wegner and Edward Wormley.

Biographies
Shigeru Ban (1957–)

Born in Tokyo, Shigeru Ban studied architecture in the United States, graduating from the Cooper Union School of Architecture in 1982. He worked with the architect Arata Isozaki before establishing his own practice in Tokyo in 1985. Ban has served as a consultant to the UN Refugee Agency on disaster relief projects. One of his largest commissions to date is the Pompidou Centre building in Metz, France (2010).

Shamir Shah (1964–)

Interior designer Shamir Shah was born and grew up in Kenya. He studied architecture at Yale University before founding Shamir Shah Design in New York in 1999. Projects have included many residential commissions with a high level of bespoke design as well as hotels and commercial projects, including a flagship store for Jonathan Adler (see page 270). His company also designs own-label furniture.

The living room (*above*) features
an Arne Jacobsen chair and artworks
by Nathaniel Price. In the dining area
by the kitchen (*right*), the dining table
is a bespoke piece by Shamir Shah
and the latticed screen is by artist
Malcolm Hill. The butterfly art
installation in the main living
area (*opposite*) is by Paul Villinski.

Rios Clementi Hale

Bohnett House / Beverly Hills, Los Angeles, USA, 2009

The evolution of trust between designer and client can bring about some extraordinary results. The bond between architect Mark Rios and his long-standing client David Bohnett has developed over the course of a dozen projects. Key among them is Bohnett's home in the Flats district of Beverly Hills, a striking, elegant and playful combination of the 1930s style of the original structure, a specially assembled collection of 1950s and 60s furniture and a contemporary edge.

It is a glamorous house befitting its heritage, set within a neighbourhood of Hollywood legends including Lucille Ball and Jack Benny. Sitting on a double lot, open to the street without any hedges or fencing, it is a well-known fixture in this part of Los Angeles. Designed by an unknown local architect in the style of Paul Williams, architect to the stars, the 1,100 square-metre (12,000 square-foot) house of white-painted brick sits in generous grounds complete with a swimming pool, tennis court and guest house. Here, Rios and Bohnett experimented with colour, pattern and furnishings to create a home that is both sophisticated and highly individual.

'It was an opportunity to take on a fun and interesting architectural and design project, and ensure that the house remained an icon in Beverly Hills,' says Bohnett. 'We were looking for each room to have its own character but for the house to also tie together as a whole. To do that, each space needed to be distinctive without being inconsistent with the overall design. It was a balancing act but also fun.'

An original terrace on the upper level of the building was reintroduced but otherwise there were few structural changes to be made. The marble flooring was retained in the entry hall but in many of the key living rooms the flooring was replaced with dark timber boards to tie the spaces together.

The majority of the furniture in the house is from the 1950s and 60s, for the most part acquired at auction over the three-year course of the project. Rios and Bohnett collaborated on a collection that includes pieces by Billy Haines, Edward Wormley, Giò Ponti and Karl Springer. A number of striking pieces by the celebrated Italian designer Piero Fornasetti (see page 106) stand out in the collection, including the screen in the entry hall and a set of table and chairs with marine motifs in the family room.

Pattern, colour and wallpapers are used to great effect in key spaces across the house: the kitchen, for example, was transformed from an ordinary

and functional area into a glamorous space that is also suited to entertaining. Rios reinvented the existing cabinets by repainting them in lemon lacquer tones while adding a vibrant wallpaper and a mirrored ceiling. The breakfast room and dining room were designed as a contrasting pair, the former being lighter for daytime use and the latter much darker for the evenings, lined in richly textured leather wall panels. The two spaces are lightly divided by 1950s vintage screens but can be combined for larger gatherings, creating a sense of flexibility.

The library is a more intimate yet striking retreat, where the existing wooden walls were lacquered a shining crimson, forming a colourful backdrop to a collection of vintage Hollywood photographs. A bespoke geometric black-and-white carpet provides a contrast to the dramatic impact of the red walls.

The house achieves that difficult balancing act of inventing a whole sequence of highly individual retreats while lightly tying them together, with highlights afforded by powerfully individual pieces of furniture.

Biography
Rios Clementi Hale

Rios Clementi Hale Studios is a multi-disciplinary practice founded in 1985 by Mark Rios, Julie Smith-Clementi, Frank Clementi and Robert Hale. Projects have involved architecture and interior design as well as landscaping and furniture/product design. Rios Clementi Hale has worked on many residential schemes, education buildings, hotels and corporate briefs, including projects for a number of Hollywood studios. Rios Clementi Hale also creates furniture and products for the notNeutral design company.

The loggia of the house (*left and opposite*) has the sophisticated air of a tailored sitting room where one can enjoy the fresh breeze and a view of the grounds. The striped wallpaper is by Perennials and the sofa and chairs in grass green are by McKinnon & Harris. The coffee table is a reproduction of a 19th-century Italian design.

The various rooms within the house have a different character according to their function. Evening spaces such as the library (*right*) and dining area (*opposite below far left*) are defined by rich, deep colours, while other parts of the house are lighter and fresher. In the sitting room (*opposite above*), select furniture pieces include a Fornasetti cabinet and a circular coffee table by Giò Ponti, who also designed the twin armchairs and matching sofa by the fireplace.

Marcel Wanders

Casa Son Vida / Mallorca, Spain, 2009

The work of Marcel Wanders is characterized by wit, humour, playfulness and innovation combined with a sense of drama. He draws inspiration from many different sources across the history of design and fuses eclectic ideas to make something fresh and new, sometimes adding a layer of Pop art kitsch. Wanders seeks to make design joyful and exuberant, but he is also fiercely ambitious and determined that his work should be pleasing and poetic as well as functional and thoughtful.

Casa Son Vida in Mallorca was one of Wanders's first residential commissions as he began to broaden his portfolio beyond furniture and product design. A combination of an existing building and a dramatic, swirling, biomorphic addition by the firm tecArchitecture, the house was initially commissioned by a developer who approached Wanders to create the interiors. Against the crisp, white architectural backdrop, Wanders introduced waves of pattern and colour, splashes of bright mosaic, sculptural elements, bespoke flourishes and many self-designed pieces of furniture for Poliform, Moooi, B&B Italia and others.

A key challenge that had to be addressed in the design process was the combination of the square forms of the original structure and the sinuous nature of the new elements, and how to furnish these fluid spaces. 'The shape of the new building is quite difficult to react to because it's so biomorphic and three-dimensional,' says Wanders. 'What we tried to do was make a clear distinction between the furniture and the more architectural elements. The furniture is really apart from the building, but we also created finishes that are part of the architecture.'

In the master bedroom, a supporting pillar was disguised as a sculpted centrepiece holding candles, while a Boffi bath was placed like a museum artwork in a gallery. A dressing table to one side sits right next to a vast, circular, wall-mounted mirror. The kitchen combines sophisticated functionality with Wanders-design units that draw inspiration from 19th-century French designs. Elsewhere, in more private areas such as the media room or the master bathroom, Wanders introduced bursts of pattern and vibrant colour.

Wanders was particularly concerned that the spaces should work together as a whole, paying attention to transitional spaces such as the main entrance hallway, where a futuristic, shimmering sculpted tree, toplit by a ceiling light, marks the gateway between inside and outside.

'You are in a square, open to the roof, with the tree at the centre of it, so that it feels as though you are almost in a piazza,' says Wanders. 'It is a very magical way to play with the transition from outside to inside. There are poetic ways to connect space, and it's essential to create a whole environment rather than just a series of rooms.'

Lively and in parts eccentric, Casa Son Vida is a product of great imagination. It is tied together and works with the contrasts between soothing open spaces and more intense visual experiences. It is a luxurious and lyrical building.

'We wanted to do something really unique,' says Wanders, 'something that would make the owner really happy living here. The house had to be like this because of the place that it is, the surroundings, the people, the parties. I love to make things that people can enjoy.'

Biography
Marcel Wanders (1963–)

Born in Boxtel in the Netherlands, Marcel Wanders studied in Eindhoven, Maastricht, Hasselt and Arnhem, graduating in 1988. He began working as a product and furniture designer, and founded Wanders Wonders in Amsterdam, which became Marcel Wanders Studio in 2001. He has designed for many leading design companies including Cappellini, Poliform, Flos, B&B Italia and Baccarat; his Knotted Chair (1996) for Droog is one of his best-known designs. In 2001, Wanders also co-founded the Moooi design label. Projects include the Mondrian South Beach Hotel in Miami and the Kameha Grand Hotel in Bonn, as well as private residential commissions.

An extraordinary tree sculpture by Wanders defines the entrance area of the house (*opposite*) as a 'magical way to play with the transition from outside to inside'. The artwork on the side of the house (*above*) is by British artist Leon Cullinane. (Photographs by Gaelle Le Boulicaut)

The circular red sofa in the sitting room (*left*) was designed by Wanders, as were the grey Moooi sofa and matching armchair. The chairs in the dining area (*below right*) are also part of the Wanders range for Moooi while the chandelier is from Baccarat. The mosaics in the bathroom alongside the bedroom (*below left*) are by Bisazza, and the bed is by Wanders for Poliform. The kitchen (*opposite above*) is a modern version of a French period look; the master bedroom with its sculpted central pillar (*opposite below*) features a Boffi bathtub floating in the room with a bespoke shower head. (Photographs by Gaelle Le Boulicaut)

Greg Lynn

Bloom House / Los Angeles, USA, 2009

In the age of digital dynamism, architect and designer Greg Lynn has become well known as a masterly shapeshifter. His work is biomorphic, sinuous and fluid, and relies on computer-aided design to produce bold and experimental forms with a sculptural quality. Like Claude Parent (see page 148) and his ideas of the *fonction oblique* back in the 1960s, Lynn rails against convention and the right angle.

For many years, Lynn's message seemed to be largely channelled through installations, lectures and his own books rather than buildings. Some marked him down as a theorist, but the Bloom House in Los Angeles proved a significant progression from computer screen to reality, developing Lynn's furniture commissions and ideas about interior design on a larger scale within a house that contrasts a linear, conventional exterior with rooms full of curves and character.

The story of the commission itself is unusual: the idea for the house was first suggested by film and television director Jason Bloom, who went on to marry Jackilin Hah, a designer from Lynn's own office. Hah Bloom became not only the client but also part of the design team and project manager.

'The house became a workshop for realizing some innovative ideas we had in the office,' says Hah Bloom, who now has two young children. 'We built a lot of models and tested some pieces through full-scale mock-ups. It is a very bespoke house.'

The glass front of the house is pierced at ground level by a glowing fibreglass lantern that runs along the ceiling like an upturned abstract canoe. The sitting room is dominated by an extraordinary oval fireplace that seems to emerge from the walls like a burning egg, with a built-in banquette and a Ravioli Chair designed by Lynn.

The journey towards the kitchen at the rear of the house offers further surprises as one passes a curving plaster pod (rather like an installation in itself) that holds Hah Bloom's home office. The kitchen itself is perhaps the most accomplished room of all, with moulded, pure-white Corian used to create an intricately crafted kitchen island, cabinets and drawers, where handles seem to push outwards gently and seamlessly like a collection of closed eyelids.

The breakfast area has the feel of a futuristic diner, with bright-red cushions on the banquettes shining out against the crisp, clean finishes of the walls and furniture. Upstairs, the master bedroom is dominated by a bespoke bamboo bed with a built-in headboard and bedside tables. The beauty of the crafted wood echoes the work of George Nakashima and Wharton Esherick (see page 54) as much as that of Lynn's biomorphic contemporaries. The master bath is a shrine to luxury, with a moulded Corian wash stand, cocoon bath and shimmering mosaic tiles.

'The Bloom House is a showcase for how to make a moderate-size house seem voluminous and intimate at the same time,' says Lynn. 'And the materials and shapes also show what is possible using ergonomic curves and surfaces. I was interested in finding a new kind of clean, integrated minimalism that did not depend on expensive materials and luxurious finishes.'

Biography
Greg Lynn (1964–)

Born in Ohio, Greg Lynn began drawing and sketching ideas from an early age. He studied architecture and philosophy at Miami University and Princeton University, and opened his own architectural office in California in 1995, working on buildings, furniture designs and installations. Among his completed projects is the Korean Presbyterian Church of New York (1999). Many of Lynn's ideas about form and the nature of digital architecture have been circulated through theoretical projects, teaching and his writings.

A bespoke fibreglass lantern forms a striking centrepiece to the house, running along the ceiling of the main living area (*opposite above*) and emerging from the façade of the building (*above*). The oval fireplace is another focal point, thrusting out from the wall of the living room, which includes a bespoke banquette and Ravioli Chair. Touches of vibrant red stand out against the white walls and surfaces.

The fireplace in the sitting room (*opposite*) forms a unique, sculptural focal point, and the red hue of the bespoke banquette is a foil for the purity of the white walls. The bed in the master bedroom (*above left*) is another bespoke design by Lynn. In the master bathroom (*below right*), white Corian was used to make the sink unit.

David Collins

MahaNakhon Apartment / Bangkok, Thailand, 2010

In a dynamic, sleepless and epic city like Bangkok, the idea of a home as a calm and peaceful refuge becomes highly seductive. This is the thinking behind designer David Collins's first MahaNakhon apartment in Bangkok, a prototypical luxury home set within a distinctive new seventy-seven-storey tower. Fusing the sophistication of upscale serviced Manhattan apartment blocks with Thai-inspired colours and textures, this escapist retreat is a hymn to luxury, tranquillity and the power of bespoke design.

Designed by German architect Ole Scheeren, the MahaNakhon tower houses a hotel with just over 190 serviced luxury apartments. David Collins first worked on these interiors in a show flat for the tower, which is located in a prime position between the city's Silom and Sathorn roads.

If space is luxury, the apartment embraces this idea with its generous, elegant entrance hall and large living room, lightly divided into separate zones for sitting and entertaining. The main living space is characterized by calming notes, with its parquet floors and crisp white walls a backdrop to a palette of soft, enticing blues used for the upholstery, rugs and artworks. The dining room to one side of the sitting room is in a recessed gallery and forms an

extraordinary space with customized panelled walls in embroidered deep-navy silk.

'Thailand is very much about colour and texture – the glazes on the ceramics, the reflective quality of Thai silks – and these were the kind of things that I found inspiring,' says Collins. 'There are allusions in the fabrics, rugs and the whimsical tie-dye curtains in the living room, and all the artwork is by Thai artists. But we didn't want the Thai influence to be too obvious. It's more subliminal.'

What is especially striking is the highly bespoke nature of much of the furniture, light fittings and textiles in the apartment, with more than seventy-five original designs and custom pieces created by David Collins Studio. From custom velvet sofas and satin chairs to coffee tables coated in shagreen leather, these original pieces help define the apartment's character and add a rich variety of textures of a sensuous, tactile beauty.

The apartment's luxurious aspect is carried over into the more functional spaces, such as the kitchen, where the walls are coated in silver-grey silk and the floors and worktops are made of crisply cut marble. With enough space for both a breakfast table and a striking, sculpted chaise longue, the kitchen goes well beyond the functional and becomes a space for

relaxing and entertaining as well as cooking and preparing for guests.

The master suite has been designed by Collins as a contained miniature apartment, with a bedroom large enough for a seating area and a dressing table, and a bathroom indulgent and spacious enough to compare with those of a fine hotel. This is an apartment that introduces a philosophy of flexibility and redefines the ways in which different spaces in the home can be used.

'We have changed our aspirations and want something more sophisticated than a room with a bed and a wardrobe,' says Collins. 'The bedroom could be a place to have breakfast, to take an afternoon nap, while wardrobes have become dressing rooms with a quality, lighting and finish comparable to high-end fashion stores. And the bathroom is something akin to a spa experience.'

In the sitting room (*below*), much of the furniture is bespoke and designed by David Collins, including the two armchairs and the twin coffee tables. The dining area (*opposite*) is positioned in a recess to one side of the living room and includes bespoke panelling, a custom rug and a dining table with a silver sycamore top and lacquered navy dining chairs in polished metal and leather.

Biography
David Collins

Collins is best known for his interior designs for high-end hotel and restaurant projects around the world, as well as various residential designs. He was born in Ireland and grew up near Dublin, where he studied at the Dublin School of Architecture Bolton Street. He founded his own practice, David Collins Studio, in London in 1985. Hotel projects include the Lime Wood Hotel in the New Forest National Park, UK, and The London NYC in Manhattan, while restaurant designs include The Wolseley and Nobu Berkeley St in London. Collins's work involves a highly tailored, holistic approach that embraces architecture, interiors and furniture design.

The colour scheme of the sitting room (*opposite above*) is fresh and vibrant, with an emphasis on blues and whites with yellow accents. The yellow chairs are custom Collins designs in satin and the circular straw marquetry table is also a bespoke piece. Great emphasis is placed on detailing; the luxurious master bathroom (*opposite below right*) features marble floors and a bath by Agape. The master bedroom (*right*) has a four-poster bed designed by Collins with posts wrapped in leather cord; the silk velvet sofa is another custom piece.

Marc Newson

Newson Apartment / London, UK, 2010

Marc Newson's London apartment was directly inspired by the Hitchcock thriller *North by Northwest*. It was the Swiss chalet in that classic film that steered the designer's ideas for the home he shares with his partner, fashion editor Charlotte Stockdale, and their daughter, Imogen. Situated on the second floor of a vast Edwardian former mail-sorting depot, the building might have lent itself to a loft-style treatment, but that was the very last thing Newson wanted.

'Lofts are large and cold,' says Newson, who also owns a house in Paris. 'We wanted to preserve a sense of volume but at the same time create an atmosphere and warmth, which is quite difficult to achieve in such a large space. That's the thing about chalets – they are naturally cosy no matter how big the space. That house in *North by Northwest* became a reference point for this apartment and inspired the river rock wall. I had to import the rock from Nova Scotia.'

This wall of rounded stones became a dominant feature in the design of the double-height living room, bringing a great sense of texture and drama. It surrounds a fireplace flanked by Scandinavian Svenskt Tenn sofas, upholstered in a leafy-green textile design by Josef Frank, a designer whom Newson admires. These organic flavours, along with the blonde oak floors, contrast with the more futuristic quality of other architectural elements in the apartment, which include openings and internal windows carved into the curving walls that form the upper level of the apartment and overlook the living area and kitchen below.

The kitchen itself is brought to life by cabinets and a triangular island, coated in a shiny, soothing retro pistachio green and topped with Carrara marble. 'I love this particular shade of green,' says Newson, 'I had read somewhere that a couple of scientists had determined that this was the real shade of the universe (incorrectly as it turned out). I even had my vintage Aston Martin DB4 painted in that hue.'

In a home that offers a choice of discoveries, the library comes as a particular surprise. It was Stockdale's request, as she had grown up in a house with a library, and it was designed as a traditional wood-panelled room using salvaged oak panels. The room also features a zebra-skin rug and sofas upholstered in a Colefax & Fowler tweed. Perhaps more in tune with the public perception of Newson's dynamic style of design is the master bathroom, which is lined in striped marble, carved and shaped to form a seamless, curvaceous surface. It is one of Newson's favourite spaces in the apartment.

There are a small number of Newson's own-design furniture pieces, but they are subtly scattered throughout the house rather than given particular prominence. Among them is his marble Voronoi Shelf, two Micarta chairs, a Diode lamp and a few other pieces. For Newson, however, the greatest success lies in the fact that the space is not a loft-like exhibition hall, but has the feel of a family home.

'Having a young family guided the design to a large extent,' says Newson. 'Space was a priority. Just before this, we were living in a five-floor townhouse with only two rooms on each floor, so seeing Imogen running around this place is amazing.'

Biography
Marc Newson (1963–)

London-based designer Marc Newson has established a unique position as a contemporary designer who is in great demand in the commercial sphere but also the creator of highly collectable, limited-edition pieces of furniture that sell as artworks. Born in Sydney, Newson studied sculpture at the Sydney College of the Arts (SCA) before moving to Tokyo, Paris and finally London, where he established his design studio in 1997. His work includes aircraft design – he is creative director of Qantas Airways and designed the insides of the A380 planes – as well as watches, clothing, cookware, bicycles, boats, binoculars, bags, furniture and interiors. Newson also teaches, and his work is exhibited internationally. His futuristic, dynamic and sinuous style of design has been widely imitated.

The mountain chalet atmosphere of the apartment is largely created by the double-height fireplace wall of rounded river stone (*opposite*). The design of the apartment was a collaboration between Newson and Squire & Partners architects. The sofas are covered in a Josef Frank Svenskt Tenn fabric, and the two Micarta chairs are by Marc Newson. The mezzanine containing bedrooms and guest accommodation forms a sculpted bridge above the open-plan sitting and dining areas (*overleaf*).

The kitchen (*left*) is picked out in a pistachio green with Carrara marble for the counter tops. Streaked marble is used to powerful effect in the bathroom (*opposite above right and opposite below left*), and the Low Voronoi Shelf console (*opposite above left*) is also made from marble. The library (*opposite below right*) was designed in a more traditional style, with oak-panelled walls, for Newson's wife, Charlotte.

Bibliography

Author's note: where quotations have no references in the text, they are generally sourced from interviews or correspondence with the architect, designer or client of the house in question, or from materials supplied by them.

Adriaansz, Elly et al., *Brinkman and Van der Vlugt: The Sonneveld House*, NAi Publishers, 2001

Alini, Luigi, *Kengo Kuma: Works and Projects*, Electa Architecture, 2005

Allan, John, *Berthold Lubetkin*, RIBA Publications, 1992

Baron, Armelle, *Axel Vervoordt: Timeless Interiors*, Flammarion, 2007

Bell, Quentin and Virginia Nicholson, *Charleston: A Bloomsbury Country House and Garden*, Frances Lincoln, 1997

Bergé, Pierre et al., *Maison Jean Cocteau*, Somogy Art Publisher, 2010

Blundell Jones, Peter, *Hans Scharoun*, Phaidon, 1995

Bo Bardi, Lina et al., *Lina Bo Bardi*, Instituto Lina Bo e P. M. Bardi/Edizioni Charta, 1994

Bognar, Botond, *Kengo Kuma: Selected Works*, Princeton Architectural Press, 2005

Bowles, Hamish et al., *Vogue Living: Houses, Gardens, People*, Alfred A. Knopf, 2010

Bradbury, Dominic, *The Iconic House: Architectural Masterworks since 1900*, Thames & Hudson, 2009

——, *New Natural Home*, Thames & Hudson, 2011

Brooks Pfeiffer, Bruce, *Frank Lloyd Wright*, Taschen, 2000

Byars, Mel, *The Design Encyclopedia*, Laurence King, 2004

Campbell-Lange, Barbara-Ann, *John Lautner*, Taschen, 2005

Cecil, Mirabel and David Mlinaric, *Mlinaric on Decorating*, Frances Lincoln, 2008

Cohen, Jill et al., *House & Garden's Best in Decoration*, Condé Nast Books/Random House, 1987

Conran, Terence and Stafford Cliff, *Terence Conran's Inspiration*, Conran Octopus, 2008

Coquelle, Aline, *Palm Springs Style*, Assouline, 2005

Craig, Theresa, *Edith Wharton, A House Full of Rooms: Architecture, Interiors, and Gardens*, Monacelli Press, 1996

Cygelman, Adèle, *Palm Springs Modern*, Rizzoli, 1999

Duncan, Alastair, *Art Deco Complete*, Thames & Hudson, 2010

Eerdmans, Emily Evans, *The World of Madeleine Castaing*, Rizzoli, 2010

Eisenhauer, Paul (ed.), *Wharton Esherick: Studio and Collection*, Schiffer Publishing, 2010

Etherington-Smith, Meredith, *Axel Vervoordt: The Story of a Style*, Assouline, 2002

Faber, Tobias, *New Danish Architecture*, Architectural Press, 1968

Ferrand, Franck, *Jacques Garcia: Decorating in the French Style*, Flammarion, 1999

Fiell, Charlotte and Peter, *Design of the 20th Century*, Taschen, 1999

Goodmand, Wendy and Hutton Wilkinson, *Tony Duquette*, Abrams, 2007

Greeves, Lydia, *Houses of the National Trust*, National Trust Books, 2008

Hampton, Mark, *Legendary Decorators of the Twentieth Century*, Robert Hale, 1992

Hansen, Marika et al., *Eliel Saarinen: Projects 1896–1923*, Otava Publishing, 1990

Hess, Alan, *The Architecture of John Lautner*, Thames & Hudson, 1999

——, *Oscar Niemeyer Houses*, Rizzoli, 2006

Hicks, Ashley, *David Hicks: A Life of Design*, Rizzoli, 2008

Hicks, David, *Living With Design*, Weidenfeld & Nicolson, 1979

——, *Style and Design*, Viking, 1987

Jackson, Lesley, *Robin and Lucienne Day: Pioneers of Contemporary Design*, Mitchell Beazley, 2001

Jodidio, Philip, *100 Contemporary Architects*, Taschen, 2008

Laaksonen, Esa and Ásdis Ólafsdóttir (eds), *Alvar Aalto Architect: Maison Louise Carré, 1956–63*, Alvar Aalto Foundation, 2008

Lahti, Markku, *Alvar Aalto Houses*, Rakenn Ustieto Oy, 2005

Neil Levine, *The Architecture of Frank Lloyd Wright*, Princeton University Press, 1996

Lewis, Adam, *Albert Hadley: The Story of America's Preeminent Interior Designer*, Rizzoli, 2005

——, *The Great Lady Decorators: The Women Who Defined Interior Design, 1870–1955*, Rizzoli, 2010

Lovatt-Smith, Lisa, *The Fashion House: Inside the Homes of Leading Designers*, Conran Octopus, 1997

Lucan, Jacques et al., *The Function of the Oblique: The Architecture of Claude Parent and Paul Virilio, 1963–69*, AA Publications, 1996

Lynn, Greg, *Form*, Rizzoli, 2008

McCarter, Robert, *Frank Lloyd Wright: Architect*, Phaidon, 1997

McCartney, Karen, *50/60/70 Iconic Australian Houses*, Murdoch Books, 2007

McDowell, Colin, *Matthew Williamson*, Rizzoli, 2010

Massey, Anne, *Interior Design of the 20th Century*, Thames & Hudson, 1990

Mauriès, Patrick, *Fornasetti: Designer of Dreams*, Thames & Hudson, 1991

Mead, Christopher Curtis, *The Architecture of Bart Prince: A Pragmatics of Place*, W. W. Norton, 2010

——, *Houses by Bart Prince: An American Architecture for the Continuous Present*, University of New Mexico Press, 1991

Minshaw, John and Celina Fox, *John Minshaw Designs*, Frances Lincoln, 2009

Mitchinson, David et al., *Hoglands: The Home of Henry and Irina Moore*, Lund Humphries, 2007

Morris, Alison, *John Pawson: Plain Space*, Phaidon, 2010

Niemeyer, Oscar, *The Curves of Time: The Memoirs of Oscar Niemeyer*, Phaidon, 2000

O'Hagan, Helen, Kathleen Rowold and Michael Vollbracht, *Bill Blass: An American Designer*, Abrams, 2002

Oliveira, Olivia de, *Subtle Substances: The Architecture of Lina Bo Bardi*, Gustavo Gili, 2006

Passebon, Pierre, *Jacques Grange Interiors*, Flammarion, 2009

Peltason, Ruth and Grace Ong-Yan (eds), *Architect: The Pritzker Prize Laureates in their Own Words*, Thames & Hudson, 2010

Postiglione, Gennaro et al., *One Hundred Houses for One Hundred Architects*, Taschen, 2004

Powers, Alan, *Modern: The Modern Movement in Britain*, Merrell, 2005

Rashid, Karim, *Evolution*, Thames & Hudson, 2004

——, *I Want to Change the World*, Thames & Hudson, 2001

——, *Space: The Architecture of Karim Rashid*, Rizzoli, 2009

Reading, Malcolm and Peter Coe, *Lubetkin and Tecton: An Architectural Study*, Triangle, 1992

Russell, Margaret, *Designing Women*, Stewart, Tabori & Chang, 2001

Saladino, John, *Style by Saladino*, Frances Lincoln, 2000

——, *Villa*, Frances Lincoln, 2009

Scott, Grant and Samantha Scott-Jeffries, *At Home with the Makers of Style*, Thames & Hudson, 2005

Serle, Geoffrey, *Robin Boyd: A Life*, Melbourne University Press, 1995

Sills, Stephen, James Huniford and Michael Boodro, *Dwellings: Living with Great Style*, Little Brown, 2003

Smith, Michael S., *Houses*, Rizzoli, 2008

Stefanidis, John, *Living by Design*, Weidenfeld & Nicolson, 1997

Street-Porter, Tim, *Hollywood Houses*, Thames & Hudson, 2004

——, *The Los Angeles House*, Thames & Hudson, 1995

Sudjic, Deyan, *John Pawson: Works*, Phaidon, 2005

Syring, Eberhard and Jörg C. Kirschenmann, *Hans Scharoun*, Taschen, 2004

Tarlow, Rose, *The Private House*, Clarkson Potter, 2001

Tasma-Anargyos, Sophie, *Andrée Putman*, Laurence King, 1993

Tinniswood, Adrian, *The Art Deco House*, Mitchell Beazley, 2002

Todd, Pamela, *Bloomsbury at Home*, Pavilion, 1999

Trocmé, Suzanne, *Influential Interiors*, Mitchell Beazley, 1999

Ueki-Polet, Keiko and Klaus Klemp (eds), *Less and More: The Design Ethos of Dieter Rams*, Gestalten, 2009

Venturi, Robert and Denise Scott Brown, *Learning from Las Vegas: The Forgotten Symbolism of Architectural Form*, MIT Press, 1977

Webb, Michael, *Architects House Themselves*, Preservation Press, 1994

——, *Modernist Paradise: Niemeyer House/Boyd Collection*, Rizzoli, 2007

Weintraub, Alan, *Lloyd Wright: The Architecture of Frank Lloyd Wright, Jr*, Thames & Hudson, 1998

Wharton, Edith and Ogden Codman, Jr, *The Decoration of Houses*, The Mount Press/Rizzoli, 2007

Wilkinson, Hutton, *More is More: Tony Duquette*, Abrams, 2009

Williamson, Leslie, *Handcrafted Modern*, Rizzoli, 2010

Wolf, Vicente, *Learning to See*, Artisan, 2002

——, *Lifting the Curtain on Design*, Monacelli Press, 2010

Wright, Russel, *Good Design Is for Everyone – in his own Words*, Manitoga/Russel Wright Design Centre/Universe, 2001

Yeoward, William, *William Yeoward at Home*, Cico Books, 2010

Gazetteer

This listing contains addresses and contact details for houses open or accessible to visitors.

Note: access conditions to the properties below vary widely, so please make sure to contact the institution in question to make arrangements before visiting.

Any houses that are featured in this book but not mentioned here are strictly private and not open to the public.

Castle Drogo – Edwin Lutyens
Drewsteignton
Exeter
Devon
EX6 6PB
UK
T: +44 (0)1647 433 306
www.nationaltrust.org.uk

Charleston – Duncan Grant & Vanessa Bell
Firle
Lewes
East Sussex
BN8 6LL
UK
T: +44 (0)1323 811626
www.charleston.org.uk

Château du Champ de Bataille – Jacques Garcia
27110 Le Neubourg
Normandy
France
T: +33 (0)2 32 34 84 34
www.duchampdebataille.com

Dragon Rock – Russel Wright
Russel Wright Design Center
584 Route 9D (PO Box 249)
Garrison
New York 10524
USA
T: +1 845 424 3812
www.russelwrightcenter.org

The Frick Residence – Elsie de Wolfe
1 East 70TH Street
New York
10021 New York
USA
T: +1 212 288 0700
www.frick.org

The Glass House – Lina Bo Bardi
Instituto Bo e P. M. Bardi
Rua General Almério de Moura, 200
05690-080 São Paulo
Brazil
T: +55 (11) 3744 9902
www.institutobardi.com.br

Haus Schminke – Hans Scharoun
Kirschallee 1B
02708 Löbau
Germany
T: +49 (0)35 85 86 21 33
www.stiftung-hausschminke.eu

Hollyhock House – Frank Lloyd Wright
4800 Hollywood Blvd
Los Angeles, California 90027
USA
T: +1 323 644 6269
www.hollyhockhouse.net

The Homewood – Patrick Gwynne
Portsmouth Road
Esher, Surrey KT10 9JL
UK
T: +44 (0)1372 476424
www.nationaltrust.org.uk/homewood

Hvitträsk – Eliel Saarinen
Hvitträskintie 166
Luomo FI-02440
Finland
T: +358 (0)9 4050 9631
www.nba.fi/en/museums/hvittrask

Maison Jean Cocteau – Madeleine Castaing & Jean Cocteau
15 rue du Lau
91490 Milly-la-Forêt
France
T: +33 (0)1 64 98 11 50
www.jeancocteau.net

Maison Louis Carré – Alvar Aalto
2 chemin du Saint-Sacrement
78490 Bazoches-sur-Guyonne
France
T: +33 (0)1 34 86 79 63
www.maisonlouiscarre.fr

The Mount – Edith Wharton
2 Plunkett Street (PO Box 974)
Lenox, Massachusetts 01240-0974
USA
T: +1 413 551 5100
www.edithwharton.org

Sonneveld House – Brinkman & Van der Vlugt
Museumpark 25
3015 CB
Rotterdam
The Netherlands
T: +31 (0)10 4401 200
www.nai.nl

Villa Demoiselle – Louis Sorel & Tony Selmersheim
5 place du Général Gourand
51100 Rheims
France
T: +33 (0)3 26 61 62 56
www.champagne-demoiselle.fr

Villa Esche – Henry van de Velde
Parkstrasse 58
09120 Chemnitz
Germany
T: +49 (0)3 71 533 10 88
www.villaesche.de

Walsh Street House – Robin Boyd
290 Walsh Street
South Yarra
Melbourne
Victoria 3142
Australia
www.robinboyd.org.au

Wharton Esherick House/ Museum – Wharton Esherick
PO Box 595
Paoli
Pennsylvania 19301-0595
USA
T: +1 610 644 5822
www.whartonesherickmuseum.org

Interiors by Style

Marcos Acayaba, Milan House, São Paulo, Brazil, 1975, page 168

Eduardo Longo, Casa Bola, São Paulo, Brazil, 1979, page 190

Bart Prince, Joe & Etsuko Price Residence, Corona del Mar, USA, 1989, page 218

Ministero del Gusto, Maison Ministero del Gusto, Marrakech, Morocco, 1998, page 252

Karim Rashid, Rashid House, Scarborough, New York, USA, 2004, page 284

24H Architecture, Dragspelhuset, Lake Övre, Sweden, 2006, page 306

Marcel Wanders, Casa Son Vida, Mallorca, Spain, 2009, page 326

Greg Lynn, Bloom House, Los Angeles, USA, 2009, page 330

Marc Newson, Newson Apartment, London, UK, 2010, page 338

Theatrical
Lorenzo Mongiardino, Peretti Tower, Porto Ercole, Italy, 1985, page 22

Duncan Grant & Vanessa Bell, Charleston, Firle, East Sussex, UK, 1916, page 42

Jean Cocteau & Madeleine Castaing, Maison Jean Cocteau, Milly-la-Forêt, France, 1947, page 92

Tony Duquette, Dawnridge, Beverly Hills, Los Angeles, USA, 1949, page 96

Piero Fornasetti, Villa Fornasetti, Milan, Italy, c. 1955, page 106

John Lautner, Garcia House, Los Angeles, USA, 1962, page 134

Ricardo Bofill, La Fábrica, Barcelona, Spain, 1975, page 172

Eduardo Longo, Casa Bola, São Paulo, Brazil, 1979, page 190

Anthony Collett, Collett House, London, UK, 1982, page 198

Jacques Garcia, Château du Champ de Bataille, Normandy, France, 1992, page 230

Todd Oldham, Oldham House, Pennsylvania, USA, 1997, page 248

Ministero del Gusto, Maison Ministero del Gusto, Marrakech, Morocco, 1998, page 252

Jonathan Adler, Adler/Doonan Apartment, New York, USA, 2001, page 270

Matthew Williamson, Williamson House, London, UK, 2007, page 308

Marcel Wanders, Casa Son Vida, Mallorca, Spain, 2009, page 326

Picture Credits

Index

Acknowledgments

To Cecily

Dominic Bradbury and Richard Powers would like to express their sincere thanks to the many owners, interior designers, architects, guardians and custodians of the houses featured in these pages for their generous help and support. Without their assistance this book would not have been possible. We are grateful to the many design practices mentioned in the book and to their staff, who have helped us again and again during the production of this publication.

Particular thanks are also due to Karen Howes and The Interior Archive for all their support and for the many contributions to *The Iconic Interior* by Interior Archive photographers, especially Mark Luscombe-Whyte, Simon Upton and Fritz von der Schulenburg.

We would also like to thank the following for all their assistance with the production of this book and photography of the houses contained within it: John Allan & Avanti Architects, Association Alvar Aalto France, Mathilde Beaujard, Odile Botti, Michael Boyd, Faith Bradbury, Neil Buhrich, Hatta Byng, Stephane Chomant, Cecilia den Otter, Anne Dorthe Walther, Lisa Dube-Scherr, Paul Eisenhauer, Liz Elliot, Annabel Friedlein, Jacques Garcia, Judy Glass, Maria Gomis, Jeffrey Herr, Instituto Lina Bo e P.M. Bardi, Mark Jespersen, Sarah Kaye, Coralie Langston-Jones, Victoria Larson, Tony Lee, Laurence Macadam, Sandrine Mahaut, Marmol Radziner Architects, Karen McCartney, John McIlwee, Danielle Miller, Lori Moss, Zeynep Musoglu, David Nicholls, Asdis Olafsdottir, Jessica Olshen, John Pardey, Martin Penrose, Elfreda Pownall, Matthew Riches, Helen Risom Belluschi, Rebecca Ross, Philippa Rowson, Mike Rundell, Kirsten Schenk, Jane Seamon, Victoria Shorr-Perkins, Amanda Talbot, Julie D. Taylor, Yuki Tintori, Sophie Toh, Michael Webb, Neale Whitaker, Hutton Wilkinson, Patsy Youngstein, Starrett Zenko and the staff of the RIBA Library.

Special gratitude is due to Gordon Wise and John Parton at Curtis Brown and Peter Dawson at Grade Design, together with Lucas Dietrich, Adélia Sabatini, Katharina Hahn and the rest of the team at Thames & Hudson, without whom this book would never have been born.

Library of Congress Cataloging-in-Publication Data

Bradbury, Dominic.
The iconic interior : private spaces of leading artists, architects, and designers / Dominic Bradbury ; with photographs by Richard Powers.
   pages cm
Includes bibliographical references and index.
ISBN 978-1-61769-005-1 (alk. paper)
1. Interior decoration—History—20th century—Themes, motives. 2. Interior decoration—History—21st century—Themes, motives. I. Title.
NK1980.B69 2012
747.09'04—dc23

                2012007221

First published in the United Kingdom in 2012 by Thames & Hudson Ltd, 181A High Holborn, London WC1V 7QX.

Printed and bound in China
10 9 8 7 6 5 4 3 2 1

ABRAMS
THE ART OF BOOKS SINCE 1949

115 West 18th Street
New York, NY 10011
www.abramsbooks.com